Blood into Water

Social Fictions Series

VOLUME 38

The titles published in this series are listed at *brill.com/soci*

Blood into Water

A Case of Social Justice

By

R. P. Clair

BRILL

SENSE

LEIDEN | BOSTON

All chapters in this book have undergone peer review.

Library of Congress Cataloging-in-Publication Data

Names: Clair, Robin Patric author.
Title: Blood into water : a case of social justice / by R. P. Clair.
Description: Leiden ; Boston : Brill Sense, [2021] | Series: Social
    fictions series, 2542-8799 ; volume 38
Identifiers: LCCN 2020044640 (print) | LCCN 2020044641 (ebook) | ISBN
    9789004446236 (paperback ; acid-free paper) | ISBN 9789004446243
    (hardback ; acid-free paper) | ISBN 9789004446250 (e-book)
Subjects: LCSH: Environmental justice--Fiction. | Nicaragua--Fiction.
Classification: LCC PS3603.L3454 B58 2021 (print) | LCC PS3603.L3454
    (ebook) | DDC 813/.6--dc23
LC record available at https://lccn.loc.gov/2020044640
LC ebook record available at https://lccn.loc.gov/2020044641

ISSN 2542-8799
ISBN 978-90-04-44623-6 (paperback)
ISBN 978-90-04-44624-3 (hardback)
ISBN 978-90-04-44625-0 (e-book)

Copyright 2021 by R. P. Clair. Published by Koninklijke Brill NV, Leiden,
The Netherlands.
Koninklijke Brill NV incorporates the imprints Brill, Brill Hes & De Graaf,
Brill Nijhoff, Brill Rodopi, Brill Sense, Hotei Publishing, mentis Verlag, Verlag
Ferdinand Schöningh and Wilhelm Fink Verlag.
Koninklijke Brill NV reserves the right to protect this publication against
unauthorized use. Requests for re-use and/or translations must be addressed to
Koninklijke Brill NV via brill.com or copyright.com.

This book is printed on acid-free paper and produced in a sustainable manner.

ADVANCE PRAISE FOR
BLOOD INTO WATER

"In her newest work, Clair uses fiction and narrative to teach readers about the complex intersections between societal and corporate materialism, intense emotion, and close relationships. Clair weaves together multiple, and oftentimes conflicting, voices to create a work that presents an excellent and compelling story, while unveiling a pedagogical tool that can be used to stimulate readers. The characters come to life as the story unfolds. I applaud Clair's ability to render an evocative story that has the power and richness to give voice to the lived experiences of those that work together, as well as those who are dialectically opposed from each other. I envision this book as a practical yet provocative text for use in courses focusing on organizational and interpersonal relationships. It is an absolute must read!"
– Adrianne Kunkel, Professor of Communication Studies, University of Kansas

"I do find the book riveting, and very hard to put down. I think the level of detail is simply fascinating. It might be appropriately placed in a communication ethics course. In the past, I would have made it an option for honors students in my large organizational class of 240 students, but now those large sections have been broken into much smaller ones. If I get to teach the environmental communication course again next year, the book [*Blood into Water*] along with the *Zombie Seed* would be a good fit."
– Joseph Scudder, Professor of Communication, Northern Illinois University

"This is an amazing book. It is beautifully written. Clair is a superb storyteller. Her weavings of life histories are rooted in her characters' day-to-day living which serves to broaden the reader's understanding of the people she has created for this beautifully written work of fiction. Whether it's the wails from a heartbroken mother or the off-

put sense of humor driving a person's corporate greed, Clair takes us on a journey where along the way we find ourselves gasping for air at many turns in the road. I love this book. Well done!"
– **Leonard Cox, Center for Oral History, Columbia University**

CONTENTS

CONTENTS

ACADEMIC INTRODUCTION

Blood into Water is a novel that weaves together the past and the present, from Mayan legends to contemporary stories of corporate greed. The story follows a mother and son, Sofía and Miguel Rodríguez, as they team with reporter Caleb Barthes to uncover a corporate scheme of exploitation. Barthes has been sent to Nicaragua on an investigative assignment to look into water rights and privatization plans. He learns far more than he expects about the environmental, political, and cultural issue from Professor López, his assigned contact person. López takes the reporter and Miguel on a trip across the country so that they might better understand the culture and the critical issues associated with water. In the meantime, Professor Delta Quinn of Purdue University accepts a position with an all-female team of archeologists and anthropologists to explore the cave where the most recent Mayan stela has been discovered. According to contemporary archeologists, the stela is inscribed with a tribute to the Lady Ikoom, a queen of the Maya Snake Clan who lived during the 6th century C.E., a time period in which it is believed that droughts led to warfare that contributed to the near extinction of the Maya. I have taken liberties and created imaginative legends as a back story for the Lady Ikoom in which obtaining water, a precious gift from the gods, forces her to undertake heroic challenges for her people. The same could be said of Sofía, who in the absence of her son and Caleb, is drawn into the role of a leader, which like the Lady Ikoom, seems to be her destiny—to lead and protect her people. Protecting and caring for others is laced throughout the book, from the stories of the Lady Ikoom and her people to how Caleb's sister Mona cares for an abused child, as well as her brother in his time of need. Relationships are tested—mother-son, brother-sister, friend-friend, lovers and a people to their culture. But it is Sofía who may most embody the brutal poetry of life, love, loss, and resilience.

Nevertheless, Sofía was/is not the intended protagonist of the novel. This novel is a sequel to *Zombie Seed and the Butterfly Blues:*

A Case of Social Justice in which Delta Quinn was the protagonist and Caleb Barthes was her romantic interest who far too often saved the day with somewhat unrealistic heroics. Delta saw him as a hero. In this sequel, I created Caleb as the flawed protagonist who journeys into unknown territory, assumes superiority, and falls from his pedestal. Simultaneously, I did not want Sophia and her son, Miguel to be marginalized as they represent the true story that inspired the novel. Thus, I chose to open with Sofía and Miguel, but turn quickly to the character of Caleb. After completing the novel, I wondered, who will readers think is the protagonist and how might I answer that question. Dr. Natalie Lambert, a communication and data analysis expert, wondered the same thing about Shakespeare's *Romeo and Juliet.* She questioned, is the story about both of them equally, or is one or the other the protagonist? Using 'big data' analysis she determined that it is Romeo who is mentioned far more often than Juliet. I also conducted a data-mining search and discovered that based on the criteria of frequency of names mentioned, Caleb is definitely the protagonist with over 500 mentions (Delta = 391, Miguel = 341, Sofía = 182 and with Mamá added there are 200 mentions for Sofía). In addition, the character of Mona Bathes, Caleb's sister and Delta's advisee, who played the part of comic relief in *Zombie Seed and the Butterfly Blues* has been given her rightful representation as a more fully developed character. While Mona retains her comedic charm, she also enacts the role of adviser to her adviser, caretaker to her foster child, and the only one who can save Caleb from himself. Mona is mentioned 161 times. But there is one final word-character-subject of concern that was important to me to assess and that is "water." Whether in Spanish or English, water issues are at the forefront of this novel. I open the novel with the word, *agua,* in order to make that point. The data mining acknowledged its importance continuing throughout the novel. 'Water' is mentioned 450 times (additionally, rain = 122 and tears = 41, *agua* stands alone but is also embedded within *Nicaragua* and *Managua*, making the calculations more difficult, but the symbolism more acute). Finally, as a writer I have purposefully moved from the previous protagonist (i.e., Delta) to the present (i.e., Caleb) in order to employ what is called

Extended Narrative Empathy (ENE), a theory that I developed (see Clair & Mattson, 2013; Clair et al., 2014, 2016) and felt was enacted in the award-winning (both the Pulitzer Prize for fiction and the National Book Critics Circle award) book titled, *A Visit from the Goon Squad* by Jennifer Egan (2011) which I read after developing the theory. The theory encourages looking beyond the protagonist to see how each person or character acts as a protagonist from a different perspective, even the antagonist can be viewed as the protagonist. By engaging in the perspective shifting, people/readers can develop empathy for others and acquire a more complete understanding of a story/the narrative.

Current debates over cultural appropriation versus empathy-driven appropriate cultural representation are of key concern in this novel, as well as the previous novel. In *Zombie Seed and the Butterfly Blues*, I intentionally created a diverse cast of characters, especially racially and ethnically. Delta's bi-racial background opens the door to diversity and the cast of characters enter through it (female and male, African-American, Indian, Chinese, and Euro-American, gay and straight, and so on). In writing the current novel, I was faced with how to write Sofía and Miguel with cultural appropriateness and as little appropriation as possible. I relied on multiple methods to create both the characters and the setting. Ethnographic methods began with interviews of people who had lived in Nicaragua (e.g., Geyselle González). Geyselle helped me in the initial stages, read early drafts of beginning chapters and a short story based on the novel. She reached into her recent memories and described water collection, school desks, and more. In addition, I interviewed a researcher who conducted extensive research in Nicaragua but prefers to stay anonymous. I gathered archival documents, read histories, traveled via the internet, and watched personal videos as well as documentaries on Nicaragua. With respect to Delta's travels in the novel, I undertook travels to Belize, crossed the country as described, and took a day trip to Tikal (Mayan orthography—*Tik'al*). Several people reviewed this book before its publication and each had comments about the cultural representation and specifically about language. Some wanted me to include more of the unique beauty of the Nicaraguan language;

one wanted me to delete it and considered it a form of cultural appropriation. I chose to delete specific poetic references in respect to the culture; in other words, I err on the side of caution, respect, and cultural humility (Tervalon & Murray-García, 1998). I have taken the advice of Stephanie Carlo on inserting Spanish spellings of first and surnames with a couple of exceptions (I kept the name Geyselle as is, as this is how Geyselle González spells her first name). I did not add an accent to Renée Chavon's last name as I didn't want her character to necessarily be of Latina ancestry. Although I hope I made all of the other editing corrections that Stephanie Carlo (a professional editor and friend) provided, I take full responsibility if there are any forgotten edits or typos. In short, I hope that I have provided cultural justice to the language, characters and country of Nicaragua.

Blood into Water was originally inspired by the true story of the "Bolivian Water Wars" in which a corporate conglomerate, in cahoots with the government, tried to privatize the water of Bolivia. The corporate position was that clean water provided by the government, but sourced through a private organization, like Bechtel, would provide low cost access to clean water. The opposition movement argued that the corporatists demonstrated intense greed as they encouraged the government to make it illegal for the poorest peasants to collect and drink rain water, not an uncommon practice (Schultz, 2010). The story at first seems like good v. evil, but these situations are far too often more complex than what first meets the eye. Farmers spearheaded a social movement to end Bechtel's control, but their interests are rarely discussed—they too would have had to pay for water, irrigation consumes huge amounts of fresh water. The novel recreates these issues in a different country and under different circumstances, and does so for a reason. Nicaragua offers a unique setting for students in terms of history, politics, economics, and culture. In *Blood into Water*, the reader becomes aware of this environmental issue as well the people caught between two stories—the corporate narrative and the social movement. Students of environmental communication, organizational communication, rhetoric, social movements, and cultural studies should find much to discuss based on this novel. Students of corporate communication should find the research details in the novel concerning international and national business law revealing. These, too, are based on in-depth research that comes alive in the story. Organizational communication courses, whether discussing marketing, business law, corporate culture or corporate colonization, should benefit from the novel.

Furthermore, the novel laces legends of the Maya into its background. Students of narrative, archeology, and anthropology will find the mixture of fiction and fact worth parsing out through discussion and research. Actual recent digs in Guatemala inspired the background story of the Lady Ikoom. And the true story of the discovery of stela 44 by Guatemalan archaeologist, Griselda Perez, will fascinate students of archeology. In addition, women's studies students will likely appreciate that the story of the all-female team portrayed in the novel is grounded in reality (Discovery, 2013). Although researchers have not found artifacts of the Maya in Nicaragua, the novel is set there for several reasons. It is believed that lesser known groups provided carved columns and other support for the Mayan temples, which were made in geographic areas that are situated today within the borders of Nicaragua. These little known facts should be of interest to students of archeology, history, and even engineering.

In short, this novel is meant for the college classroom. It offers students a creative text dealing with an environmental issue that leads to a social movement. It demonstrates the entanglement of the personal and the public and it reaches into the past to make an historical connection with the present. Anthropologists, archaeologists, historians, rhetoricians, sociologists, psychologists, as well as scholars of business, organizational communication, interpersonal communication, cultural studies and environmental studies will easily find a place in the curriculum for this novel.

Finally, the most compelling aspect of the novel may be found in the universal humanity of it—the joys and struggles of the characters and their interpersonal and cultural relationships. From intercultural studies to interpersonal studies this book asserts a message about humanity that should be studied in the humanities and beyond. Aspiring novelists and students of literature will find the novel an example of how arts-based research moves from in-depth investigation to a literary work and others should find it informative of a world which they may not be familiar.

ACKNOWLEDGMENTS

I wish to thank my friend Jill Vaught and my husband Tim Hack as well as my son Shea Hack for their helpful criticism, editing and general support of my work. I especially want to thank Geyssel González, my Nicaraguan translator, cultural consultant, and (on-line) friend. A thank you to Professor Alejandro Cuza-Blanco for correcting a few of my Spanish errors. An enormous thank you with my personal gratitude to Stephanie Carlo, who provided extensive editorial advice by checking all Spanish and editing the entire novel. I am also very grateful to Professor Joseph Scudder of Northern Illinois University for his expert editorial comments on everything from bird watching to checking my details on geography, cave diving, and mining. My gratitude is unending to those friends who have supported my writing over the years especially, Pam and Jim Finucane, Leonard Cox, who hosted my previous NYC book debut at Barnes & Noble for *Zombie Seed and the Butterfly Blues: A Case of Social Justice*, the prequel to the current novel. Jasmine Tan, who also sponsored a lecture/presentation for me at Manhattan College. A special gratitude to my family. There are so many of you and I love you all—Cory, Melissa, Calle, Shea, Emma, and Katie, plus, Candy, Kate, Jo, Elizabeth, Bob, Jim, and Drew plus partners Bob, Rich, Kathie, Susan, Joey (and all my nieces and nephews). I have also received support from my husband's immediate family and life partners and their children and extended families (especially Susan and Sarah). In particular, thanks to the entire Hallahan family, especially Bobbi and Bud, who provided literary resources on the topic of water. Thank you all so much. I am fortunate to have all of you in my life. I am also indebted to Ralph and Ginny Webb as well as Harry and Dena Targ and Stacey Connaughton for their support of my social justice novels. Most importantly, my thanks to Patricia Leavy (talented author, professor, editor, and so much more), who believed in my abilities to produce a worthy novel and sequel. And to the entire Brill | Sense team, including John Bennett and especially Jolanda Karada for catching both large and small errors, advising me on the cover, selecting endorsements and giving the whole book a clean aesthetic. My gratitude to Keith Berry (professor/writer and genuine human being), who introduced me to Tony Adams, who introduced me to Patricia Leavy. Ah, networking! Without a doubt, great company in which to be. Specifically, with respect to the current novel, *Blood into Water*, I am grateful to Professor Ernest "Chip" Blatchley III for his lectures on water, water sanitation, and sharing his insights in civil and environmental engineering and allowing me to audit his course. And I am grateful to Maria Helena Trujillo for sharing her personal story of being kidnapped in Columbia with other student journalists and asked by the kidnappers to tell their story. I hope she will turn her experience into a full novel someday. Maria Helena's story inspired me to include the chapter on "pirates." My learning about the Bolivian Water Wars inspired me to develop the novel and in particular "corporate pirates" who 'steal' water. This project was supported by a generous fellowship to The Center of Artistic Endeavors from the College of Liberal Arts at Purdue University. Writing the novel required cultural visits to Belize and Guatemala, which I could not have completed without my husband Tim Hack. Thank you for being my travel partner through life.

PRELUDE

In Deep Time,

The Lady Ikoom held the sharp pointed end of a piece of jade against her hand. Standing stoically, she pressed it through her skin, puncturing her palm and drawing a line of blood. She winced slightly, almost imperceptibly. Then turning her palm over, she let blood droplets fall into the deep pool of sacrificial waters.

In Current Time,

…Miguel mustered the courage to walk back into *el barrio* with a bloody nose.
…Delta felt raindrops against her face and tasted blood in her mouth.
…Madera committed himself to the idea that water is gold and winning is everything.
…People shouted, "Water is Life—*¡El agua es vida!*"
…Sofía felt it, then turned her blood-soaked hand over; the blood wasn't hers.
…Caleb tried once more; he reached out his hand. She slapped it away.
…Mona understood, without a word being spoken, that…

Time moves as ocean tides,
Flowing in and out.
Needs float on surface waves, undulating
currents of change,
remain the same,
Blood and Water, Water and Blood
Love and Loss, and
Love…
Blood, not water,
Remains, yet,
Tides forever
change.

Sofía spoke and then wrote:

"Tears speak our truth, a water that washes our souls."

PART 1

NICARAGUA: THE LAND OF FIRE AND WATER

CHAPTER 1

MIGUEL AND SOFÍA

"*¡Agua, Miguel!* We need to fill the water jugs before you go to school," Sofía called to her son.

She lived for mornings!

Mornings began with the brightness that only Miguel could provide. And this morning was no exception.

She felt his presence before he entered the courtyard where she sat working on the mending. His broad smile and quick step demonstrated the vitality that only adolescents can exude under such heat and humidity. And always, whether with joy or sorrow, anger or jealousy, gratitude or longing, her son's emotions arrived on the air currents like a strong eagle. She loved his youthful enthusiasm. Even if it were a day to mope, Miguel would do it with flair, flopping dramatically at his mother's side, bringing a smile to her face. This morning was indeed one of those mornings, Miguel swooped in full of playful energy laced with tenderness.

"Mamá, you have the most beautiful smile in all of Nicaragua." He grabbed a piece of fruit from the basket on the counter and wound up for a pitch.

"The *zapote* is for dessert."

"*Madre*, you're the most beautiful woman in the world. *Mi hermosa madre.*"

She shrugged and went back to sewing.

"I swear it," he promised holding a hand to his heart.

"You're full of little lies," she told her son, returning to the work in her lap. Her long, shiny, black hair fell forward gently draping her profile, concealing a gentle smile.

"I'm full of love for my mother," he insisted, suddenly taking a position on bended knee, directly in front of her. At this, she couldn't help but to break into a full smile, before dipping her head once again to her sewing.

"Ah, I've seen the smile," he boldly announced. "And it's exquisite."

"I have no front teeth," she retorted.

"You don't have to have any teeth to have the most beautiful smile in the entire world. The smile comes from your heart. The smile lives in your eyes. Who needs teeth? Teeth are overrated," Miguel made this last comment as he sank his own strong, white teeth into the reddish gray rind of the plum-like fruit—*zapote*—that he held in his hand.

"Whose mending are you doing?" the boy queried as he chewed.

"Don't speak with your mouth full. And what does it matter who it belongs to?"

"If it's mine, you're a saint. *Reina concebida sin pecado original,* Mother without original sin," he added with hyperbolic flourish and the sign of the cross.

"Don't be irreverent. And if it's someone else's mending?"

"The dogs! They don't pay you enough."

"Oh, so you're the only one deserving of my talents?"

"That goes without saying." The skinny boy, dressed in khaki pants and a red and yellow striped t-shirt, spun his body around, pivoting on one foot and finishing his move in a rapper pose—gang signs, cocked head, pouting lips, and all. He took another bite of the unpeeled *zapote*, the deep pink pulp coloring his lips.

"Where do you learn such dance moves?"

"I have my ways." He started to reach for a second zapote before even having finished the first.

"Those are for after dinner," she scolded again of his eating the sweet fruit. He replaced it.

"Who made up that rule?" He held the first, half-eaten *zapote* in his hand as if it were a baseball, fingers gripped on the edges of the uneaten-side of the fruit. Miguel wound up for a pitch and gave an imaginary release, before returning the sweet snack to his white teeth.

"Be careful you don't swallow any seeds."

"No worries. I'm invulnerable, like Superman. I'm impervious to poison and to pain."

"Where did you learn *that* word?"

"*Superman?* From the comic books."

"No, *impervious.*"

"Ah, the other comic book."

"Do you learn anything at school?"

"Yes, at lunch time I learn which comic books to read."

She smiled again, shook her head and then tenderly scoffed, "Go on now or you'll be late for school. Where is your desk? Where are you books? These things don't come cheap."

"No, I have business today."

"Business!? No, no business. No monkey business. You go to school. I want you to get an education. Then you can get a good job and support us."

"I'll support you. I'm going to be a famous baseball player in the United States, but first business and then baseball."

"First school and then studies. And if you play baseball, you should do it for the glory of your own country—Nicaragua." Miguel's mother knotted the thread and bit the end of the string with her lateral incisors. She didn't want the boy to be a baseball player; she dreamt of his becoming a doctor, an engineer, or even an ambassador to the United Nations. She helped him with his English by speaking it as much as possible.

With the exception of her missing two front teeth, Sofía, without a doubt, would be named the most captivating woman in *el barrio*. "*Hecho,* done," she announced and tossed the shirt into the basket on her left. Another basket, filled with mending, sat to the right of her.

"What happened to your desk? Your uncle will be hurt."

"My desk is too small for me and besides I'm graduating this year. I'll sit on the floor. And Uncle Guillermo will be happy that I gave the chair to a younger boy…"

She lifted another white shirt from the basket, thinking about the day her brother brought the light weight rattan chair with a side arm, on which one could place a workbook, for Miguel to use at school. Not every child could afford to have a desk; some students sat on the floor. His uncle had mended the desk and even enlarged it by weaving

7

additional rows into it over the years. Her head dipped under the memory and realization that at fourteen years of age, Miguel is no longer a child. He looked younger than his years, as did she. Sofía appeared far from thirty-four years old, perhaps it was the tiny waist and slender frame or her large eyes and full lips that added to her youthful appearance; as for Miguel he could easily pass for eleven or twelve, but was proud to be fourteen and graduating from eighth grade.

"...for a good price," Miguel finished his sentence and interrupted her thoughts. "I could be quite a businessman."

"You sold it?! Quite the salesman, selling desks to children." She turned the shirt inside out and glanced at him with disapproval. "It was a gift to you."

"It was too small."

"You should've given it to one of Uncle Guillermo's younger children."

He paused not having thought of this himself, but quickly responded to her, "No, the schools are buying desks these days. So the fact that I sold it shows what a good businessman I am. Uncle Guillermo will be proud of me. I can sell anything." He paused again ever so briefly, thinking hard and fast, strategizing as to what would turn his mother's thoughts away from his deed, and then added, "I could be like the *Americanos Estados de Unidos*. They could sell the air to the birds, and water to the mermaids, if they chose to do so."

"And they would overcharge them."

"The birds?"

"*Sí*, and the mermaids. It's dangerous to get into bed with capitalists and their ideas. They're greedy, too greedy."

"It's a new world, mamá. Everyone is getting into bed with everyone else. Look at the U.S. and Russia. And now, U.S. businessmen only need a Nicaraguan partner to set up factories in Nicaragua. Someday perhaps we'll be as rich as the *Americanos Estados de Unidos*."

"I think there's a bit more to it than that *and* we're rich in other things. We don't need to be like the *Americanos Estados de Unidos*."

"Amardo says that you can get whatever you want out of the trash in the United States. People in the States are so rich that they throw away their old things every spring and buy new ones. You can get furniture, TVs, computers, whatever you want. Just go pick it up and it's yours. And I've heard that baseball players make more money than anybody." His voice rose with excitement.

"Humph. How would Amardo know what it's like in the United States? Has he been there?" she asked him sarcastically while reaching into the basket on her right.

"He knows people. Reynaldo's mother is in the States. She calls him on his cell phone every month. Reynaldo tells Amardo, and he tells me."

"What is Reynaldo doing with a cell phone? No, wait, don't tell me. I don't want to know. Don't hang around with Reynaldo."

"I'm hanging around with Amardo. He tells me about the States." The boy switched the topic again saying, "We should go." Miguel purposefully veered the topic away from Reynaldo, a wanna-be gang member, of whom his mother clearly disapproved. Not so long ago, Miguel had proudly told his mother, *Reynaldo can pocket around fifty dollars a month from selling drugs,* only to receive a slap across his cheek. She'd never struck him before. But the thought of him selling drugs both frightened and revolted her. Miguel's mother didn't want her son near gang members.

"Really, we should go," Miguel insisted.

"To the United States? How would we get there? Too dangerous. Too expensive. Too many capitalists. What do you want to do, hop a train and take a vacation at Disneyland? *Hola*, Mickey Mouse." The thought of them shaking hands with Mickey Mouse's three giant fingers made her laugh. Her toothless smile radiated like sunshine filling the small room.

"Mamá, Nicaraguans do not take *vacations* in the United States." She had meant to make him laugh and he knew it, but that was his job—to make *her* laugh.

"I'll call it what I like, *vacation*, is as good a choice as any other description. They visit for a while before being deported, that's a kind of vacation," with that said, she softened her toothless expression. The thought of her son trying to take the long journey to the U.S. terrified her. *It's dangerous, so many people die trying to make the trip*, she thought. *Or families are fractured, split up.* The thought of losing her son, even being separated from him, ripped her soul in half. She couldn't bear the idea. She thought of how in the past Latin families, especially from the more conflicted countries—El Salvador, Guatemala, and so on, did it to themselves—mothers, fathers, whoever, left their children to go to the U.S. for jobs, always promising to send money and return or send for the children later. Fractured families had become all too common. Then men started using children to get across the border. Now, the fracturing of families is coming from another angle, the U.S. has been ripping babies from their mothers' arms. The stories were on the local Nicaraguan news. All of it broke her heart. She could not bear the thought of ever being separated from Miguel. She changed the subject.

"Back to the here and now. School!" she demanded of him.

"Today school can wait. I need to make some money for us."

"We don't need money; I make enough," she countered with authority.

"When I take you to the United States, I'll buy you new clothes. No more washing and mending other people's clothes. They have machines to wash clothes in the U.S. And I'll buy us a flat screen TV."

"We have a TV."

"But we have no electricity."

"Details," she countered with a small shrug.

"No, we could have our own generator, if I make more money. I'll go to school tomorrow," he promised.

Sofía Rodríguez sighed, a half-hearted sigh, as she gave into her son's wishes. She was not as strict as she pretended, nor as noble as others made her out to be; the extra money wouldn't hurt. And both she and the boy knew this.

He loved when their interchanges reached *the sigh*. Some days it took more coaxing, more love, more performance on his part, but always when he heard her sigh, he knew that he had won his mother's heart and his own way.

"If you become rich by the end of the day, buy some *jocote (jocode)* and *ahuacatl* (a waktl) at the market and maybe more *zapotes,"* Miguel's mother added.

"*Ahuacatl*? Don't speak Aztec to me."

"*Aguacate (aguacatee)*, Avocado. If you become rich, I would like an avocado."

"*Sí*, you'll have all the avocados you want."

"Buy at the end of the day, when the produce is cheaper," she instructed.

"*Sí*."

"And, Miguel," she paused for effect, "no drugs." Sofía looked directly into his large brown eyes as she said this.

"Mamá, I'm surprised at you. Disappointed even. You know I don't do that sort of thing. You know me better than that. Now, I must be about my business."

"Oh, wait! Help me with the water before you leave." They would be too tired in the evening to fill the heavy water jugs and besides, running water might not be available at the spigot at the end of the day. They needed to move quickly before the government turned it and the electricity off for the morning.

So went the mornings.

Evenings were different. For Sofía, they felt heavy and dull under the exhaustion and humidity of the long, hot day. But every night, after sending Miguel to bed, she would lay her head on the pillow, close her eyes to the lonely night, and say to herself, *I will live for the morning, for my son.*

CALEB

Caleb lived for adventures! Although he never said so. It was always couched in the reasonable explanation. He knew this was the lie he was living but whenever the truth got close to the surface, he blanketed it with his life's cover story.

I'm on assignment, he would tell anyone who asked. But not this time. This time the assignment was the secret.

Adrenaline stoked expectations, fueled his body and mind, even though he had been 'on assignment' enough times to know that the thrills were few and the mundane encounters many.

Disliking only the fact that every story contains the minutia, the bureaucratic, the sensible details and boring constraints, made him sigh. Or maybe he was just tired. The plane had landed and was now rolling slowly, coasting along a hot tarmac. "Please remain seated, ..." He hated how such things slow the story down, especially "for your own safety." *Bullshit,* he thought. *It is never for the people's safety; it is always to protect the company—liability. Of course, they never announce "Please remain seated; it's for the company's financial safety."* He smiled as he imagined someone announcing that over the P.A. It didn't matter though, no one was listening, or at least no one was paying attention, as no one was following the instructions. Few passengers could be convinced of the rolling possible danger. And those who were still seated were more engaged with stretching than thinking about safety. As for Caleb, life wasn't meant to be lived safely.

"Please remain seated until the plane has come to a complete stop," a disembodied voice spoke through the intercom, for the second time; the phrase had been first spoken in Spanish and then repeated in English. "This is for your safety and the safety of the passengers around you." Like so many others, Caleb had already unbuckled his seat belt and stood in a stooped manner under the overhang. Waiting. At last, the plane jerked to a final stop.

Stretching into the aisle, angling his head out from under the overhang, watching those ahead of him side stepping this way and that as they unloaded overhead bins and collected their belongings, Caleb also began the disembarking process. Along with a plane full of passengers who had arrived mid-morning at Augusto C. Sandino International Airport in Managua, and after taking a red eye flight from Chicago, due mostly to the lengthy layover and his determination to stay awake, Caleb now stood bleary-eyed. He never slept while traveling, not anymore. He had learned his lesson more than five years ago when he had taken a train at night from Barcelona to Madrid where he had fallen asleep using his backpack as a pillow, carefully protecting it from theft by having wrapped the shoulder strap around his arm. No one had stolen the backpack; however, securing it to his arm didn't keep thieves from slicing a thin opening in the pocket and lifting his passport, papers, and wallet. He never made that mistake again. He would sleep later.

Now, he stood cramped by the tight seats and overhang for carry-on luggage. Perspiration dripped down the back of his neck and under his arms. He reached into the seat pocket, checking for whether he had finished the water in the plastic bottle. The heat on the plane caused the last drops to condense against the inside walls of the clear container, bottle fog ensued. He shook it nonetheless, removed the cap, tipped it full upright and tapped the last droplets into his waiting, open mouth.

He traveled light, still wanting to be able to keep his possessions close at hand—via carry on. But at the last minute, the airlines determined that his duffel bag was too big for the overhead bins, forcing him to check it. He pulled out his phone, charger, and packet of information that his friend and mentor, Tracker, had given to him and put those in his inside jacket pocket before handing over his duffel bag. He kept a pad of paper and pen in the side pocket—old-fashioned back up—the mark of a well-trained reporter. Sunglasses in the other side pocket. Clothes and shoes can be replaced easily enough, he had thought, but the packet containing his passport, hotel address, and the contact information for Professor López could not.

Nicaragua hit him like a blast furnace when he finally exited the plane. He felt the hot air suck the last breath of air-conditioned airplane oxygen from his lungs and replace it with an equatorial effusion. As if he had just emerged from a dark cave, the brightness of the sun seared the tarmac and bounced into his retinas causing him to squint. No need for a canopy today. The skies were psychedelic blue. Tiny flecks of light danced in the air. He fished out his sunglasses and put them on as he made his way down the metal stairs that had been rolled into place and secured for the disembarking passengers.

He followed the crowd toward the first customs check point. Passports first. Luggage later. Tired travelers stood in sluggish lines waiting for their papers to be reviewed. Caleb pulled his passport out of his inside jacket pocket that he carried over his arm, and looked at the cover—a dark navy blue with gold lettering, PASSPORT written at the top, the eagle with arrows in one set of talons and an olive branch in the other, *E Pluribus Unum* lettered on the ribbon flying behind the eagle, *United States of America* lettered at the bottom. He studied it as if he'd never considered the details before; he was tired.

"Next."

Caleb placed his passport on the counter. The uniformed officer opened it with exaggerated flourish, as if annoyed that it was not already on the proper page. He flipped past pages stamped in various colored inks—Spain, Netherlands, U.K., Greece. He flipped again to the first page—photo. The immigration clerk glanced down, glanced up, turned the passport page, glanced down, glanced up. "Caleb Barthes?"

Caleb nodded.

"Illinois?"

Caleb nodded again.

"Chicago?" the officer guessed.

"Yes."

"Birthdate?"

"August 10, 1980," Caleb answered.

"Reason for coming to Nicaragua?"

"Educational," Caleb answered.

"Educational?" The authority figure sought details with one word, intonated with disbelief and an accusatory glance.

"I'm meeting a professor from the university to learn more about water issues in Nicaragua, especially water reclamation and purification." Tracker had told him not to give away his reporter status.

The uniformed officer shifted his glance as well as his tenor.

"*Dios nos dio agua,*" the guard announced, adding, "Watch what you do with your *educational information.*"

It sounded like a threat to Caleb, a threat that he didn't understand. Nevertheless, he mentally filed the incident with other information that had been given to him about water issues before he had left Chicago. As for his Spanish-speaking abilities, they were limited as he was a bit rusty. He made out the words *Dios* and *agua*—God and water. But, then again, he thought, maybe it was just his brain fog that kept him from catching the rest.

"How long will you be in Nicaragua, the land of lakes *and volcanoes?*"

Again Caleb heard an ominous warning in the officer's emphasis, especially as he had said, *and volcanoes,* but could not process the hidden meaning. Images of water and fire passed through his mind's eye, shimmering azure pools and turbulent cauldrons of burning reds and yellows tinged in blue.

"Ten days," Caleb answered.

"Where will you stay?"

"The hotel *Vellejos.*"

"You have a reservation?"

"Yes."

The customs agent looked down once more at the photo of Caleb Barthes, handsome with dark brown hair waving slightly across his forehead, blue eyes, the color of the Caribbean Sea, pale skin, a hint of a smile. He double checked the image against the bleary eyed, six foot, one-inch traveler who stood before him.

"Okay," he said tersely, before stamping the page, closing it and handing it back to Caleb. And then, without welcoming Caleb to Nicaragua, the officer dismissed him with a curt, "Next."

"Oh," the officer called him back. "Don't forget to stop and get your tourist card." The officer pointed to another window, with another line, where another agent sat on a stool attending to visitors.

"No, I'm not a tourist. I'm here for—"

"No difference. Pay at the next window. Twelve dollars. U.S. money. Carry the card with you at all times. This is for your safety."

Caleb sighed.

MIGUEL MEETS CALEB

"Hey, *Norte-Americano*, you put a look on your face like you know where you're going. I like that about you. Confident. Already I like you. We should be friends," Miguel cajoled.

Caleb turned to find the Nicaraguan boy walking along side of him, trying to keep up with Caleb's long stride. Caleb didn't respond. He continued in search of the baggage claim after having collected his tourist card.

"I can show you where to go," Miguel told him.

"I know where I'm going," Caleb answered with only a quick look at the boy. Young, slender, copper skin, brown eyes and dark hair that he had flipped from his forehead.

"Sure. Sure. You follow the pictures to baggage claim, but what then? What then?"

"Then I get my baggage."

"Yes, but you already passed the baggage, Cowboy," the boy told him. Caleb turned and looked behind and then in the opposite direction."

"*Sí*, those suitcases over there, they are the luggage from your flight."

Caleb had walked past the bags thinking that they were a collection of lost luggage. *Where is the carousel? Is the Managua airport really that small, that there is only one place to collect your bag?* he wondered.

"I see you taking in broad glances of our modern international airport, searching. Searching for what, I ask myself. Ah, he needs to rent a car. He needs to go to a bank. He needs to find his hotel. But first, luggage, and then the car."

"Motorcycle."

"*Sí*. That's exactly what I was thinking, that you are a modern cowboy who needs a motorcycle. From Texas, right? Am I right?" Miguel circled around Caleb like an excitable puppy.

"How did you get in here?" Caleb wondered how the boy got past airport personnel.

"I have my ways. But mostly I am a lost boy searching for his mother. I am irresistible, no?" Miguel looked with wide, orphan-like eyes. "Now, where did you say you are from?"

"Chicago."

"Chicago!" Miguel said with enthusiasm. "A gangster."

"Not a gangster."

"You don't have to be coy with me, Al Capone. I'll keep your secret."

Now Caleb let a small smile slip across his lips. "Shouldn't you be in school?"

"School?! No, it's a holiday."

"Is that so? What holiday is it?" Caleb joined a small crowd that had begun their wait for luggage.

"Help an Americano Day. I plan to assist you."

Caleb didn't want assistance. His head was beginning to throb from the lack of sleep, dehydration, and the incessant jabbering of the juvenile at his side. In addition, he realized that he needed to be on guard from this little Nicaraguan artful dodger.

"I'm practically the ambassador of tourism." The boy watched as Caleb's face drew tighter. Miguel changed his posture and his tone, saying, "Please, I want only to practice my English." Caleb's countenance softened, even though he knew this was just another ploy. The boy's English was nearly perfect. The reporter sighed and pretended to fall for the ruse.

Caleb Barthes, the Chicago journalist, leaned against a pillar, and said, "They took my bag from me at the last minute. Will it be here among these bags?"

"I will find it and make sure it is safe." With that said, Miguel looked up and down the rows of bags.

"What color is it?" he asked Caleb. "Is it here yet? I will carry it for you."

Caleb scanned the area and shook his head. His bag was not in view.

Miguel opened the door with impunity to the outside where employees scuttled bags from the tarmac to inside. Calling out to the airport baggage handler in Spanish first, "*¡Mi amigo le gustaría equipaje!*" And then the boy translated the phrase calling out again, "My friend would like his luggage." Miguel turned to Caleb, asking, "My English, pretty good, no?"

Baggage handlers shouted at the boy. He turned to Caleb and gave him a wink; he then waited, glancing toward the door. "You'll see," he told Caleb in English. Then he called through the opening again, in Spanish first, saying: "*Hoy sería bueno.*" "I told them, *Today would be nice.*" Miguel then reopened the door and stood holding it as if being a good helper.

"*Vámonos,*" one of the bag handlers shouted, "before I call the authorities." Caleb heard another voice, saying something like *Sofía's hijo* and the conversation ended. Within seconds Miguel was standing beside Caleb. "Soon, you see, soon, your bag, I bet you a million *córdobas*, it'll be next, Cowboy," Miguel told Caleb.

Caleb looked at the boy. He couldn't be more than eleven or twelve years old, Caleb thought.

"I'm not a cowboy."

"Gangster?"

Caleb grinned.

"See, I knew you were a gangster from the moment I set eyes on you. Clyde Barrow. Handsome. Daring. Lover to Bonnie Parker. *Famosos fugitivos*—Bonnie and Clyde.*"

Caleb smiled. His distemper and headache began to subside. "How do you know such things?"

"My mother and I watch old movies. We know lots of things. What color is your bag, Clyde?"

"Brown, with a baseball cap hooked to the straps."

Miguel looked concerned. He leapt toward the door, opened it, and shouted to the workers, "*Mis compadres*, would you look for my friend's bag? It's brown and has his baseball cap attached. He is an important baseball player from Chicago. So don't steal his cap."

"We're not thieves," a voice yelled back in Spanish and a few seconds later the bag with a baseball cap appeared in the hand of an airport worker who set it down and shook his head at the impish boy.

"Ah, I'm relieved; I've saved your cap," Miguel said with Caleb's duffel bag in tow. The agile boy then swung it into Caleb's waiting hands. "Thieves. You must watch out for thieves," the boy asserted strongly, before adding, "I'll take good care of you, my friend." He led the way.

"Now, we'll go and get you a motorcycle."

"What about customs?"

"What customs?"

"Don't they have to check my bags?"

Miguel laughed. "People try to smuggle things out of Nicaragua—cocaine, heroin, illegal immigrants. What would you smuggle *in* from the U.S.?"

Caleb was too tired to think about it. He shook his head, shrugged his shoulder.

"Come. Come. This way to the motorcycles."

NICARAGUAN TRANSPORTATION

"Wait, this way takes us out of the airport," Caleb objected, turning in the other direction toward ground transportation, rentals.

"No, no, you don't want to rent your car at the airport," Miguel said.

"Motorcycle," Caleb corrected.

"*Sí, sí,* motorcycle. Even still they'll overcharge you. It's not that they are thieves or even capitalists but they will charge you more, much more. Google it, if you don't believe me."

Without a word Caleb googled the airport prices in comparison to off-site prices and confirmed that the airport rental services charged 15% to 20% more than city dealers. The boy was telling the truth.

"And you say they are not capitalists," Caleb sarcastically questioned the boy.

"No, no, of course not, they have the right to charge more. After all, they're also selling the convenience, *sí*? And I'm just trying to help you save money. Everyone knows that *Americanos Estado Unidos* like to find the best deal, yes? We'll take the bus—*Transport Nicaragua*. Very cheap. And you'll see *the real Nicaragua.*"

The real Nicaragua, Caleb thought, *the genuine, authentic Nicaragua. Is there such a thing in this era of globalization? Generations of colonization followed by internal strife, battles over capitalism or communism—imported theoretical practices like imported beer or Coca-Cola. The real thing. To quench your thirst.* The thought triggered Caleb's literal thirst; his throat grew more parched as they made their way through the terminal toward the bus stop. *Ah,* he spied a water fountain, pressed the lever, but no water sprung forth.

"No water?" he asked his ambassador of tourism.

"What do you expect, we are a third world country; Marx never promised us a rose garden. Even if there were water, I'm not sure you should drink it."

"I think Marx promised lots of things from communism," Caleb added.

"Oh, you're as bad as my mother. There is no such thing anymore. Communism. Capitalism. It's all jumbled together. More like social-corruptalism."

Caleb smiled. He couldn't argue that point. The boy was growing up postmodern.

"So what should we do to keep the world safe?" Caleb asked the boy as he thought of the history of communism being transported and imported from Marx and the young Hegelians in Europe to Lenin's Russia and Mao's China, and finally back again, westward to the colonized lands of Cuba, Venezuela, and Nicaragua. The word, *Sandinistas,* floated across Caleb's mental map. *A word that still frightens the older generation,* Caleb thought.

"How do we save the world?" Miguel repeated before answering, "Baseball."

"Baseball?" Caleb smiled again as he hadn't thought of baseball in association with Nicaragua or communism or capitalism for that matter. *Hhmm.* He tried to piece together the disparate vision of Sandinistas playing baseball, but the image wouldn't stick; it made no sense. His disjointed thoughts were easily interrupted as they approached the bus and he spied the words, *Transport Nicaragua,* painted on the side of an old, refurbished school bus that had been painted white to cover the standard school bus yellow. *A hand-me-down from the global north?*

The boy spoke quickly in Spanish to the driver and handed him the fare. Caleb watched the transaction. Then they boarded the bus, made their way to the back and settled in for the ride.

"A whole córdoba to ride the bus?" Caleb asked as they nestled into their seats.

"No, no, not usually. Usually, it costs fifteen cents, but he will take us to the car rental, which is not a usual stop. This is why I pay him more, for better service, for you, my friend."

Caleb looked straight ahead. The bus was nearly full of riders. The backs of the metal bus seats were painted bright red and the backs of short Mestizo girls' heads could be seen just above the seatbacks.

Black ponytails bounced with the bumpy ride. The bus driver made another stop and three more people boarded—two men and a woman. One was a middle-aged man who stood with his wares bundled into a large plastic bag the size of a dry-cleaner bag. The man balanced his burden on one shoulder as he made his way down the aisle. A short, round woman followed him down the aisle and plopped exhausted into a seat. The third new passenger, after having taken the last seat, adjusted a tin-foil-lined tray filled with baked goods, in his lap. Cinnamon aroma wafted through the air on the warm breeze that came from open windows.

Each seat had been taken and one man was left standing when the bus stopped and picked up several more commuters, all shorter in stature than the six foot, one inch, Caleb Barthes. All carrying wares, or food, or clothing. One man held a cardboard box filled with bottled water. With no seats left, he took his place in the aisle along with two women carrying bags of laundry. Caleb would have offered his seat to the women, had they not been separated by several other travelers, including the man holding the box of bottled water. Caleb stared at the water and unconsciously licked his dry lips.

Miguel noticed, "I'll get you one." In response Caleb pulled a twenty from his wallet. "No, no, put that away," the boy insisted quickly, forcing the bill back toward Caleb's wallet and glancing around to see if anyone had noticed. Caleb shoved it into his pocket, deciding not to bare his wallet again. Miguel made the inquiries in Spanish and then gave the man one *córdoba*. Bottled water was passed back.

"Do you want one?" Caleb offered.

"No, no, I'm fine," the boy lied. Caleb drank the water without hesitation. He paused only once before finishing most of it. And only then could he focus on the details of the bus, beyond what little he had taken in at first.

The red metal seatbacks glimmered with chipped paint, but no rust appeared on the metal bars. Torn seat cushions showed loose stuffing beside his leg, the rips were small. The floor of the bus appeared dusty, and quite dry. The ceiling, which he noticed as he drained the water bottle, had been painted a salmon color. The front of the bus had been painted sea green and the high dash and window frame around the driver's front window had been decorated with stickers of cartoon characters—Sylvester the Cat, Tweety Bird, Yosemite Sam. *How old is this bus?* Caleb wondered. A rosary hung from the mirror. A scapular behind it. He could no longer see the back of the driver's head, as more passengers embarked and none had disembarked. As his view became more and more restricted, he allowed himself to relax into the smells of the bus—fried bread and fresh fish, accompanied the cinnamon aroma he'd registered earlier, all of this was occasionally disturbed by someone's flatulence. One man farted loudly and others laughed. Caleb smiled at the thought of it—mankind united by a simple action, an uncontrolled fart unleashed into public space, answered with laughter.

Perhaps, this is the real Nicaragua as the boy had promised, Caleb thought. True enough he would probably not have had this experience if he had taken a taxi to the Hilton hotel—Managua—as so many tourists might do. In experiencing an authentic Nicaragua, he felt superior, not to Nicaraguans, but to other writers, other reporters, his story would excel with realistic details of the *global South. A place and time which moved via refitted and repainted buses from the U.S. with Looney Tunes cartoon characters keeping watchful eyes on Mestizos as they go about their daily business, a people, like any other, only complicated by centuries of colonization.* He played with the sentences in his mind, considering how he might use them in a future article while his head bounced in rhythm with the road. His eyes closed. He drifted in and out of sleep, jerking awake every few seconds to check his belongings.

"Our stop," the boy said. The two made their way to the front of the bus and exited down the sticky, rubber-covered steps. Caleb followed Miguel through a parking lot and into a small office, where the boy negotiated the rental price of the motorcycle.

"How long?" he asked Caleb.

"How long?" Caleb repeated the question instead of answering it.

"How long are you staying in Nicaragua?" Miguel sounded impatient, the dealer needed to know.

"I don't know," Caleb told him.

"You have to know," an indignant Miguel demanded. "What did you tell the immigration officer who checked your passport?"

"I told him ten days."

"Ten days then," Miguel finished brokering the deal. "You pay now," the boy told him. "Does he take credit cards?" Caleb asked.

"Of course, he is a reputable dealer. What do you think, we are a third world country?"

"Of course not," Caleb politely lied as he finalized the payment and signed papers for the rental. Apparently, it was okay for the boy to make sport of his country, but very impolite of Caleb to question the status of Nicaragua.

The boy's amiable nature returned as they rode through the streets of Nicaragua. He sat behind Caleb and shouted into his ear, "You and I, we are like Che Guevera and Alberto Granado, no?"

"Only if I'm Che. He was the more handsome," Caleb pointed out.

"Now I know you need food and more water, you must be suffering from heat stroke. I'm clearly the more beautiful of the two of us."

Miguel closed his eyes and smiled at the fresh feeling of freedom, the wind in his face, as he rode the motorcycle that descended the slight hill. *The real hills are inland,* the boy thought, imagining what it would be like to fly, with emotion, down the Nicaraguan hillsides on the back of his own motorcycle. Nearing the bottom of this little knoll, he opened his eyes.

"Turn left."

Caleb leaned to the left as he took the turn. Miguel leaned gently with the flow.

"Stop up here on your right."

"Is this where my hotel is located?" Caleb asked as he pulled the bike to the right.

"No, no. This is where the market is located."

"I don't want the market; I want to go to my hotel."

"I understand. I understand. You're tired, but trust me you need some commodities."

"What commodities?" Caleb sighed despondently and gave little attention to the boy's answer. Instead, he dismounted the motorbike, pulled his phone from his pocket and tapped on the *maps app*.

"Still you don't trust me? I'm offended, my friend. Didn't I get you a better deal on the motorcycle than you could've gotten for yourself? Didn't I pay for your bus ride—one *córdoba*? And when you found the water fountain at the airport without enough pressure to supply you with a drink of water, didn't I find the bottled water for you that I bought with the last of my own money? What would you do without me? And I believe it is I who must consider whether to trust you? You haven't yet asked to go to the bank where you could exchange your U.S. dollars and pay me back for the water or the bus transport that I bought for you."

Caleb let Miguel carry on as he checked his current location against the address of the hotel.

"Here, at the market, we'll buy, for you, more water and a few avocados and sapodillas. You're probably hungry right now. Tortillas are plentiful in the market. You also need matches and candles. Maybe some toilet paper."

Caleb gave the boy a quizzical and skeptical look.

"I saw over your shoulder the name of your hotel. It's not exactly the Hilton, *amigo*," Miguel quipped. "Who made these reservations for you, anyway?"

Caleb thought of his friend and mentor, Tracker, who had planned on coming himself, but due to unforeseen health problems, was forced to stay in Chicago. The sixty-year-old Tracker, fluent in Spanish, and familiar with Nicaragua, had made reservations at a 'cheap' hotel, only warning Caleb that the giant insects he would encounter are not really cockroaches. Caleb had questioned him further, *and if they are not really cockroaches, what are they really? Ah,* Tracker had said, *if only we could unmask them, but they are afraid of the light and they move very fast.* And then Tracker had added, *No worries, really. They're harmless, for the most part.*

Caleb, now believing he would need water, food and candles wondered just how rustic this hotel would be, but he didn't ask his new-found minister of tourism, the boy at his side, who still babbled about how much Caleb relied upon his skillful services. Instead, Caleb quietly imagined the worst. After all, Tracker was frugal even when the *Chicago Tribune* was picking up the tab, but this time the newspaper had made no promises as Tracker had been unable to convince the editor that he would really find the story he was seeking. Even more reason to be tight, Tracker would have felt, especially since he had promised to reimburse his young friend, Caleb, on his return. Now standing in the hot sun, on an unmarked street, Caleb wiped sweat from his forehead. *Perhaps, the boy is right; maybe, I do need a few 'commodities.'*

"You are hot, no? Of course you are hot. Nicaragua has only two temperatures: hot and hotter. Come, come. Let's get you some more water." Miguel led the way. Caleb followed, walking the motorcycle around the corner and into the Managua marketplace.

THE MARKET

Managua marketplaces are alive—bursting with color, teeming with smells, bustling with people, rippling with movement, burning to be consumed. This marketplace lived on *Calle Miramar*, Caleb noted the street name after spotting the address on the front of a store. A fact that seemed less important to him the more he let himself be surrounded by the ambiance of the market. It called to him. Through the Caribbean music and savory smells, the bright colors and curving paths between the kiosks, the market welcomed the visitor, embraced him and simultaneously seemed completely unaware of him.

Make-shift lean-to's divided one booth from the next and trailed down both sides of the street. Tents protected vendors from the prickly heat of a piercing sun. Umbrellas, of every stripe and color, stood high, shading fruit and vegetables. Customers wound their way from stand to stand in no particular order. People passed him on the left and on the right as he walked the motorbike slowly through the throng down the center of the street. He stood a good head taller than the people of the market; and yet, he felt smaller than the whole affair, as the market washed over him like a giant wave of color and sound and smells. He followed his little companion as the street turned into a maze of booth-lined pathways.

A plump woman with dark hair and white blouse jostled past him, balancing a turquoise tray on her head with watermelon slices poking out of the top, green rind and pink pulp. It made him turn slightly, only to discover a new vision. Another woman, with bronze skin and shiny black hair, stood bagging tomatoes from her stand for a customer. Her hand collected the red fruit from the top of the wide pyramid of tomatoes and placed them in a clear, plastic bag. Caleb watched the vendor as she quickly flicked her wrist, swinging the transparent baggy around, tightening the top like a noose before knotting the bag full of tomatoes for the customer. Money was exchanged without a word, as if customer and vendor had read each other's minds. The language of the market is either noisy with negotiation or silent with acceptance.

The boy picked up a *zapote*, weighed it in his palm, and assessed its color. "We can do better," he said. He moved on. Caleb followed him from stand to stand where the scent of onions and pineapples wafted in the air, one smell replacing the next, barely giving the brain time to process the scents, where beans and rice sizzled next to meat and the smell of grilled chapattis whetted the appetite. Avocados and *zapotes* complemented each other like Christmas decorations—red and green, where beans and yams spoke of earth and dirt in the best of ways, where piles of plantains and big-bulbs of garlic announced their status as necessities and peppers reigned supreme. Ah, the peppers—bell peppers, jalapeño peppers, cherry peppers, small serrano peppers, cayenne peppers, tabasco peppers, *rocoto* peppers, and the hottest of them all, at least at this market stand, the *habanera* peppers filled the booths and colored the stands. Peppers sat in boxes and in baskets, on burlap and on newspaper, but the hottest hung from fishing lines strung across the back of the stands, dangling heat—blazing red, green, orange, and pink.

"There," the boy pointed. Caleb looked in the direction of the pointed finger and saw only a basket stand. The whole color of which appeared to be burlap brown, with the exception of the tiny woman's hair and turquoise blouse. Surrounded by a sea of hemp, her shiny black hair streaked with silver, and bright print blouse stood out against the weaving, even if her skin did not. Tanned and wrinkled with age, her skin appeared lined like the baskets that she wove. Her fingers moved hemp threads deftly, crisscrossing into diamond patterns. Caleb turned to his companion, Miguel, with quizzical eyes.

"No, no. There!"

Then Caleb saw it—the next booth, a tortilla stand—to which Miguel had pointed. Caleb inhaled deeply. His mouth watered. Steaming griddles stood in front of the booth; heat seared the combination of chopped onions, tomatoes, sweet peppers, rice and tiny bits of chicken that sizzled on the grill. Caleb needed no further directing. He led the way now; his hunger pulling him toward the grill.

As they came closer, they watched the grill master, a heavy set man, wearing a bright yellow t-shirt, as he flipped the ingredients, chopped them, and flipped them again with the side of his large, stainless steel spatula, moving the morsels around and around and bringing them back together, corralling them into one flavorful combination. The swish and clicks of the *espátula* kept rhythm like a salsa dance. A short woman, worked quickly by the grill master's side, removing warmed tortillas from the grill with her fingertips and laying them on a countertop. They worked in tandem—the grill master slapped a spatula full of the grilled mixture into each tortilla and she quickly rolled and wrapped them. Miguel ordered one and handed it to Caleb. The woman reached out her hand.

"Quick, quick, I'm out of money; do you still have the $20.00 bill?"

Caleb had kept the $20.00 in his pocket, safer than always pulling out one's wallet. He handed over the money without a second thought to his little minister of tourism and greedily sank his teeth into the spicy and flavorful tortilla. Once a sense of satisfaction swelled through him and between bites, Caleb insisted that the boy get one for himself. Miguel spoke in Spanish, ordering a second tortilla and negotiating an exchange rate for Caleb's money with the vendor. He gave Caleb the change and they ate as they walked. Once sated, they made their way through the stands, buying avocados, *zapotes*, plantains, tomatoes, garlic, peppers, bottled water, fried bread, candles and matches, and one roll of toilet paper. All of which Miguel carried in a burlap sack bought from the elderly weaver, whom Caleb had seen earlier.

The marketplace had wrapped its arms around them, fed them, nourished them with foods and flavors, with colors and smells, and with music and energy. Life-giving, sustaining, like mother's milk, *la leche*. For the first time today, Caleb felt nourished, comfortable, relaxed. This time, it was Miguel who reminded Caleb that they had responsibilities.

"It's getting late. We need to go to the bank and then your hotel," Miguel told Caleb.

"Hotel, first," Caleb insisted. "I want to know I have place to sleep." He'd now been awake more than twenty-eight hours. He googled the hotel, glanced at the map on his phone, looked up to check the street signs, there were none. They had turned so many corners weaving their way in and out of booths that Caleb thought they had surely changed streets.

"What street is this?"

"The street with the marketplace—*Calle Miramar*."

"And the cross street?"

"The street that leads to the marketplace."

"Yes, but what's the name of it?"

Miguel shrugged.

"Well, do you know how to get here?" Caleb showed the boy the name of the hotel again.

"Sure, sure, I know this place."

"Are you positive?"

"*Sí*, positive. But I don't think you'll like it."

"I'll be the judge of that," Caleb remarked and thought that all he needed is a pillow for his head. Caleb had slept on enough hard floors or in the open on the earth and dirt of places like Afghanistan to be less than picky; and now, his exhaustion was catching up with him quickly.

CHAPTER 6

THE MOTEL

Caleb kick started the Yamaha and then the boy climbed onto the motorbike behind him. Balancing the burlap sack of groceries and Caleb's duffel bag, Miguel's light frame bounced on the backseat of the motorbike. Caleb shifted gears. Miguel juggled the armful of packages, tightening his grip as the bike jerked forward. At last, they breezed along the road.

After navigating through the streets of Managua, passing cinderblock buildings and strip malls with restaurants, ice cream stands, pharmacies, and clothing stores, after passing parking lots and weaving through streets lined with low-built, sun-drenched homes, they arrived at a dusky rose-colored building—a motel, where a handful of barefoot children played in the unpaved parking lot, kicking a semi-deflated ball amongst themselves. Aside from the children, the place looked deserted of occupants. The long, low building with blue doors every twenty feet or so were closed to the noise of the children playing. Only two cars sat idly in the lot. A mangy dog lay listless in front of the office door, the only open door at the motel. Caleb parked the bike and went inside. Miguel followed.

A man who appeared to be in his forties sat at a folding table, his head resting on the tabletop.

"*Hola*, are you in charge?" Caleb asked.

The man lifted his head. He looked from Caleb to the boy. Miguel spoke in Spanish, "*¿Eres el gerente?*"

"*Si.*"

"I have a reservation," Caleb told him. The manager looked to the boy.

"He has a reservation. It's not tricky! *Reservation-reservación.*" Miguel said to the man.

The manager burped and laughed simultaneously. And then laughed some more. "Ah, a reservation," he repeated. "That is funny." The laughter needed no translating.

"What's so funny?" Caleb asked Miguel with a straight face.

"Do you want me to ask him?"

"Yes, and tell him my friend said that he made a reservation for me at this motel," Caleb instructed. Miguel translated.

Once again the man laughed and then spoke in Spanish.

"What did he say?" Caleb asked. Miguel swallowed hard and then translated. "He said, your friend has played a joke on you. No one has made a reservation at this motel, ever."

Caleb swallowed his irritation. "Well, ask him if he has any vacancies."

"He also wants to know, who is your friend that made you a reservation?"

Caleb thought of his mentor, the seasoned reporter, Tracker, who had given this assignment to him, but he didn't answer.

"Never mind, I think I know," the manager said in Spanish with a smile and shake of his head. Miguel didn't bother to translate.

"Ask him again if there are any rooms available."

Miguel translated again and Caleb watched as the manager stood slowly, encumbered by hard belly fat; he recovered a set of keys from a hook on the wall. The intrusion on his quiet afternoon had lost its humorous side. His laughter had subsided and turned into a serious squint as he left the office and walked outdoors to face the broiling sun. Miguel and Caleb followed the manager as he walked to the end of the motel, where without using the keys that he had brought along, he opened the blue door with a brusque shove. *Apparently, the keys are for show only,* Caleb thought and gave a side glance to his little buddy. Miguel responded with a shrug and a raised eyebrow.

"I like the way they jingle," the proprietor offered as explanation and laughed again, regaining his good humor. The manager ignored the door knob and pushed the door wider before stepping back for Caleb to see. The cinder block walls met a dirty cement floor. A twin size mattress on box springs took most of the space, allowing for only a small nightstand and chair to share the remaining square footage. A window, of tempered-fire block glass, let a dull ray of light into the room, beyond that of what the open doorway produced, and in the softened sunbeam, flecks of dust danced with abandon.

The room reeked. The top sheet had been loosely draped over the bed, no bedspread existed; no need. Pillow? One. Lifeless, flat pillow. No air conditioner. Not even a fan. Caleb crossed the room with a quick couple of steps and threw back the threadbare sheet.

Holy Shit! They're huge! Caleb thought as he watched the giant, hard-shelled insects with creepy feelers quickly making their escape. The tripod sprinters ran in different directions for cover from the sun. At least a dozen of these tropical bugs, of esteemed size, rushed for the crevice between the bed and the wall. Others went under the pillow. Caleb recalled Tracker's words, *'they're not really cockroaches.'* *No shit*, Caleb now thought, that would be an understatement of radical proportion. *These things are the size of armadillos*, he thought.

"Where are the facilities? The toilet? The shower?" Miguel demanded.

The manager stepped halfway out of the door, sighed and pointed with his head down to the other end of the motel from where they had just come.

"Communal?!" Miguel questioned, announced, and judged deficient all at the same time. "He is a U.S. Americano, he needs a bathroom, a shower. Some running water, for heaven's sake!"

Again, the manager only shrugged off Miguel's passionate demands.

"We have, what we have," the manager said without emotion.

"Come on, my friend," Miguel said to Caleb. "We can do better," Miguel scoffed at the manager and led the way back to the motorcycle.

"If you change your mind, my name is Geovany Vellejos, you can remember that much, eh Americano?" the manager said, adding "I think you will be back."

Caleb and Miguel left *Vellejos's* motel. Miguel knew exactly where to take Caleb.

THE PRESIDENTIAL SUITE

"Sure, yes, you can stay at the Hilton, $100.00 or $200.00 a night. You're a rich U.S. Americano. Okay, turn here, turn right. Now pull over, right there." Miguel guided Caleb through the streets of Managua and to a different destination. Caleb realized they were in a residential area with no hotels in sight.

"Where are we?"

"At the home of my mother."

"Your house?"

"*Sí*, we must stop. My mother will be worried about me. I should've been home hours ago."

"Then we go to a different hotel," Caleb had been unable to pick up a signal on his phone; the battery desperately low; otherwise, he would have left his companion at the doorstep and been on his way.

"*Sí, sí*. Then we'll go to a magnificent hotel. The Princess Hilton. You'll like it. It's pink."

Caleb dismounted the bike. He took in the view of the house and yard in front of him. His eyes traveled the sidewalk, passing by three sleepy cats, up the steps, which were lined with potted plants, to see the porch with hammocks strung on either side of the front entrance of the cinder-block cottage. Unlike the houses on either side of it, this one stood framed by a startling array of colorful fauna. Caleb, a city boy, didn't recognize the cucumber, garlic, and sage. The marigolds he had seen before, but the low green catnip that acted as ground cover was new to him. Sofía's utilitarian garden did more than provide spices for their food and decoration for the small yard; it acted as a barrier to pests. Her home was the only one on the street that never suffered from cockroaches; her son never complained of mosquito bites when he slept in his hammock on the front porch; and, the cats kept more than rodents away between their naps.

"Come, come. It'd be rude not to meet my mother," Miguel called from the front steps. Caleb sighed.

The sun was setting behind the houses across the street. Caleb grabbed his duffel bag. Miguel already held their burlap sack full of avocadoes, *zapotes*, peppers, onions, plantains and a few other items from the market, he waited for Caleb before entering the house. The door stood ajar; Miguel pushed it wider and called out for his mother, as if they were walking into a large hacienda.

"*Estoy aquí; no hay necesidad de gritar.* I'm right here; no need to shout," she said, coming from the back of the small house, from the kitchen to the living room. The living room, painted burnt umber with a mustard-colored trim had a couch and a small television, along with two additional chairs.

"This is my mother, Sofía Rodríguez," the boy told Caleb. The woman wiped her hands on a towel which she then threw over her shoulder. She extended her damp hand and Caleb shook it. "Caleb Barthes," he said introducing himself, he tried not to stare, but her dark chocolate brown eyes, brunette hair, and golden skin all seemed to glimmer with hues of the setting sun.

She kept a cautious and curious eye on the stranger before glancing toward her son for an explanation.

"Yes, yes, I know what you're thinking. He's a cowboy, a vulture capitalist, an Americano who comes to take advantage of the beautiful shore lines and picturesque lakes and volcanoes of Nicaragua. But no, you're wrong. He's a gangster from Chicago who needs a hide out."

Sofía couldn't help but let a small smile cross her lips, almost fully giving away her toothless status to a stranger. Caleb smiled back at her, just barely noticing the absence of her two front teeth; instead, he focused on the way Sofía's dark eyes sparkled gaily, even as she scoffed at her son.

"See, he is traveling incognito as a baseball player." Miguel pointed to the baseball cap hooked to Caleb's duffel bag.

"I'm a reporter, from the *Chicago Tribune*." She was letting him into her home, the least he could was tell her the truth.

"His friend made a terrible mistake—booked him a room at the hotel cockroach. The *Vellejos* motel," the boy explained. His mother shook her head. Miguel continued, "I told him that he could stay with us."

Caleb turned with mild surprise at the boy's comment. Sofía's smile disappeared and her eyes widened. Then she spoke reproachfully to her son in Spanish, "*Él parece agotado.* He looks exhausted. How long have you been dragging him around the streets of Managua?"

"She wants to know if you would like to see the guest room," Miguel told Caleb.

Sofía rolled her eyes gently and smiled softly, this time without showing even a hint of her toothless grin, as she turned her back and led the way to the boy's bedroom. She waved her hand as she stepped into the room to show Caleb. There, a twin bed, clean and carefully made, covered with a thin, print spread, with white sheets poking out from underneath, took up one side of the room. A nightstand, small and simple, but hand-painted with a Mayan sun design and geometric stylized-flowers bordered the bed; upon it stood a small lamp. Two school workbooks lay stacked under the lamp, a candle by its side. Miguel crossed the room and quickly scooped up the books. Miguel turned Caleb by the arm to see the one poster that decorated the wall.

"*El Presidente*," the boy said as if to introduce Caleb to the man depicted on the poster, adding, "Not Daniel Ortega. No, no, this is Dennis Martínez, the famous Nicaraguan baseball pitcher, who played for the Baltimore Orioles, Montreal Expos, Cleveland Indians, Seattle Mariners and Atlanta Braves." Caleb suspected that the boy could rattle off Martínez's career stats as well, but instead of allowing the boy to do so, Caleb interjected, "All-star. World Series champion. Pitched a no hitter in 1991 against the Dodgers."

Miguel's eyes widened with delight. "You're no poser, just carrying a baseball cap. You really know your baseball! Yes, yes, he was the first Nicaraguan to play for the U.S. majors. He retired the year I was born. I must take up where he left off." Miguel puffed up his chest, beaming with pride as he added, "I will play in the U.S. one day."

Miguel's mother shook her head; she shared another smile with the tall and handsome *Norte-Americano*, and again, she didn't show her lack of teeth, her lips curled like a ribbon into a sweet smile.

"Your mother may not agree," Caleb quipped.

"My mother, she is a socialist. You know how they are. Anyway, we call our guest room *'El Presidential Suite'*. Very nostalgic, no? It is for our American visitors. Better than the pink Hilton Princess Hotel."

Caleb smiled again.

"Let the man sleep, Miguel." Sofía's tone came across as taut as a tightrope, balancing hospitality for her guest with discipline for her son. It was clear that she would have a word with Miguel in the next room, momentarily. But before she left the room, she studied Caleb Barthes, as he glanced around the simple yet colorful furnishings, until he came full circle and their eyes met. Landing on each other's gaze, like butterflies on sage, brief with fleeting possibilities. He held his glance with confidence; it was she who looked away first, sweetly flustered. He noticed the warmth rise into her cheeks.

"Okay, okay you sleep now. You've had a rough day," the boy said, noticing the adults silent exchange. Miguel then traversed the room and pulled the cotton curtain across the window, shading remnants of the day's tropical heat. "C'mon, Mamá." He led the way; his mother followed, leaving Caleb alone in the room, facing José Dennis Martínez Ortiz, winding up, ready to pitch.

CALEB, SOFÍA AND MIGUEL

Caleb awoke to the rich aroma of coffee and red beans and rice. He lay in the comfortable bed with the last vestiges of sleep slipping away—dreams with disconnected details. His mind tried to catch the remnants, an image of the desert, blue skies, a soldier making coffee over an open fire, and then he was driving, lost, a beautiful Nicaraguan woman rode passenger, and without speaking, said to him, *Let me show you the way*. And then the sound of a gun exploded in his head. The coffee spilled. The soldier dove for cover. Bang! Two more bangs followed. Bang! Bang! The bat hit ball.

Knocking, not banging, not shooting, not baseball, a knock woke him. *Where...?* He jerked forward. The hard knock came again at his door. *Knocking, not shooting.* Caleb wiped sweat from his forehead as he realized he had slept as hard as the insistent knock that came from the other side of the door. He widened his eyes. He blinked the poster of *El Presidente* into focus. The wind up, the pitch, the crack of a bat...

"Hurry, *Señor*. You must get up now." Miguel banged again on the door, before opening it. "You shower now," he said, pulling Caleb from the bed by his hand and leading him to the bathroom shower stall. "Soap," the boy said, placing the bar of dark soap into his hand. "Towel," he told his guest as he hung the weathered, thin terry cloth towel over a rod. "Quick, quick, my mother has breakfast waiting for you."

Miguel slid the shower curtain aside and turned the faucet knob. A weak drizzle of water fell from the rusty showerhead onto the red tile floor of the stall. The shower curtain was an unnecessary accessory, and rarely seen in Nicaraguan homes of this style. The boy tested the water's warmth with his hand as if he were a gentleman's gentleman.

"Okay, okay. You shower now. As nice as the Princess Hotel, no?"

Miguel left the man to his morning ritual and joined his mother at the back of the house in the kitchen. She stirred the red beans and rice before breaking eggs into the mixture and scrambling all of it together.

"Get the water jugs," she told Miguel as she folded the eggs over repeatedly, intentionally breaking the yolks.

"He's nice, eh?" Miguel hoped for agreement.

"Hurry, you need to fill those jugs before the water gets shut off again."

"He seems friendly and smart," Miguel tried to persuade her.

"What makes him smart?" Miguel's mother quipped.

"He's a journalist. Journalists are smart."

"A baseball reporter," she scoffed.

"Hey, baseball reporters are smart, too. Lots of numbers, lots of math," Miguel defended. She smiled.

"Hey, Lucy!" the boy said it as if he were Desi Arnaz playing Ricky Ricardo, "You put your teeth in."

"A woman's prerogative," she said. He started to say something. "Not another word," she warned.

Miguel took a longer look at his mother. She wore a white blouse, her favorite print skirt, hoop earrings and heels, not her usual flat sandals. For the first time, he realized his mother, a thirty-four-year old woman, with striking brown eyes and soft midnight-colored hair, might have a life beyond being his mother. He started to speak, "You haven't worn the dentures in—"

"Not another word, I said," she held up one finger for silence. "Finish filling the jugs and then get ready for school."

"I am ready."

"Exams soon?"

"Plenty of time before exams."

"Good morning," a refreshed Caleb appeared on the scene and offered greetings. His hair, still wet, waved across his forehead. He had dressed in a wrinkled, white shirt, and a pair of blue jeans. He stood barefoot. Casually, rolling up the sleeves of his shirt, he complimented the aroma of the dark beans, *ah caffeine.* "The coffee smells good."

"It won't live up to your dreams," Sofía warned him.

"Why is that?"

"They send the best coffee beans abroad. It's one of our chief exports." And as she poured him a cup of the second-rate brew, she added, "I'd like to have Nicaraguan coffee some day in a Parisian café."

He smiled, sipped the coffee. "So you're a romantic?"

"All Nicaraguans are romantics," Miguel answered Caleb before his mother had a chance. The boy was still busy at the spigot, filling plastic jugs with water.

"And realists," she added.

"What are you doing?" Caleb directed the query to the boy.

"Filling water jugs. If we don't do it now, we'll have to walk to the water plant with buckets and carry them back."

"Really?"

"*Si*, my mother is very clever, she can carry three buckets, one in each hand and one on her head."

"Miguel, this is not something that will impress our guest."

"I bet he couldn't do it on a dare."

"I'll bet you're right," Caleb agreed. He sipped the coffee; he'd had worse.

Sofía pulled plates from the cupboard and began dishing up the red beans and rice along with scrambled eggs and flat bread. After serving her son and guest, she joined them at the table.

"So, what brings you to Nicaragua?"

"I'm investigating water issues."

"Water," she said "Ah, the great unsolved mystery."

"What do you mean?"

"My mother needs water for her work. She's a *lavadora,* a laundress and seamstress, but also a poet and a socialist. When there is no electricity my mother writes poetry by candlelight, in a notebook that I gave her for her birthday. She never complains about washing clothes in a tub or even at the lake, beating other people's clothes against a rock until they are clean. She comes from the loins of the Sandinista." Miguel said it with flourish.

"He exaggerates," Sofía said.

"About the loins of the Sandinista or poetry by candlelight?" Caleb asked.

"No, about pounding clothes on a flat rock. We have wash tubs and *pilas* in the city and there are even a few laundromats in Managua, but not in the rural areas. We might be Sandinistas but we are also modern people." Caleb noted that by modern people, she meant they had wash tubs and wash boards not washing machines and dryers. That's when it dawned on him that clothes hanging from clotheslines and barbed wire fences were more than a colorful touch, they were a part of living in Nicaragua.

"Living in a third world country is—" Miguel's sentence remained unfinished, interrupted by his mother.

"It's not so bad," Sofía said.

"She will simply say, *everyone must do their part*. But when the water doesn't come, she says, *Why?! I do my part. The water should do its part.*" Miguel mimicked his mother's words and threw his arms in the air. The boy looked to see her reaction to his gentle, comic imitation of her. She smiled good-naturedly. Her smile complete with gleaming white teeth. Miguel continued, "We have the largest lake in Central America yet water from the pipes flows haphazardly. We're never quite sure when we'll have water nor does the government ever give us a good explanation. That's why my mother calls it 'the great unsolved mystery.' I think it's an engineering problem. Whatever it is, we have to store water and prepare for black-outs of electricity, too."

"Ah, so this is why we needed the candles?" Caleb thought aloud of the purchase they made at the marketplace.

"*Sí.*" Miguel shoveled a forkful of eggs, beans, and rice into his mouth.

"How often does the electricity go out?" Caleb queried.

"Oh, every day, my friend, every day. Usually, they turn the electricity off at night, but sometimes during the day also. I think we need engineers to fix the problem," Miguel repeated his assessment, before taking another bite.

"Which is why you must get ready for school. You are the future of the country. *Vámonos.*"

"Almost done," he said of his breakfast, but he took the next bite slowly and chewed it all before speaking again.

"*Señor* Barthes is staying in the country for ten days. I should show him the way to the Hilton this morning. Unless, ..." he took another forkful of food into his mouth and then let the word, *unless*, hang in the air for either of the adults to pick up.

"No, you are going to school today. I won't hear another word on the matter," Sofía commanded.

"Sandinistas are all about education," the boy said with a mouthful of beans.

"This is true," Sofía confirmed with pride.

"Is anyone opposed to education?" Caleb had a way of posing questions so that they sounded as if he was both debating a point and agreeing simultaneously. It also bought time and information; his knowledge of the Sandinistas was limited.

"The Sandinistas remodeled the system, created literacy programs, organized education for the poor. In ten years they more than tripled college attendance. Today, we are a very literate country. My son can grow up to be a doctor, an engineer, or a scientist."

"I want to be a baseball player," Miguel was unwavering. Sofía sighed.

"Oh, that reminds me," Caleb changed the topic. "I have a meeting with a scientist while I'm here, and I'm not sure..." Caleb pulled out his phone. No connection. He pulled out a note pad from his hip pocket, flipped the pages, "*Universidad Politécnica de Nicaragua.* Could you tell me where to find it?" He stumbled over the pronunciation and looked apologetically from Sofía to Miguel.

"*Sí*, yes, I know where this is and can guide you there," Miguel offered.

"No, you are going to school today," she told Miguel and then turning to Caleb, she added, "I can show you the way. The *Universidad Politécnica* is another Sandinista achievement. When is your meeting?"

"Tomorrow, I think," Caleb said. "Tracker wasn't completely clear on this. I should call to confirm."

"You should take him to see the sites while you're there. Monument of Peace," Miguel suggested, knowing his mother would approve of the recommendation. "Or take him to see sites today and tomorrow. Oh, and *Señor* Barthes, you'll see many hotels over there, too. Very nice, yes, but, if you stay with us, I can be your guide and translator on the weekend. My mother and I are very good at English. And when school lets—"

"I want you studying this semester."

"She is a task master," Caleb inserted.

"He has his final exams in November. Then he can relax over vacation. He'll graduate in November and begin preparation for more intense coursework."

"The end of November?" Caleb asked.

"Yes, vacation here is from the end of November to the beginning of February. This way everyone can enjoy the Feast of the Immaculate Conception, *La Purísima,* the first week in December," Miguel told their visitor. Sofía's expression took on the delights of the festival and she began describing the parades, the singing and dancing in the streets, music everywhere, delicious foods, until Miguel interrupted her and spoke directly to Caleb, "Señor Barthes, stay with us. It would be our pleasure to have you. Besides, the hotels are overpriced."

"Are you sure? I'd be more than happy to stay with you, but of course not without paying room and board."

"Sure, sure," the boy said. "Do you see twenty U.S. dollars a day as reasonable?"

"Yes, wonderful."

"And for food another five," the little negotiator added.

Miguel extended his hand and they shook on the deal, but Caleb did not release his grip without adding. "But not without your mother's approval." Caleb looked to Sofía whose dark hair had slipped over her eye. She smoothed it back and nodded her assent.

"And would you take notes for me when I meet with the professor?" he asked Sofía, not the boy. "I don't know if he speaks English. I can pay you for your help as a translator."

She started to offer to do it without payment, but Miguel jumped in on her words, "I would be—"

"Okay, okay. The deal is done. Mamá, will take you to see the sites today. Cowboy, you'll like the lakes and volcanos. Tomorrow, to see the professor. She'll take notes and you can pay her. Then, I'll become your guide starting Saturday. You'll want to stay much longer than ten days. Much longer. My mother will tell you stories of Nicaraguan history. Stories that you'll love. History and culture."

PART 2

AN ANCIENT STORY: THE ADVENTURES OF THE NOBLE LADY IKOOM

CHAPTER 9

IKOOM AND KUT'L

Deep Time

Ikoom sat crossed-legged on a flat boulder that jutted outward over the rocky terrain. Perched just above Ku'tl, she watched as he painted a glaze onto a hand-crafted vase. On the urn, a story of a hunter unfolded in circular fashion. The pictorials began with the young man's sighting of a white tail deer. The second image showed the young hunter surrounded by empty bowls as he called upon the deities with upward and outstretched arms. The third image portrayed the hunter, arm extended, holding his *atlatl* and taking careful aim at the deer. The fourth scene depicted the triumphant kill via the aftermath—the white tail deer is draped over the hunter's shoulder; he carries it victoriously back to his community. In this image the deer's head hangs in death, a drop of blood falls from its tongue, and a heart-shaped, tiny, white cloud with three parallel lines extend from the cloud.

"What's that?" Ikoom asked him.

"The last breath," he answered without looking up from his work. Ku'tl turned the vase again. Next the hunter is seen placing the cleaned bones of the deer and the polished skull carefully within a shrine. Turning the vase again revealed the face of the white tail deer with which the narrative had begun, and with which the deer had first aroused the young hunter's hunger. Ku'tl lifted his head and looked up at Ikoom. Her dark hair was woven into a single platelet with a long, colorful ribbon intertwined; the braid fell loosely over her shoulder. Her breasts were bare, as was the custom, and her long skirt was bunched into her lap. She held a tiny flower in her fingers and twirled it.

"You're quiet today," he said.

It's true, she thought. She had been quietly contemplating her fate, wondering what the gods would have in store for her and how she should tell Ku'tl. After a long moment's thought she spoke.

"When my mother moved me from cradled arms to the side of her hip, she gave me a gift."

"This is true of all Maya children," Ku'tl said, adding, "My mother gave me an obsidian chip for an *atlatl* spear along with a chisel and a paint brush, so that I might be a warrior, a hunter and an artist of the noblest class. And now, I show my talents as an artist and hunter," he announced with some braggadocio as he held up the nearly finished water urn for her to praise, but Ikoom only smiled softly. Then she cast her glance downward again onto the delicate and dying violet she held between her fingers. She wasn't sure why she had plucked it; she had never before killed a flower.

Ku'tl heard the silence and knew that it was meaningful. *Something is wrong. But what?*

"What is it, Ikoom? What gifts did your mother present to you?" he asked with patient interest and empathetic concern.

"A paint brush like yours, cloth of many colors, and…" her voice trailed off in mid-answer; she paused. He waited. Maya girls of the elite class often received a paint brush for painting and cloth or ribbons for weaving.

"And?" he asked at last.

"And…" she said, taking a deep breath.

"And what, Ikoom?" This time he asked with growing impatience and concern. He leaned toward her.

"and obsidian incense."

This answer gave Ku'tl pause. His eyes opened wider as the implications narrowed in his mind to one meaning.

"They want you to speak with one of the gods?"

She nodded.

"Which one?"

"Not one, but two."

"Who?"

"Chaac and Ixchel."

"Both?" With each word she spoke, Ku'tl became more suspect, more worried. It would seem Ikoom had been selected as an infant to represent the people when she became a young woman. She had seen fifteen summers now. A time for revelation. Both boys and girls were selected but no one was told until they came of age. Now, Ikoom would face a fate of both honor and danger.

"Yes."

"Where?" He hated to ask and already felt an anger rushing into his lungs.

"Into the well."

He shook his head, not in disbelief, but in defiance. He had never told her, but he had already determined to make her his wife. "No," he finally said.

"No, you mustn't; you don't have to do this," he argued.

"If I don't, the dishonor will destroy my family." There were tears in her eyes.

He couldn't speak. He knew that few survived the well and of those who had survived they either died soon after or became oracles who could speak only to the deities and then give cryptic messages to mortals.

Ikoom forced back tears; she wouldn't let them fall down her cheeks. "I'm honored to have been chosen," she continued bravely, yet her voice cracked slightly. "But I need you, Ku'tl."

"Anything," he promised her. "Anything. Just tell me what you need."

"Ku'tl, be my distraction. Please, sit by the well and tell me tales of glory and mystery and adventure; keep my mind off the deepness, the darkness and the coldness of the well. Will you do it?"

"I promise upon my last breath to be your distraction."

"Ku'tl, I don't want you to get into trouble."

"I don't care. I'll stay by the well and tell you stories all night long."

"I'm supposed to endure *The Deep* alone."

"No one survives alone and I won't be in the well with you. There is no rule about having someone sit vigil."

***

The day came for Ikoom to be wrapped in knotted vines and lowered into a deep well by the conjurer of the gods. She was dressed in her best finery; her hair was wrapped in ribbons and wound around her head into a lavish wreath. Her parents presented her to the priest and he set about to burn obsidian incense in small bowls around the parimeter of the deep well. His weathered hands shook slightly as they set each bowl of incense on the ground. Once finished, he undertook the task of preparing Ikoom. He tied the vines securely under her arms and around her waist, tugging at them to be sure they would hold. Then he enlisted the service of two young men to lift the girl and then lower her into the dark well. The priest whispered to her—*The Deep holds the mysteries and their answers. Listen to The Deep. Ask the gods for rain.* Friends, relatives and city dwellers watched with hope in their hearts that her youthfulness would either entice the gods to save her or take her, but in either case, to give them the rain they so desperately needed. Before her eyes dipped below the rim of the well, Ikoom looked about the scene, searching for Ku'tl in the crowd. She didn't see him. A rush of terror flooded through her veins and chilled her body. She felt a panic rising in her throat—*Ku'tl, where are you?*

The priest's assistants lowered her slowly downward. She felt the loneliness of *The Deep.* She could see nothing except darkness below her, and a small shaft of light above her, which grew smaller and smaller as she was lowered deeper and deeper and deeper, until…

Everyone heard the splash of water. The priest instructed the young men to secure the vines and then he began praying; the people prayed with him.

Ikoom also heard the splash, but she alone experienced the coldness of the water. Her body jerked involuntarily as her skin met the cool liquid. Her muscles tightened against the shock of the alternate temperature. She dangled waist deep within the dark, cold water. Afraid to speak; afraid to move; afraid to breathe and afraid not to breathe, Ikoom continued to focus entirely on one concern: *Where is Ku'tl? Why hadn't he come?*

***

Once darkness began to set in and all was quiet above her, Ikoom felt the intensity of absence; she was filled with emptiness. Abandonment surrounded her like a specter's shawl—ghostly and eerily.

"Ku'tl!" she cried out, so frightened by *The Deep*. But no one answered. Her bare legs tread water even though she was suspended by sturdy vines. Tiny bumps, from the chill, covered her arms. She looked up and called out again to no avail. The sun had slipped westward. Soon it would be completely dark. *Surely Ku'tl will come under the veil of night. He must be waiting so that others won't see him*, she determined. She held tenaciously to that thought and the tough vines that suspended her.

I shouldn't have asked him to come at all, she chastised herself. *I'm dedicated to helping my people and this is an honor. I need to bravely call upon Chaac and Ixchel. But of course, the gods and goddesses have far more important things to do than to notice me. I must let them know that I'm here if they should desire to tell me the secrets of rain and what I must do to help restore the reservoirs.*

"Chaac, hear me! I am here in *The Deep* within your mysterious being." Her voice echoed within the well; it reverberated off of the irregular, grey stones that circled upward toward the shaft of disappearing light.

"Chaac, hear me! I'm here," desperately she called again. "Tell me what message you wish me to carry back to the people."

The poetry of *The Deep* filled her, chilled her, surrounded her. Ikoom's voice and thoughts moved through her and against the stone walls of the well:

Echoes trailed away without response.
She continued to tread water, trying to keep her legs warm.
She grew cold. Colder.
The light disappeared from view.
Darkness fell
upon
The
Deep
Deep
Well.

Ikoom longed for the view of one star, but none appeared. As *Deep Time* passed, her arms and legs grew numb and her energy dissipated. A weakness began to cover her like a limp, wet, cold blanket. Floating in the darkness, she lost her sense of connection to the world above. She entered *Deep Time*. She became one with *The Deep*. Her head dropped back. Her raven-colored hair hung heavy with the weight of water; over time, the ribbons came loose and they streamed on the surface of the liquid. One touched her face; she jerked awake. *How long? How long have I been asleep?* She looked above. *Stars!* The discovery brought her joy. She still lived in the world even if she hung suspended in *The Deep*.

"Chaac, I am your daughter! Hear me! I'm here now calling upon you!"

"Ikoom!" The voice above echoed downward, a strong whisper.

"Ku'tl, you came." She instantly recognized his voice.

"Ikoom, I couldn't stay away, but had to wait. The priest told me that if I speak to you, I would be…"

Ikoom heard a thud. Like an axe cracking against a heavy tree branch. Silence followed. The sound and silence reached her with sickening awareness. That awareness repeated itself, echoing in the night. Someone had struck Ku'tl. He had been caught trying to help her. And now all was gone. She remained still. Wondering if a priest stood above her at the edge of the well. No sound followed. Nothing but the noise of her own quivering arms and legs against the water, met her ears. The emptiness was vast. A sickening hollowness filled her stomach.

I never should have spoken to Ku'tl, she thought. *What have I done?! I've betrayed my friend, I have betrayed my family, and my duty to Chaac.*

She began now to think of how Chaac had betrayed his own brother by committing adultery with his brother's wife. She thought of Chaac's great tears over an act that can never be undone, and how those tears replenish the earth as rain, but for some reason Chaac has stopped crying. *His tears once fed the earth and brought maize into the world. I must speak with Chaac, listen as he tells his story, and find a way to make him cry again.*

"Oh, Chaac, I'm sorry!"

Still all was silent and her thoughts returned to Ku'tl. *It's my fault.* She took a deep breath. *It's all my fault. Everything is ruined.* Tears formed in her eyes. She tried to force them back.

"I'm sorry, so sorry."

She envisioned what had happened to Ku'tl. She hoped that the priest had only struck Ku'tl unconscious. *No,* she would not even consider that Ku'tl might be dead. But as she made this declaration it only proved the point that she was thinking otherwise, that it might be true. She must force such thoughts away, she told herself. *Oh, Ku'tl,* she cried softly. *I must find a way to save him,* she thought.

"Chaac! I am here. Now!" Her voice strong and shaky simultaneously, her lips quivered and yet words demanded that Chaac visit her. *I mustn't think about Ku'tl. I must give myself up entirely to the gods.* "Chaac, forgive me! I am here!"

"Chaac! Hear me!"

But Chaac didn't answer. *Deep Time* entered her mind; she slipped into another realm of being. She floated in an abyss. Without dreams. Without consciousness. Without time. Without place. Without warmth. She slipped into unconsciousness until…

"I am Chaac! I hear you!" *The Voice* filled the well, shattering her slumber, like thunder on a summer's night. Deep, with regal resonance, *The Voice* called to her.

Ikoom opened her eyes. A ledge now extended from the wall of the well and there stood Chaac, with the body of a gigantic man covered in scales and with a face of strength and maturity. His armor spouted a reptilian nose and bulging round eyes, which he had set regally upon his head. He carried an axe. He spoke with a commanding and petulant voice. "Why have you called me? What do you want?" Ikoom, startled by his imposing size, frightening features, and angry tone remained speechless.

"Speak!" Chaac demanded.

Gathering her wits, she told him, "I want to be your companion."

"You're lying. You want to be Ku'tl's companion. You've betrayed me. Tell me again, what do you want?"

Tears welled in Ikoom's eyes. She had failed herself and the people. She had betrayed Chaac and it was her fault that Ku'tl might be dead. She couldn't answer the god of rain.

But Chaac was not without mercy and he took pity on Ikoom as he saw the tears gliding down her cheeks. Empathy ensued. Chaac had lived a life of *Great Tears*. He lost his brother's love. So deep a despair he felt, knowing his brother would never forgive him, that by now he had relinquished all his tears. The god of rain now existed drained; he could no longer cry. The well of guilt and hope was dry. Seeing her tears reminded him of his past transgressions. But no tears emerged.

"Please, do what you will with me, but save Ku'tl," she begged.

Perhaps, he thought, *I should forgive this girl her failings. But is she worthy?* Chaac took a deep breath and squared his giant shoulders.

"Find Ixchel and then find me once again. Then and only then, will I tell you how you can make amends, but if I allow Ku'tl to live, you may not speak to him ever again. And if you meet the challenges of the *Chasm*, then I'll share the mysteries of *The Deep*. But first, you must survive the *Island of Women*."

Chaac disappeared with a thunderous noise and a crashing light. Then, in darkness once again, Ikoom experienced opposing emotions: gratefulness—for having been given a second chance, and a dreadful trepidation—for having been given a second chance. Overwhelmed, she passed into unconsciousness again.

***

Ikoom felt her body rising. Her eyelids fluttered open and closed again as the light became more intense. Chaac was sending her back upward to earth. She looked up, squinted against the brightness of the sun. Two men hauled her over the side of the well, scraping her knees. The numbness saved her the pain. The priest stood above her. She could barely stand. Ku'tl lay on the ground. Dead or alive, she couldn't tell. She looked away.

"What did Chaac tell you?"

She tried to respond, but her blue-tinged lips only quivered. The priest threw a warm gown around her shaking form and led her to a boulder warmed by the summer sun's intense rays. The drought appeared all around her—browning, brittle grass broke under her feet as she moved on shaky legs toward the rock. Ikoom kept her eyes turned downward against the brilliance of the sun. Shriveled plants exfoliated their leaves beneath her feet. Little white mystic flowers withered on the ground, having fallen from the tree. Only a few sweet violets lived in the shade of the boulder, like the one she had twirled between her fingers the day she had told Ku'tl of her mission; the violet grew as a tiny reminder of possibility.

"What did Chaac tell you?" the elder repeated as he handed her a cup of warm liquid with herbs. She sipped. He waited. The crowd drew closer. Her form shook from exposure in the deep, dark well. Her lips continued to quiver for some time. A hush came over the crowd. At last, she spoke.

"He told me to prepare for the challenges of the *Chasm*. But first, I must go to the *Island of Women*." A small gasp issued forth from the group gathered around the girl. First, they were surprised at her lucidity and then by the extreme sacrifice that Chaac had demanded. No woman had ever returned from the *Island of Women*. And no one had ever entered the *Chasm* and returned to tell of it. Gathered around it—yes, burned incense at its opening—yes, but enter it beyond the mouth of the cave, accost the subterranean gods, and live to speak of it, this was unheard of among all of Mayan history. No one could remember the last time the people had had to resort to sending an emissary to the *Island of Women*, much less to the *Chasm*—the great gulf that separates the mortals from the gods. Only the priest had actually seen the skeletons that line the ledges of the cave that leads to the Great Chasm where Chaac lives.

PART 3

CALEB AND MIGUEL

SOFÍA AND CALEB

Sofía gave Caleb a history lesson on the Aztec and Maya influences on the people of Nicaragua—discussing the languages, the foods, and the geopolitical history. Slipping from a stylized-historical tour guide persona only occasionally to speak of the current problems: pollution of the lake by toxic run off from industrial waste or how the government is dealing with threats of acid rain that come from rupturing plumes of steam rising from the volcanos; otherwise, she maintained a docent-style distance and a nearly Victorian decorum on their first day together.

They'd been walking all morning, under pleasant skies on this late October day. She gestured to a spot under a tree, overlooking Lake Managua. They sat in the grass.

"Is this what you used to do?" Caleb asked her. She cocked her head.

"Were you a tour guide at one time?" he asked.

"No," she scoffed, not as if it were a silly idea, but more that it was unthinkable. "I don't like rich Euro-Americans. Those are the people who come for tours."

"Do you think of me as a rich tourist?"

"I'm not sure what to think of you," she countered.

"So why are you putting up with me?"

She turned away from him and gazed out over the lake. "My son likes you."

"I like him. He's an artful dodger. An extremely lovable one, of course."

Sofía raised an eyebrow at the description of her son.

"Artful dodger, a scamp who picks people's pockets, a Charles Dickens character," Caleb explained.

"I know who he is, I question whether that is a good character-ization of my son, Artful Dodger betrayed Oliver Twist, didn't he?"

Caleb smiled and nodded, impressed that she knew the book. She chose not to show her conflicted feelings, insulted by his stereotype of her as an illiterate, third-world peasant and yet simultaneously pleased that he suddenly respected her for her awareness of literature. Her mood fell to the former.

"Americans, so arrogant. Do you think you are the only ones who read?"

"My apologies," he said sincerely. She accepted the apology and softened her tone as she admitted he wasn't completely wrong about Miguel.

"My son *is* an artful dodger of sorts, but he's also as innocent as Oliver Twist. Perhaps, he's picking your pockets, but he'd never betray you. He steals your heart more than your money. And he is so alive with so many different emotions. I wish I could capture him in a poem, but I've tried and I can't quite find the words to do him justice, yet. He is my every joy. My life. He is the blood that flows through my veins."

"I think those words are poetry. Does he inspire most of your poetry?"

"He's a part of me and so a part of every poem I write, even if it's not directly about him. Whether it's about labor or love, Miguel is in everything I do. Whether it's about a love or loss, about the stars above or the soil beneath our feet, he's in everything I see; he is my life. My blood." Her voice was lyrical, her eyes moist.

"May I read some of your poems?"

"Why?"

"I, because, I want to get to know you, your culture, Nicaragua."

"You want to know two things about me, Cowboy," her tone shifted. "I can see it on your face, in your eyes." Caleb tipped his head questioning.

"You want to know, where is Miguel's father? And what happened to my teeth?"

Caleb nodded to her observation. Never had he been read so quickly and so well. He hadn't realized until she said it, but those two questions had been sitting unspoken at the edge of his tongue since he first saw her beauty ruptured by the absence of the two front teeth and since he first realized there was no man in the house. He waited to see if she would answer the questions or not.

"Both questions can be answered in one word, *Contras*."

"Contras?"

"After the Sandinistas took the country back, the Contras were angry and frustrated. One night a group of them came to our home. Trained in the School of the Americas, I believe, they wanted to frighten my father. My father had been given a small parcel of land by the Sandinista government. Contras believed it was their land. I was young, very young and everything happened so fast." Sofía paused. She glanced away, beyond the here and now, traveling back to memories of long ago. She saw it unfold before her, again. At last she shared.

"They were standing in our house. The Contras. Suddenly one of the men took the butt of his rifle and aimed for my father's stomach; I rushed in front of my father as the man launched the weapon forward. The rifle butt cracked into my two front teeth. I heard my mother's screams as I saw lightning all around me and then blood spilling from my mouth. So much noise and confusion, and pain." She paused for a moment, still reliving the nightmare. She looked up at Caleb. His eyes filled with sympathy and horror as he pictured the scene of Sofía as a child being brutally hit by the butt of a rifle. It took him a moment to frame his question.

"Your father, he must've been beside himself. What did he do?"

"With guns pointed at him, what could he do? He could do nothing. Those are times when women can do the most. My mother shoved the man away and told them all to get out, now that they had had their revenge. She pushed the men toward the front door. She shamed them—saying, *revenge by hurting a child!?* They left. Their damage done."

She remained quiet for a moment, resting from the memory, before she added, "As for Miguel's father, that's a different story, my story. Not for you. And one that I'll keep close to my heart."

"Of course, I'm sorry. I didn't mean to...," Caleb stumbled through an apology. It was Sofía who rescued them from the dark mood.

"I was surprised to find that you aren't fat," Sofía quipped.

"Fat?" he laughed.

"U.S. Americans, aren't they all obese these days?" she queried with a smile.

Caleb returned the smile. "Well, not all. Just most." He stood and took her hand to assist her up and then they began to walk again. Lake Managua disappeared from view as they meandered alongside the busy road.

"I really would like to read your—" Caleb's inquiry was cut short by a loud bang. They both turned toward the noise. An out-of-control truck headed straight at them.

After swerving off the road, the driver overcompensated and the truck barreled forward, directly toward Caleb and Sofía. Caleb grabbed hold of Sofía and dove over the hillside. They rolled down the embankment. He protected her head, cradling it in his hand, as they rolled over and over until they came to an abrupt stop against a tree. Her ankle hit the tree; but, his arm bore the brunt of the collision as they bounced once more against another tree before coming to a complete stop.

"Are you okay?" he quickly asked.

"*Sí, sí.* I'm okay," she said catching her breath. Then she extracted herself from his embrace without a romantic lingering glance. Sofía sat up, held her ankle, and added, "But was that really necessary?"

"I thought it was," he answered, thinking he had just saved her life. His hero status suddenly in question. He helped her up. She limped up the incline and back to the road where they discovered the delivery truck had suffered a tire blow out. The driver walked toward them. Sofía greeted him. He apologized profusely. She turned to Caleb.

"Okay, Cowboy, you want to be a hero, help the man with his flat tire. Trust me, you'll learn about my culture, about Nicaragua."

Caleb left Sofía by the roadside nursing her injury. He asked the man if he wanted help changing his flat tire. The man appeared to speak no English. Sofía shouted translations from the roadside where she leaned against a lamppost. The driver graciously accepted and apologized for causing an inconvenience to them.

"Where is the spare?" Caleb asked.

After a few more exchanges, Caleb came to realize that the man had no spare. Caleb looked to Sofía. She waved him down the road as if to say *be on your way.* Caleb followed the truck driver. They walked out of Sofía's view.

Good fortune ensued. The gas station owner's brother had a matching tire and he could bring it to them at the gas station. But haggling over the price took some time and in the end Caleb made up the difference. His very presence had caused the inflated price. He didn't realize this at first, but eventually he caught on by the way that they looked at him and then back to the driver. Dickering and pointing.

Caleb and the truck driver sat down to wait. After twenty minutes or so, Caleb bought a round of coca colas for the three men. Eventually, the owner's brother arrived on foot rolling the large tire into the gas station. After paying for the tire, Caleb and the driver took turns rolling it back to the scene of the calamity. They also took turns carrying the borrowed jack. The metal grew hot under the afternoon sun.

Sweat poured down Caleb's neck and back as he assisted the driver who jacked up and braced the back of the truck, wrenched lug nuts free, heaved the shredded tire away and lifted the replacement into place. Sofía watched patiently and when they were done, she put in a request.

"Ask him if we can have the flat tire," she said.

"I'm not the one who speaks Spanish," he told her.

"Ask him," she repeated. Caleb sighed.

"Amigo, may we have the flat tire for our trouble?"

"*Sí, sí.*"

"People here sometimes understand more English than they let on," Sofía explained later when Caleb joined her on the side of the road.

"And how do you plan to get that back home?" Caleb asked her.

"I can hold it on the back of the motorcycle."

"I've always wanted a swing to hang from the *bucayo* tree in the courtyard, something good can come from something bad, no?"

"You are a romantic."

She smiled, a toothless grin, hidden by dentures.

CHAPTER 11

CALEB AND THE FAMILY

Early evening cast a warm glow over the sun-drenched courtyard at the back of Sofía's home where she now sat watching the American work. The *bucayo* tree dropped a blood-orange-colored petal or two as a breeze stirred. The humidity, as usual, hung like a heavy blanket in the air. Caleb had helped her into a chair, her ankle still slightly swollen.

"What are you looking for?" she asked him as he opened the low storage cupboards built into the wall.

"A basin that I can fill with water so that we can soak your ankle."

"You U.S. Americans, always so wasteful. I don't need a whole basin of water. Just wet the towel," she said, pointing to a worn terry-cloth dish towel hanging on a rod. He followed her instructions, soaked the towel, wrung it out and brought it to her. He knelt by her ankle, lifted her foot gently by the arch and slowly began to wrap the injured foot. He glanced from her ankle to her eyes checking to make sure he wasn't hurting her. But with each glance their eyes lingered longer. She saw concern in his eyes for the second time that day.

She glanced at his hand on her knee. Then her gaze traveled along her soft, golden-brown thigh. His gaze followed. She longed for his fingertips to take the same path. She wanted him to slide her skirt farther up to reveal her upper thigh. To touch her.

He wanted to slide his hand upward toward the top of her thigh. He wondered, were her eyes saying, yes? He glanced again. Her lips parted slightly. She took a small breath.

"*¡Mamá!* I'm home," shouted Miguel from the entrance.

Caleb stood quickly, taking the towel from around her ankle, rather abruptly. She laughed.

"Out here," she called to her son.

Caleb found himself at the wash tub, dipping the towel in water again and lightly wringing it out as Miguel came in and gave his mother a hug. She kissed him on the lips and the forehead. Then shared the story of their adventurous afternoon at his request. Sofía then sent Miguel to invite Uncle Guillermo and his family to dinner.

"The U.S. American wants to cook for us."

Caleb's eyes widened with surprise but he also relished the challenge.

"Under your guidance," he added.

"Of course, of course."

She directed him to the cupboard where she stored the dried food; he returned with a bag of white rice grains and pre-cooked beans.

"What will we make?"

"*Gallo Pinto*, for starters." She pointed to a pot and then told him, "One cup of rice, two cups of water." She stood, delicately placing her banged up foot into her sandals before carefully limping to his side. She took him by the arm, walking to the grill.

"The wood goes in here," she told him as she pointed to the opening of the brick oven that stood across the courtyard from the large sinks. The top of the oven was currently covered by a grill. The grill could be exchanged for a heavy brick lid converting the grill into an oven. She could use the stove to boil rice, fry bread, or bake desserts. Caleb admired the versatility of the oven.

"Guillermo made it for me."

"Your brother?"

"*Sí*, he is good at building things."

"I look forward to meeting him," Caleb said.

"This is good because if a man wants to get to know a Nicaraguan woman, he must first get to know her brothers."

"Ah, I see. And how many brothers do you have?"

"I have three."

He stepped away. "Where is the measuring cup?"

"Who needs such things?"

"But you said, one cup of rice, two cups of water."

"Hand me the pot."

Caleb handed her the pot. Sofía set it on the stove. She held her palm over the pot, poured rice into her cupped hand four times and each time she let the grains fall into the pot. "Now the water," she instructed. Caleb brought her a water jug. "Go ahead. You pour; I'll tell you when to stop." He poured the water as she studied his face, strong lines, straight nose, wide smile—

"Oh, stop!" She looked at the ratio and judged that she needed more rice now to match the water. She added another handful. "Okay, Cowboy. You like onions, peppers, what else? You like it hot, spicy?"

"Yes, yes."

Caleb built the fire and Sofía sliced the onions and diced the peppers. Once the fire was strong, Caleb put a lid on the rice pot and then made his way to stand next to the true chef. He leaned his head over her shoulder. "What next?"

"Out front along the sidewalk you can pull up a garlic bulb, break off some sage and bring in a little mint. Oh, but first, the dried pepper, there, will you help me with it?" She pointed to one that hung from a fishing line that was strung above the sinks. "Chop to the tiniest degree. Then, we'll crush it. That makes paprika."

Music, from the neighbor's house abruptly blasted *Aziatic punta* tunes. The Garifuna influenced contemporary songs made both Sofía and Caleb smile. Sofía danced gingerly, protecting her injured ankle, but with spirit, nonetheless. When the music switched to *Bob Marley and the Wailers* they both moved to the beat.

"Every night, a free concert," she told Caleb.

After crushing the peppers, he wiped his hands on his jeans and headed out front to gather the herbs that she wanted. He returned, without the garlic, admitting that he didn't know what it looked like. She smiled and took him by the hand. She hobbled toward the front door and on outside.

She shooed the cats out of the way and showed Caleb the winding swan-like stem of the garlic plant. She wrapped her hand around it and yanked. At the base sat the small bulb, covered in fresh dirt. She brushed it off. He took in the aroma.

"Garlic," she pronounced.

"So much to learn," he commented. She pointed out the herbs, which he had only guessed at before picking. The only ones his olfactory recognized for sure were the garlic, mint, and sage. Other herbs in the garden were new to him.

They returned to the courtyard kitchen. She found the water and rice boiling and moved it to the edge of the grill and prepared a griddle with oil. She warmed the flat bread that she had fried the day before, placed the bread in a basket and covered it with a towel. The music continued to play, she heard Miguel call out over the rhythms, and with him, her brother Guillermo, his wife Geyselle, and their four children.

"¿Que pasa, mi hermana?" Guillermo shouted as he entered the courtyard, holding a bag of seasoned chicken in one hand and beer in the other. "We come with contributions." Guillermo set the package and beer on the table, hugged his sister and then he turned to Caleb, looked him up and down. And then the oldest brother turned back to Sofía, "Quiene es este?" Guillermo asked as if Miguel hadn't already told his uncle about the American visitor.

"Our house guest, Caleb Barthes. Caleb, this is my brother, Guillermo." Sofía pulled her sister-in-law closer with a hug and then introduced Geyselle. Just then the youngest child reached for the tortillas and flatbread, nearly dumping the basket. Geyselle's attention quickly turned to the child. Caleb extended his hand to Guillermo who shook it solidly. "¡Bienvenido! Lo qui lleva a Nicaragua?"

"Educational trip," Caleb answered without seeking translation. Sofía glanced at him.

"I recognize a little Spanish," he told her. "But only a little."

"Then we speak English tonight. Good practice, eh Miguel?" Guillermo headed to the grill.

"Seasoned with oil?" he asked of his sister.

"Yes, ready to go."

Guillermo put the chicken on the grill and returned to give Caleb a beer. Both men opened the bottles. Geyselle passed on a beer as she corralled the children one way or the other. Miguel played catch with his cousin. Sofía gathered plates before returning to the grill to add the seasonings.

"I thought the American was cooking for us. I was expecting hamburgers and apple pie."

Caleb turned toward the grill and took the spatula from Sofía. "Your sister is guiding me."

"Sure, you'll be the iron chef one day, if you listen to her." Guillermo took a swig of his beer. "But what did you say, why are you in Nicaragua?"

"There is a professor here who knows about water purification and my colleague in Chicago, a reporter, wants me to help him write an article on water issues in Latin America."

"He's going to attend the professor's lecture. Mamá is going to translate," Miguel said as he caught the ball and threw it back again.

"So you are a reporter, like your friend?"

"*Sí*," Caleb said. Guillermo laughed. "And now you are the one speaking Spanish." They all laughed. "Ah, beer. It frees everyone's tongue. Soon you'll be bilingual." On a more serious note, Guillermo added, "How long are you staying?"

"Ten days," Miguel said while still playing catch.

"Longer, maybe. Sofía, I called the professor today and he can't see me until next week." Caleb flipped the onions, peppers, chicken, and more in the chef's style that he had witnessed at the market.

"*No hay problema,*" she told him as she set the plates on the table.

"If you need to extend your visa, I can tell you how to do it with ease and for less money than most would pay. The border guards often ask for extra, if you know what I mean," Guillermo told Caleb.

"Meanwhile, we'll show you Nicaragua. Tomorrow you come to our house for dinner and meet the rest of the family."

"Guillermo, no," Sofía said. "One brother at a time," she added. Guillermo laughed.

"As you wish, my sister."

The dinner party went late for having young children in attendance. Geyselle carried the youngest and Guillermo carried the next youngest, the older boy walked sleepily behind his father. They parted on the front porch after saying their good-byes.

Sofía gave Miguel a kiss goodnight and the boy climbed into one of the hammocks on the front porch. Sofía returned to the courtyard to clean the remains from dinner. Caleb followed her. He helped to clear the dishes to the sink. She began washing.

"Clear sky. So many stars," Caleb commented.

A new song drifted over the backyard fence, Jimmy Cliff singing *Many Rivers to Cross*. The Jamaican blues tune lulled the nearby neighborhood with soft notes and sorrowful lyrics. Caleb took the wash rag from Sofía's hand and set it aside. He opened his hands to her.

"A dance?"

She hesitated.

"Just a dance, nothing more," he promised.

She acquiesced, taking his hand at first and then accepting his embrace.

"Just a dance."

"I promise."

"I have more brothers, don't forget."

He smiled.

They danced as Jimmy Cliff played on...*So many rivers to cross...and this loneliness won't leave me alone...It's such a drag to be on your own...*

PROFESSOR LÓPEZ

"The lecture will be given in Spanish," Professor López told Caleb.

"Do you mind if I tape record?" Caleb asked. Sofía promised to take notes and help translate the tape later. The professor kindly agreed, but added, "You may find it, well, complex, if you're not familiar with the terminology, even if it is translated to English."

Professor López then walked with his guests to the classroom; once there, he waved them toward the back of the room. He took his place at the podium in the front of the small, brightly lit classroom at *Universidad Politécnica de Nicaragua*. His students, all male, sat at long tables, their pens pressed to paper, like runners' toes on the starting block. Caleb and Sofía took seats in the back of the classroom. The professor spoke in Spanish. Sofía listened and translated in her head as he spoke as she took notes. The tape recorder caught it all.

"Well, it started innocently enough, did it not?" the professor addressed the class. "You signed up for this course with the simple intention of learning how to provide clean water to the world and then you had your eyes opened. It's not so simple.

"Well, let us begin our review. Water issues fall into several categories. Some societies suffer lack of water. Others suffer diseases for lack of clean, potable water. Others have water but no infrastructure to move it to the villages where people live. Others have drilled wells in places that have too much of one mineral or another; that is to say, where the ground is toxic. Others face the invisible but deadly effects of carcinogens in the water that they unknowingly flushed into their own water systems—*agua mala*."

For Caleb the lecture rushed on with him recognizing only a few words here and there, especially *agua*, ...*agua*, ...*agua*. For Sofía, who had never before been in a college classroom, undertaking the

Herculean task of taking notes on an unfamiliar subject, forced her hand to tighten around the pencil with anxiety.

"Our goal for this semester has been to learn how to provide potable water, free of both acute and chronic disease-causing elements. Acute illnesses due to pathogenic micro-organisms require disinfection; chronic illness due to carcinogens, radon, lead, or even disinfection by products themselves, DBP, in the water, requires careful monitoring and chemical testing."

"During the first few days of the semester we talked about two basic types of water sources—surface water and groundwater. Surface water is subject to particles and micro-organisms while groundwater is subject to chemicals. Here, for example, we must be careful of what pesticides and herbicides might be used on Nejapa golf course. Run off may seep into the ground or even into the streams, which means it is possible for us to have to deal with chemicals even in surface water. The current state of Lake Managua is another example of polluted surface water. But perhaps even more deadly are micro-organisms. Generally speaking, chemicals are associated with groundwater and micro-organisms with surface water. Recall that I mentioned the case of Milwaukee cryptosporidium oocysts, which entered the water system, in 1994, making 403,000 people sick and killing 104 persons. The protozoa are quite deadly, as few as one organism can kill hundreds of people. The origin was believed to have been due to run off from a cow pasture. Where to place the blame? The farmer? The filtration system? The cow? I don't know. But what matters is what we do about it. Turbidity levels far exceeded normal, and that has to be controlled for by the civil and chemical engineers. The Milwaukee example also reminds us that even in the richest of countries accidents can happen, filtration systems can be deficient."

Caleb recognized the word *Milwaukee* and then thought it was probably a Spanish word. He glanced at Sofía who did not know the word Milwaukee but tried her best to get the spelling down on paper.

"Of the two—groundwater and surface water, we are most concerned here, in Managua, with surface level supplies. We draw our water from Lake Managua and Lake Nicaragua. On the other hand, in north-eastern Nicaragua, villagers dig wells, collect rain water, pull buckets from rivers and streams and there they must be concerned with ground contaminants and ecological problems. Recall the story that I told you about the well-meaning missionaries who dug a well in Africa too close to the ground that was laden with salt fluorides. Within a short period of time some villagers began to suffer acute symptoms, later others suffered chronic symptoms of fluoride toxicity. Some women were unable to walk as their bones became brittle and broke under their own weight. Children suffered gastrointestinal problems. Now scientists are discovering that drugs, such as Prozac contain the fluoride molecule. So people taking Prozac will have two things to be depressed about, no? Whatever first depressed them and that they are making others sick when they piss—their urine which is filled with fluorides goes into toilets." The students laughed cautiously, recognizing that it was a joke, but about a serious matter. Sofía glanced at Caleb and made a mental note to share the joke with him later.

"Estrogens are also appearing in the water of industrialized societies, especially non-Catholic regions." The students nodded their understanding of the implication. The professor continued. "We might not face these pharmaceutical contaminants, but we could face similar situations in the future.

"So how do we remove these colloids when they have a slow settling velocity?" The professor posed the question, but did not expect an answer. Sofía looked to Caleb with concern. She wasn't sure if she was getting the chemical terminology down correctly as she took notes. But she didn't have time to let him know of her concern as the professor began speaking again very quickly.

"Chemicals collect or accumulate in or on particles, colloids. And it is our job to unsettle their comfortable existence. We need to move the water through a treatment of coagulation, to fluctuation, through a clarifier, in order to get the sludge to settle and then continue the water through a filtration system, add disinfectant, and if desired a little fluoride and phosphate. A little fluoride is good for your teeth and bones; a lot of fluoride is bad for your bones and intestines."

"In the coagulation process we need to add base elements to counteract the acidity."

"So we combine rapid mixing with ferric chloride $FeCl_3$ to H_2O to Fe3+ iron." The professor wrote the chemical element combinations on the chalk board much to Sofía's relief. "This splits the water molecule separating it into 3 hydrogens, ..." the professor held up three fingers and then pointed individually to chemical elements written on the chalk board in the front of the room. "...which is an acid with a positive ion. So, we will need to increase the charge to make the particle larger, stickier, heavier, so that it will sink. Of course we all know that negative charges repel each other."

At this, Sofía pursed her lips, as she had no background at all in negative or positive charges. Her education ended after 8th grade. She never took biology or chemistry. These issues were all mysterious to her. Nevertheless, she tried to keep up with the professor's lecture, at least in terms of writing what he said.

"Step one then is to neutralize the negative charge and then add a positive charge, but not too much, just enough to create coagulation, so that you can move onto flocculation. You need to know these formulas," he reminded his students. "Flocculation is followed by sedimentation." He wrote the formulas as he spoke. Sofía tried desperately now to keep up with the instruction. She glanced at Caleb with a panic-stricken look. He gave her a reassuring smile and nodded to the phone-recorder, indicating that they could check it all later.

"Now, what about filtering water?" The professor put forward the rhetorical question, moving once again toward the blackboard. "This removes additional particles. There are two basic types of sand filters, the slow filter and the rapid filter. To know whether the water is being effectively filtered, we must know the volume of the water, the surface area of the filter and the amount of time that it takes the water to pass through the sand; that is, we need to ascertain the velocity." Again the professor pressed chalk to board and quickly wrote formulas. Sofía felt she needed to be trilingual, her bilingual background failed to give her the rudimentary syntax for the physical sciences, especially math that incorporated letters and exponents. "Basically because we have increased the size of the bad particles through coagulation they'll be unable to make their way through the sand. Know your formula where

3 cubic per square meters per day…" the professor wrote, erased and wrote again.

"The down side to slow filtration is…"

"It's slow," a student offered.

"Yes, it's slow," Professor López smiled at the student's bold but obvious observation, "and it requires more space than rapid sand filters. Here we want sedimentation, interception, and Brownian motion. The particles can penetrate the filter bed. Ah, and don't forget to go over your notes on backwash, or how to clean the filter. So be sure to know Stokes law, the formula to find velocity, Darcy's law, which you need in order to arrive at transient groundwater flow equation, and the Pythagorean theory. Also know your formulas for disinfectant $Cl_2 \rightarrow H_2O$. The acid base reaction happens very quickly. Know chlorine, dichlorine and trichlorine."

"For the test?" one student asked.

"For life," Professor López corrected him.

"Also for rural areas where it is impossible to set up filtration centers and water treatment plants, be ready to discuss ultra violet radiation through UVB rays into clear plastic bottles. Ah, parabolas! The possibilities are endless. New uses are unfolding as we speak." He said it as if parabolas were the scientific manna from heaven. "Again, volume, surface, radiation exposure, time. About 6 hours for a half liter. Check your notes from previous lectures." He paused.

"Are there any questions?" he concluded.

Sofía put her pencil down to stretch her wrist and bend her fingers. She turned to Caleb, saying "I'm not sure how well I did, but I suspect based on my notes, we would both fail the upcoming exam."

Caleb laughed. "Fortunately for us, we're not taking the exam. And fortunately for the rest of the world, we have no intention of running a water treatment plant. C'mon, let's go thank the professor."

Those students who shied away from asking questions in front of the others now spoke one-on-one with Professor López. Sofía and Caleb waited their turn.

"Thank you, Professor," Caleb finally said when it was his turn, adding "very enlightening."

"Well, coming in at the middle must have seemed a bit overwhelming. Tell me more about your exposé, maybe I can direct you to helpful reference books."

"I'm finding with what little research I've been able to do so far, and from a lay person's perspective, that there are water issues in every country. Even countries rich in water, like Nicaragua, have water issues as serious as sub-Saharan Africa. I'm not clear why the city of Managua has water restrictions and I'm not clear on why rural areas have issues storing rain water."

"Ah yes, each situation is more complex than the next. Sometimes people collect rain runoff from the roofs and the roof tops can have bird droppings and other contaminated materials. I'm taking a small group of students to an indigenous village in eastern Nicaragua at the end of the semester. If you come with me, you'll see firsthand why the indigenous people don't have water," the professor told him.

"And as for Managua, a modern city on the edge of an enormous lake, why doesn't it have running water?" Caleb queried.

The professor spoke in Spanish at first and then switched to English. "Ah, yes, a completely different story. First, come with me to the villages of northeastern Nicaragua. And later, I'll explain how a modern city can have such difficulties in supplying water. You must know the first story to truly understand the second story. We leave after final exams and return before the Feast of the Immaculate Conception. So, we are gone about a week."

Without hesitation, Caleb agreed to accompany the professor and his small team of students to the rain forest of Nicaragua and beyond to the Caribbean coast. "The final exam is on Friday, two weeks from now. I'll grade the exams over that weekend and turn in grades on Monday. We leave the following Tuesday."

"From here?"

"Yes."

"You'll need to extend your visa, if you go," Sofía reminded him. He nodded to her and then had another thought. They had waited longer than expected for the professor's lecture and Caleb was already on day ten of his tourist visa. He would have to talk with Guillermo about the best way to get the visa extended. And he thought, *what about a translator? Although the professor speaks English. I can't expect him to translate everything.*

"Professor would you consider letting another student come along? A younger one." As the professor pondered the request, Caleb turned to Sofía. "Do you think Miguel would like to go? Could you part with him for a week or so?"

"He's more interested in playing baseball, but you may ask him."

EL BARRIO

El barrio lives in Miguel and Miguel lives in *el barrio*. Like so many Managua *barrios* Miguel's neighborhood is uniquely ordinary. It wakes in the morning but never truly sleeps; it expects disruptions as daily routines; and, it holds the residents like the humidity in the air—always on the verge of rain—soft, subdued, seductive or hard, angry, storming.

Mornings bring the sight of mothers walking their children to school, the sound of barking dogs or crowing roosters, the smells of *gallo pinto* and coffee, the feel of a light humidity on your skin evaporating under a rising sun. Children play tag with one another, tapping each other and darting backward to escape a retag; their colorful backpacks bounce against communion wafer white shirts, loosely tucked into navy blue pants or navy skirts. The younger children skip ahead of their mothers who carry sack lunches, sometimes filled with tortillas or a thermos of soup, to be eaten at picnic tables under the shade of a cashew tree. *El barrio* moves them along like a wave until they fade into the distance, replaced by the next wave. Men, who roll carefully in their hammocks, which are strung outside on porches or in courtyards on the hottest days, have given kisses to the school children as they set off. Now, they rise to meet the day, taking quiet as the cream for their coffee.

But many of the families in Miguel's neighborhood are without both cream and fathers, making it easy for teenagers to steal away, slipping into secret places, after pretending to depart for school or persuading their mothers of the need to earn money for the family, sometimes with the intention simply to play. Miguel is no exception, nor are his friends.

"What is this new occupation you have taken up?" Reynaldo asked Miguel.

"What do you mean?"

"I mean that you could make more money selling drugs with us rather than acting like a tourist guide to a gringo. You're pathetic."

"Ignore him," Amardo told Miguel, "His mood is grim."

"How much is he paying you?" Reynaldo wanted to know.

"Nothing. He pays my mother for room and board. How did you know about him?"

"We saw you arrive with him; we've seen him coming and going with your mother on his Yamaha. Where were they going?"

"He has appointments at *Universidad Politécnica de Nicaragua.* My mother translates for him."

"How much does he pay your mother?" Diego, the tallest and oldest of the group, asked with quiet interest.

"What does it matter?"

"Let's just say, I want to know," Diego kicked a small chunk of concrete. Banded geckos darted for safety under bushes and into cracks in the cement.

"We haven't finished working out the finer details."

"You're lying."

"I want to charge him enough to take my mother to Disneyland."

Reynaldo shoved Miguel. The boy lost his balance, teetering for a moment.

"What's wrong with you?" Miguel demanded.

"What's wrong with *you*?" Reynaldo countered.

"Ignore him," Amardo advised again and stepped between the two boys.

They walked in relative silence. Diego continued to kick the tiny chunk of concrete, every fifth step or so, which punctuated the sullen stillness between Miguel and Reynaldo.

"Let's go to our secret home—*Casa Escondida*—and smoke a bowl," Reynaldo suggested after a time.

"Our secret home yes, but I haven't got any hemp. We'll open a bottle of rum," Diego decided. "C'mon."

"I have to go to school," Miguel told them. "Reviews are today; exams tomorrow."

"You can have one shot," Diego said. "We'll celebrate your graduation from 8th grade."

"I won't graduate if I don't pass. I need to review."

"Everybody passes."

"Reynaldo didn't," Amardo thoughtlessly mentioned. Reynaldo glared at Amardo.

"Reynaldo became a businessman early," Diego countered. "He needed to help support his family."

They all followed Diego to *La Casa Escondida*, an abandoned structure, which still suffered the disfigurement of the 1972 earthquake that had rocked Managua—cracked walls, crooked steps, and slanted structure. Inside they had created a small home decorated with a couch that they had pulled from the garbage bin of a hotel—a prize—and a small table that they had created out of produce boxes. They stocked the drawers with candles and matches and a bottle of rum.

Diego took the first swig and Reynaldo the second gulp of the brown, bitter-sweet liquid. He passed the bottle to Miguel, who handed it off to Amardo.

"House rules," Reynaldo declared. "One drinks, we all drink."

"Let him be," Amardo said as he took a swig.

"The rules," Reynaldo stated and turned to the higher authority—Diego. "Enforce the rules," Reynaldo demanded of Diego.

"Why are you so *loco* today?" Miguel demanded of Reynaldo.

Reynaldo moved to the other side of the room. He pulled a stack of magazines and comic books from a corner. Cockroaches scattered.

"His mother has stopped calling from the United States and she has not answered or returned his phone calls," Amardo quietly told Miguel after pulling him aside.

"How long?" Miguel whispered back.

"She missed his birthday."

"Maybe something has happened," Miguel said with concern. Reynaldo heard him; he crossed the room with giant steps.

"Yes, something has happened all right. She has remarried and is pregnant with a new baby. She no longer wants me."

"You know this for sure? Reynaldo, maybe—"

Reynaldo swung at Miguel before he could say another word. The blow landed on Miguel's right eye. Miguel fell against the table.

"House rules. One drinks, we all drink. You don't drink, you suffer the penalties." Reynaldo's anger filled the room with a bitter air. Amardo reached out a hand to Miguel. Miguel brushed the gesture away and righted himself.

"Who do you think you are to be able to break the rules? You flaunt your *Americano* in front of us, riding through the barrio on his motorcycle, as if he is your new father. Has he screwed your mother yet? Or are you still negotiating the details for that, too?"

Miguel flew at Reynaldo, tackling him. The two tumbled to the ground. Reynaldo, the older, taller, and heavier of the two, quickly dominated. He pummeled Miguel's face with three quick punches. Amardo jumped into the fray to pull Reynaldo off the younger boy. But as Amardo dragged him off of Miguel, Reynaldo landed two solid kicks to Miguel's ribs. Amardo forced Reynaldo out of reach of the younger boy and held him back.

Diego attempted to help Miguel up from the ground. Miguel refused Diego's extended hand. Miguel stood and wiped the blood away from his nose. It smeared across his face. Diego extended the bottle of rum, saying, "House rules." Diego's words, given without emotion, were law. Miguel sharply whisked the bottle from Diego's hand without taking his eyes off of Reynaldo. Miguel squared his shoulders and took a swig of rum.

"Now, get out of here. Go to school," Diego told him.

"Go graduate, you little cunt! You mamá's boy!" Reynaldo yelled and then grabbed the rum from Diego and downed another slug. Amardo watched as Miguel picked up his baseball cap, slapped off the dust and left the secret house.

Miguel walked the back streets of *el barrio* where he hoped no one would see him. His eye, cheek bone, nose and lip throbbed. He felt a fire in his left side where Reynaldo had kicked him. But worse, much worse, he felt the rage of a volcano inside him. Heat boiling through his veins. Angry and confused, he couldn't go home, he couldn't go to school, he couldn't be seen on his street, and he couldn't go back to *La*

Casa Escondida. So, he went nowhere, walking and walking, on the edges of the farthest outskirts of the neighborhood.

Questions swirled in his mind. His brain continued to return to one question—how could Reynaldo say such vicious things about his mother. *My mother is a saint.* Miguel walked on until he could walk no more and then like a wounded animal he took refuge in a concealed corner by an empty building with foliage and overgrowth. He hid behind the weeds and the philodendron and hibiscus leaves. He didn't want to think about the cruel names that Reynaldo had called him. He didn't want to wrestle with the idea that maybe Reynaldo was right, maybe he did want his mother to...*No, I brought him home for the money!* Miguel beat his own head with his fists. *They don't understand. Nobody understands!*

Perhaps *el barrio* understands as it gave him a nook at the edge of his world in which to be alone, away from Reynaldo, Diego, and Amardo, away from his mother, the American, and away from school. He wanted none of it. Tears rolled down his cheeks. Snot slid from his nose. He wiped it away with his arm. It was still tinged with blood. He curled up and buried his head in the crook of his elbow. Eventually, Miguel retreated into sleep.

Hours passed before his eyelids opened. When he awakened, the shadows of late afternoon fell across his form. Miguel rolled to one knee and raised himself upward, holding his rib cage in the process. Finally, he stood nearly erect; and he headed home, without a conscious decision to do so. Instead, *el barrio* guided his feet, one step and then another, after lifting him from his place under the palm tree, behind the philodendron. *El barrio* led him along one street and then another, and another, until Miguel mustered the courage to walk back into his corner of *el barrio* with a bloody nose. He heard the sounds of early evening as he turned the corner and began walking down the street where his mother's yellow house stood out for its color and its herbs, he heard children playing and he heard the words, *Go home! Go home!*

The hollering of "Go home; go home," as a boy rounded third base, could be heard at the top of the street along with the parents' cheers for their respective teams. Home plate, a sandal, donated for the time being, by one of the parents, went flying as the boy slid into it, trying to avoid the tag. The ball was made from two balled socks, wadded up, and encased in duct tape. No one ever knew where the socks had come from, although it had been discussed at length. *Who wears socks?* They used an aluminum bat. A swing and a miss. Everyone new first base, the storm sewer drain, it remained steadfast doing its duty whether that was to protect them from torrential rains (debated at length: *The storm channels are not deep enough if climate change brings a deluge v. they're fine*) or act as the marker in the baseball game. Second base changed each game depending on who offered what for its use, last week it had been an old piece of cardboard, but that disappeared overnight. Tonight, Mrs. Pérez's metal pot marked second base. She was unaware that it had been absconded. Surely, she would not be happy if she knew. A rock on top of a piece of burlap became third base tonight, which is good, when third base was left to the honor system, too many disagreements broke out. Usually Miguel would have been at the center of such disputes, at the center of the game. This is his game. The season had opened. Instead of stopping, Miguel continued to be carried down the street by his habit of walking home. He passed two old men who sat pensively studying their chess game, ignoring the noise of the baseball game. One looked up at Miguel and then looked back to his game. A group of women gossiped on the sidewalk. They grew quiet as Miguel neared their circle. After he passed them, he heard whispers. He didn't look back.

El barrio compelled him forward. *El barrio* led him to his mother's home, down the path where the lazy cats reside and through the front door. It banged behind him, announcing his arrival. He stood silent in the archway to the living room. *El barrio* had led him home. Some days, *El barrio* can wrap his arms around you; on other days, *El barrio* turns the other way. Sometimes, *El barrio* takes you where you need to be.

CHAPTER 14

A MOTHER'S CARE

"Oh, my son! Miguel, what happened to you?" Sofía cried out as she looked up and found the battered boy standing in front of her. She quickly tossed the transcribing work aside. Stood and took his face in her hands. He winced. She turned his cheek this way and that, assessing the bruises and swollen eye. Miguel held a hand across his rib cage.

Caleb came quickly from the guest room when he heard Sofía cry out.

"Who did this to you? What happened?" Sofía questioned her son, demanding names, answers.

"It's nothing," the boy told her turning his face away.

"I'll get some ice," Caleb said. Sofía looked at Caleb and then questioned him with the same intensity she had projected toward Miguel.

"Ice? What ice? Where will you get ice?"

"From the freezer," Caleb announced, nonplused by her interrogation.

"Where do you think you are?" She turned her anger toward Caleb. He stood still, not knowing at first what he had said or done wrong. It took a moment to register—*there is no freezer. No refrigerator.*

"A wet cloth, then," he offered.

"Fine," she nodded. Caleb went to the courtyard, to the jugs of stored water.

Now speaking more softly, Sofía questioned her son, "Miguel, what happened?"

"I looked at a girl. I didn't know she had a boyfriend."

Sofía relaxed her shoulders. Her head shook gently. She clucked her tongue.

"I hope she was pretty."

Caleb returned with the moistened cloth and handed it to Sofía. He remained silent as mother and son dialogued.

"A girl. Are you sure you only looked?"

"I swear it." He crossed his heart.

"So she must be very pretty?"

"Very, but not as beautiful as my mother."

"Your mother is not very pretty right now, she has her angry face on," Sofía switched to third person unable to personalize her anger on the bruised boy. "You have exams soon, tomorrow and all next week, too." she added with concern. She gently pressed the moistened cloth to the bruised eye and then followed that by trying to wipe away the dried blood from under his nose. "These are important exams. You must pass 8th grade in order to go to high school."

"I know," he said, "I know." Miguel took the cloth from his mother's hand, before gathering his books which were on the floor in the living room. "I'll pass," he assured her. He went to the front porch with his books. Caleb followed him out.

"Take the bedroom tonight," Caleb said.

"No, you paid for the bed."

"No, it will be better for you to study. Besides, you want me to experience the real Nicaragua, *si*?" Caleb tried to bring a smile to the boy's face, but when Miguel didn't respond, he added. "This wasn't about a girl, was it?"

"*Señor* Barthes, we have a business arrangement, nothing more."

"Okay then, I'll negotiate for the hammock. Two more dollars a day. I'll not go a penny higher. I want it for a week."

Miguel swung out of the hammock, and without a word, headed inside for the bedroom. Caleb grabbed him by the arm. He took his hand and turned it palm up. Caleb dropped a pill into the boy's palm and before he could protest, Caleb closed the boy's hand into a fist around the pill.

"It'll take the edge off the pain; it's just like aspirin. I'll make sure you're up for your exams in the morning."

A PROMISE

Miguel heard Caleb call his name. He ignored it.

"Miguel, time to wake up," Caleb repeated with three short taps on the door. Miguel continued to withhold acknowledgment. He heard the door open, but pretended to sleep, his back to the door.

"Miguel, c'mon, time to shower."

Miguel rolled over and took a deep breath as he stretched his arms long above his head, but the action ended in a painful retraction of his arm around his rib cage. Miguel had been healing for a week. Today would mark the end of exam week.

"Are you okay?"

"It's nothing. I'll be fine."

"Ribs take a little longer to heal than black eyes."

"Whatever."

"Here's a towel. Your mother has fried plantains for you."

Miguel jerked the towel from Caleb's hand.

After Caleb exited, Miguel rose and went to the shower. Like a good Nicaraguan he rinsed himself, turned off the water, soaped up and then turned the water back on to rinse off. Unlike a good Nicaraguan, he let the water stream over his skin longer than usual.

Miguel blotted the towel gently against his face before looking in the mirror. Where last week, his right eye had puffed into the appearance of a swollen blowfish, today the swelling was all but gone and only a hazy yellow bruise lingered. He turned away from the image, returned to his room, and dressed.

Miguel entered the kitchen where his mother had a dish of fried plantains waiting for him. The ripened peels discarded on the counter for the time being. Her sister-in-law would make the peels into soap later, a way to earn extra money for her family by selling the soap at the market. Sofía brushed Miguel's dark hair away from his forehead and studied the bruised eye. "Hmm, not so bad," she concluded. She handed him a plate.

"Take it to the courtyard. We'll eat out there," Sofía told her son.

"I don't have time."

"Take it to the courtyard," she insisted. His shoulders slumped; he sighed, but obeyed reluctantly.

Miguel entered the courtyard where the American sat with a plate of plantains set before him. Sofía followed her son. They sat under the shade of the *bucayo* tree which cast a dappled shadow over the food. It would be months before the blood-orange flowers would turn to inedible coral beans, this week Miguel's mother would pick the buds and blooms which are edible and use them as vegetables with the evening meal, but he wasn't thinking of the evening meal.

No one spoke. A hummingbird flitted close by, drinking nectar from one and then another of the brightly-colored flowers. Miguel did not look up from his plate. The heal of his foot beat a rhythm nearly as fast as the hummingbird's wings. Sofía focused on her son.

"Last of the exams are today, *si*? Are you nervous?"

Miguel pushed the fried plantains into the rice and beans. "They're going well," he mumbled.

"Which one is today?" she coaxed conversation from him.

"I have to leave," he said swallowing a mouthful of beans and rice.

"I'd like to take you to a baseball game," Caleb offered.

Miguel stabbed three plantains with his fork and put them in his mouth.

"To celebrate your graduation," Caleb added. Miguel ignored him.

"Miguel, Señor Barthes is speaking to you," Sofía chastised her son. Miguel remained silent again.

"Miguel," Sofía repeated. The boy put his fork down with force, looked up, squared his shoulders and stared at Caleb before speaking.

"Who do you think you are? Do you think you are my father?" His sharp words were as black and spiny as the thorns of a honey locust tree. Sofía looked surprised by the boy's tongue, but before she could speak, Caleb responded to the accusation.

"No, but I would like to be your friend. A friendly gesture, that's all. I'll take you and your family to a baseball game. You know, for all that you've done for me."

Miguel gripped the side of his chair, out of view. He turned to his mother, "I'm done. I must go. I can't be late for exams." The boy pushed his chair back and lifted his plate. He strode toward the house, but stopped mid-step. Out of their view, he turned to see Caleb and his mother sharing a glance. He put his plate in the kitchen and went to get his books, which he couldn't find at first. His mother had moved them to the shelf where she kept her poetry books, Rubén Darío's book on top. Poetry. She must have been reading last night. He recalled that she had once said, *your father was like Rubén Darío, a poet and a patriot.* He lifted his textbook, a sheet of paper fell to the ground. He picked it up and read: *La familia, Tan perpetuante como la luz de la noche, tan encantadora como el amanecer ... The family, enduring as the night sky, endearing as the sunrise.* She was all the family he needed, he thought. But then read on, *...blossoming like the bucayo tree...* It gave him another thought. One about family.

He placed the sheet of paper with the poem on the shelf, grabbed his book and ran back to the doorway of the terrace where his mother and the American sat.

"Okay, okay, yes you can take my family to a baseball game. We can celebrate my graduation. That's a good idea." With that, Miguel stepped in more lively fashion, heading toward the front door, leaving Caleb and his mother to wonder, but not question, the change of heart.

Suddenly, Miguel reappeared in the entryway to the courtyard a second time.

"Hey, Americano there is a game the Sunday after graduation— *Indios* play the *Tigres.* We go, yes? My family, we'll celebrate."

"*Sí*, yes," Caleb enthusiastically agreed.

"A promise, yes?"

"Yes, I promise." Caleb swore an oath, "with your mother as my witness."

"My whole family, yes?"

CHAPTER 15

"Yes, yes, I promise, your whole family."

Miguel appeared to dart off.

Caleb and Sofía exchanged smiles, only to be interrupted once again.

"Don't wait dinner for me. I'll be late.

"Miguel—"

"Mamá, I'll be a graduate soon; I'm not a little boy. I have things to do." Nevertheless, he dashed over to her side and kissed her before rushing off to school.

MIGUEL'S FAMILY

Sunday morning brought a bright Miguel in from the hammock on the front porch. He had refused to let Caleb give up the bed for another night. Sofía had barely seen Miguel on Friday evening or all day Saturday. He had popped in long enough to report that his exams had gone well, "Nothing to worry about," he had said and then disappeared. This morning he rose early, prepared for Mass, and woke the reluctant reporter for church.

"I don't go to church," a sleepy Caleb told Miguel.

"Yes, those days are over," the boy quipped, handing Caleb a towel and dragging him from bed. "And you will meet all of my mother's brothers." A confused Caleb showered and dressed before joining mother and son for coffee.

"Miguel tells me that you've promised to set a good example," Sofía greeted Caleb. She wore her best dress with her hair pulled back, the gold cross hung about her neck, shinier than usual. She held a mantilla in her hand.

Miguel watched as Caleb silently acquiesced. The three walked to church, receiving glances from neighbors along the way. Miguel took the opportunity to say hello, "*Buenos días*" to several neighbors who glanced at them without speaking, but then nodded in return.

They walked through the large doors, took holy water, and then proceeded down the center aisle. Large, hand-painted statues of the Holy Family stared down upon the congregation, from the walls, Virgin Mary with baby Jesus statue on the left, St. Joseph statue on right. Overhead fans spun the humid air. Ladies fanned themselves with booklets, a few of them took notice of the trio—Sofía, Miguel and Caleb. Miguel selected the pew and genuflected first, Sofía followed her son, Caleb mimicked the ritual he knew from his past. They made their way down the pew and took their seats after kneeling for a short, polite prayer.

As Mass began and droned on, each of them let their thoughts drift. The sermon extolled the virtues of generosity, praised the poor on earth, and promised heaven to those who did their part. The ideology floated on wisps of incense dispensed from the brass thurible, the chains of which made a distinctive musical note in rhythm with the priest's hands.

My mother is a saint. She will receive respect from all the neighbors. No one will question her piety or her purity. She is as innocent as white clouds, hitting a ball into the clouds, el béisbol es el camino al cielo. Baseball is the way to heaven. Hitting a home run, sending a ball to the clouds with the whack of the bat is perfection... Miguel's thoughts suddenly returned to the here and now. He had no idea how his brain had gone from saints to baseball, but it had.

Sofía and Caleb exchanged a glance. She looked away as Miguel noticed them. All three held similar thoughts during the final prayers, anxiously awaiting dismissal by the priest, a release and return to the joy of the celebration. Graduation day!

"*La misa se terminó, ahora vayan en paz.* The Mass is ended, now go in peace." The priest exited with altar boys in tow.

As if restraints had been undone, the congregants let out a collective sigh and let smiles emerge. As the faithful unfolded themselves from the pews, from the sublime, from the silence, they walked and talked, moving toward the light of outdoors. Caleb stepped out of the pew and then back, allowing Sofía and Miguel to lead the way. They were part of a slow wave of people making their way to the narthex.

Sofía dipped two fingers into the holy water receptacle as they left the Church. She dripped the tiniest bit of water onto her forehead, between her breasts, left shoulder and then right, making the sign of the cross, before stepping outside. It was at the arch, the precipice between the solemn shadows and the sharp sunshine that she looked back to make sure he was there. Once again, their eyes met and this time neither looked away. Instead, he reached out and touched her moist fingertips.

"C'mon," Miguel called as he ran ahead of them. "C'mon," he yelled again from the church plaza.

They turned their attention toward the boy who called them a third time and stepped with lively energy through the crowd of parishioners. Turning back twice more to nudge them along, Miguel called out, "C'mon, c'mon."

Soon, the couple walked, with Miguel in full trot in front of them, leading them down the street toward the house. Miguel at last pointed to where a crowd was forming in front of the house. Scattered a bit, with some people on the porch and others gathering in a group as uneven as the sidewalk upon which they stood. Men and women, young and old, children and mothers, waited for Sofía, Miguel and Caleb to arrive.

"Remember my Uncle Guillermo and his wife Geyselle," Miguel told him more than asked him. Handshakes and bear hugs followed, not always in an orderly fashion. "This is my grandmother," Miguel told Caleb.

"How do you do?" Caleb offered his hand.

"Over here, we have my little cousins, Diego, Angel, and Yenny. And this is Uncle Rolando and Aunt María Paz. These are my other cousins…" Miguel was spinning Caleb in this direction and that as he introduced his relatives.

"Finally, this is my Great-grandmother Violeta." The matriarch emerged from the center of the crowd, a tiny woman with a round and wrinkled face. Her eyes sparkled.

"Great-grandmother Violeta has agreed to stay and watch the house in our absence. She'll guard your motorbike and notebooks."

"Where are we going?"

"Where are we going!? He makes a joke. You said you would take my family to a baseball game. We are going to see the *Indios* play the *Tigres!*" A cheer went up from the relatives. Miguel looked furtively around, "We are just waiting for—"

"You have more relatives?" Caleb asked in astonishment.

"Ah, here they are. At last! This is Amardo, Diego, and Reynaldo." The three boys came closer. "They are my family, too." Miguel announced firmly, putting his arm around Reynaldo, not giving his mother a chance to protest the gang member's presence and as Reynaldo started to speak, Miguel cut him off not allowing him to apologize. "So now, Cowboy, you've met them all."

Miguel spread his arms wide to indicate all his relatives and his friends, "This is *mi familia!*" Then he added, "Now we go to see *el beisbol.*"

CHAPTER 17

CALEB, SOFÍA, AND THE RAIN

Softness hung in the air above them, in the wispy clouds of the night sky. Caleb, having carried Miguel from the back of Uncle Reynaldo's Toyota pickup truck where the boy had fallen asleep on his cousin's shoulder, placed him carefully in the hammock on the front porch. The boy mumbled something and fell back into a deep sleep. Sofía smiled softly. She ushered great-grandmother Violeta, who had heard the truck and had come out on the porch, to the waiting vehicle; and then, helped her into the front cab. Caleb waited on the porch watching as Uncle Reynaldo waved as he drove off.

Caleb followed Sofía into the living room. She flipped a switch. No lights. She deftly made her way to the kitchen and withdrew the matches from the drawer. In the darkness, Sofía blindly felt for the candle on the counter, securing knowledge of its place and the position of its wick. She struck the match, lit the candle, and brought the room aglow. Under the amber ambience she retrieved another small candle, slightly larger than a votive candle, thick and wide. She lit it too before the flame of the match reached her fingertips. Each candle sat in a small, shallow dish filled with a layer of sand.

Carrying the candle bowls, one in each hand, she returned to the living room and without a word led Caleb through the dimly lit hallway to the guest bedroom. Once there she set one candle on the night stand. She held the other under her face, creating an eerie image of herself, as if she sat by a campfire waiting to hear a ghost tale. She smiled. He laughed. She moved the candle to beside her face, now providing a self-portrait with golden chiaroscuro. Her dark hair disappeared into the night on one side, while the other side emerged with amber highlights.

He reached out and took the candle from her hand and set it next to its partner on the night stand. She looked confused, for just a second, maybe two. He touched her cheek and then drew a loose strand of hair away from her face. He started to say something.

She put her finger to his lips. "Shh, the boy is sleeping; the walls are thin, the front door open."

He took her hand in his hand and kissed the finger that she had held to his lips. He searched her eyes and found a warm acceptance to his advance. She smiled softly. He brushed a strand of hair away from her neck and over her shoulder. She drew closer to him and tilted her head slightly, exposing her bare neck to him. He ran his fingers along her cheek and down her neck. He kissed her lips; she touched his cheek with her fingertips. He reached his hand to the nape of her neck and lifted her hair. The cool breeze brought with it a sigh. She drew her hands away from his face. She felt him unbutton the first button of her white blouse. He searched her eyes again for permission, eyes as moist as the humid midnight sky with stars that sparkled. She lowered her eyelids as a soft smile parted her lips. He slipped his fingers downward. She whispered something. He touched her skin ever so lightly. She kissed his neck, salty to the taste.

He unfastened the last button on her blouse and ran his hand along her shoulder. She slipped out of her skirt. He pulled his shirt over his head and tossed it aside. Her bra fell to the floor. He found her skin as moist as the Nicaraguan night and she drew closer and smelled his skin, deeply inhaling and then softly releasing her breath with pleasure. He lowered her to the bed and as his fingertips explored her body, her hands swept across his chest, the rain began to fall. She heard it through the open window—softly pattering against the strong palm leaves. She felt his shoulders, his arms, his back.

The rain grew stronger. Beating a rhythm against the ground. Without wind, it fell hard and straight. The giant droplets pelted down on the zinc roof and against the wooden porch and the cement steps that were cracked and slipping away from the foundation. Pelting harder and harder, the water splashed into the streets and against the trees and moved deeper into the earth. The pounding droplets became a singular symphony overwhelming any and all other noises of the Nicaraguan night. Like a Mayan ceramic rattle, shaken ceremoniously and seemingly without end, begging for rain, imitating the sound of rain, the night rain answered the prayers of the ancient Maya. The rain poured down. Louder and louder. The storm swallowed the passionate cries of lovers that became an eternal part of the tropical torrent, existing long after the two had fallen into a deep sleep.

> The woman rises first.
> It is the time that is her own.
> A time when men and children sleep.
> The woman rises first
> to commit herself
> to the day,
> to the work,
> to the female way.
> A woman rises first.

CHAPTER 18

ADVENTURES OF CALEB AND MIGUEL

Caleb took his turn bouncing in the back of the pickup truck; Professor López didn't play favorites. Each member of the service learning group exchanged places, from the bed of the truck to the passenger's side of the cab, except for the professor who did all of the driving. Across from Caleb sat Miguel who wiped sweat from the nape of his neck, looked up, and then smiled at the American reporter who had finagled the invitation for him from Professor López and permission from his mother to join the student group. Caleb returned the smile and nodded before reaching into the inside pocket of his duffel bag where he pulled out his notes, the ones that Sofía had transcribed for him before they left. He flipped through them, noticing the spot where they had struggled one evening to decide between the word 'flocculation' and 'fluctuation.' The truck hit another rut, bumped forward, and splashed through a puddle. The papers slipped from Caleb's hands. Scrambling, he reached out and quickly gathered them together, out of order, but safe again in his possession. But now the last page was first; on it he discovered a hand-written poem:

Managua, Nicaragua—Rain, Water and Fire

Surrounded by water and fire
To the west a
sea of peaceful waves stretches regally into eternity.
To the north
Lake of Xolotlán speaks an Indigenous language from
an era beyond memory, little bride of Lake Nicaragua.
To the south
Lake Nicaragua, the southern shawl around my shoulders,
protects me.

How could you possibly be home to sharks
while lying so near to me?
And in the east,
the sun rises from *Océano Atlántico*.
Above me
Let the rains from heaven
Pour down
Soft as a woman's cheek;
Let the rains from heaven
Pour down
Hard as a man's muscle.
Igniting fire, a ring of volcanoes.
And when, at last, they sleep,
They will breathe moist air
that grows the flora and
the fauna.

"Are these my mother's notes for you?" Miguel shouted the question to Caleb as he reached to help retrieve the papers. The noise of the rickety truck and muffler-less engine swallowed half his words.

"What?"

"Are these the notes that my mother took for the water project?" Miguel shouted again.

"Yes," Caleb answered, concealing the poem.

"Did she give you a history lesson, as well?"

"No."

"She should have," Miguel said as he balanced himself against the back of the college student next to him. He half-stood and exchanged places with another student so that he could sit next to Caleb in the back of the truck.

"I'll start at the beginning. Pay attention. There will be a test at the end," Miguel warned his traveling companion with a wink. Caleb smiled and put his notes away, carefully concealing Sofía's poem from her son's view.

"Okay, long ago, 1600 a.C., people populated Nicaragua. The people were called the *Nicarao*. *Nicarao* is also what Castro named his cigars. When the Spanish came they added the word *agua*, water. So maybe it means the people of fire and water. *Sí*?"

"Yes, I'm with you, little professor."

"Good. Someday you'll be grateful for my lectures," Miguel said with mock pomposity. "Now, the Spanish didn't come to the eastern coast of Nicaragua until after that bastard Christopher Columbus was an old dude. Two groups lived in the east: the *Mayanagua* and the *Miskitos*."

"Really? The Mosquitos?"

"Not mosquitos," Miguel said slapping his arm, "The Miskitos." he spelled it for Caleb.

"Okay, so these two groups encountered the Spaniards in the 1500s. What happened before that? Were these groups related to the Mayans?"

"Mayans! Mayans! Why does everybody want to know about the Mayans?"

"Well their name is Mayanaguas, yes?"

Miguel sighed, "Okay, maybe there was a disgruntled Maya who left his clan to the north and came south to form his own group. Or maybe he was from the Aztecs? Or maybe he was born straight up from the volcano and cooled in the lake; whatever. I am trying to tell you about the indigenous people you are about to meet. Do you want to learn or not?"

"Yes."

"So when the Spaniards' ships were lost and cast against rocky shores it was the *Miskitos* who found the lost old-timer, Christopher Columbus, in 1502 and kindly rescued him and his men who were about to mutiny. I think we both know what followed…"

"The *Miskitos* made a very bad mistake."

"Maybe so, but let's make sure we don't lose sight of who is to blame for the following atrocities."

"So Columbus and his men brutalized the indigenous people. Hanging the natives in groups of thirteen in honor of the disciples and Jesus. Raping women and killing babies," Caleb filled in the general brutal history. "I have read some of the accounts."

"But did you know the *Miskitos* have a long history and they helped to get rid of the Spaniards later? This is a good story," but as Miguel spoke these words the truck came to a stop after a sharp right that threw Miguel against Caleb's shoulder. "I'll tell you later about the pirates and the *Miskitos*, but for now, grab your gear, Cowboy. I think we have to exit the truck here."

Professor López had stopped the truck, jumped out and called for everyone to unload.

"Are we here?" Caleb asked of Miguel but it was the professor who answered the general query.

"No, no. We're merely at the first outpost. From here forward, the roads are impassable by truck."

The outpost, a simple place with one small building and an outhouse facility, sat nestled in a grove of endangered mahogany trees. An elderly man, whose face appeared the color and texture of the tree trunks, emerged from behind the building, with rope in hand, leading a donkey toward the visiting party. Without more than a brief greeting, Professor López and the man exchanged the donkey for the keys to the truck. A temporary arrangement, Caleb thought.

Caleb watched as the two plastic igloo coolers that had sat next to the professor in the middle of the front seat of the truck were carefully attached to the mule. A rope was wound several times through the opening of the container's handle and then around the mule's belly and back again. The elderly man watched through cloudy eyes as the professor secured the knots and tested the snugness of the fit with a gentle yank. Caleb watched as the old man nodded his approval.

The students finished unloading the bed of the truck, including mesh netting, two by four boards, a bag of plastic pop bottles, a bag of food, jugs of water, sleeping bags and each travelers' personal duffel bag.

"Just let me know what you want me to carry," Caleb offered.

"The tools are the heaviest, the two by four planks the most awkward. We'll all take turns," the professor told him.

They walked single file along a trail which gradually became more difficult to traverse. The steepness increased and the foliage grew thicker. Sunlight sprinkled through in a dappling manner. Two by four boards accosted plants and leaves bounced back, slapping the unwary in the face. As planned, they each took turns carrying the heavy, the awkward, and the bulky items. Each also took a turn leading the stubborn mule on their way to the next outpost. At one point, Caleb found himself walking beside the professor.

"I don't suppose the next outpost will have a place where I can charge my phone?" Caleb asked.

The professor smiled, "At the next outpost we turn in the donkey because the trails are too difficult for the animal to navigate. So, the answer is no. You will not be able to charge your phone."

"What's in the coolers?" Caleb asked nodding toward the donkey's baggage.

"Medicine."

"Any particular medicine?"

"Mostly medicine for the children, amoxicillin and such," the professor answered before adding, "When we get to the next part of the trail, after the next outpost and before we reach the ocean, you might consider wrapping a mosquito net around yourself. Just for a while. It gets pretty thick."

Caleb nodded. The professor drew close to him and spoke in a low tone. "So, you're probably wondering what you are doing here in Nicaragua."

The professor's words came as a bit of surprise to the reporter. Yes, he knew he was supposed to get water information from the professor. But he didn't realize that the professor held the secrets to his assignment in Nicaragua. However, he guessed it might be so.

"Maybe you want to know why I called our friend, Tracker. Maybe you are wondering why I didn't say anything in front of Sofía when you came to the University. Or why I slipped you a note, that said, *we'll talk later.*"

Caleb nodded. The Professor continued.

"I begin with Sofía. She has been through a lot of suffering in her life. I didn't wish to alarm her. Plus, the people seek her whenever they think they need a leader. She is their living martyr. Like the statue of the Virgin Mother, they carry her out in a procession when they think the people need to be reminded of the greed of corporations, capitalists, Americanos. I thought she deserved a break. We'll take good care of her son. And when we get back, we'll take care of the problem."

"The problem?" Caleb's mind surged with questions: *Why would a simple woman, a mother, a poet, a laundress, be called to lead the people? Lead the people where? Did this have something to do with the loss of her teeth or perhaps something to do with Miguel's father?* "What problem?"

"*Corinto.* Something is going on in *Corinto* that smells fishier than the port."

"What do you mean?"

"I was invited to the Port city of *Corinto*, on the northwest coast, to help assess the water quality at a new bottling plant—*Agua Azteca.* Have you heard of this company?"

"No."

"It is a new joint Nicaraguan-American venture here. Let me explain. In order for a U.S. company to open in Nicaragua they must be hosted or supported or partnered with a Nicaraguan citizen."

"To keep them honest?" Caleb queried.

"Yes, but it doesn't always work."

"So you tested the water. Was there something wrong with it?"

"No, that's just it. It was perfect. Each one."

"Each one?"

"Yes, they gave me three samples to do a blind test saying one was their product. And each sample had to be safe to drink, potable water."

"So, what's the problem then?"

"They spent an inordinate amount of time showing me around, giving me a tour, every nook and cranny. They have a bottling plant and a storage warehouse. They gave me the tour. They even let me look at payroll documents by nonchalantly having an accountant just happen to bring in a question about payments while I was there and then leaving me alone with the documents. Something is not right."

"Okay, but why call Tracker about it?"

"The only thing I could learn about the company is that the owner, the American owner is from Los Angeles and owns a wine-making venture, mostly imports from South America. I know Tracker. If anyone can get the scoop on whether a company is legit or not, it is Tracker. I don't want to be the expert who is used in someone else's scam if this company is dirty. People might accuse me of helping them. So that's why I called Tracker. I am sorry to hear he is not well. But what do you think? Do you think you can help me, discreetly learn about this company?"

"Okay, I get it. But why have me come all this way? Why not just send Tracker or me the info in Chicago and we do a serious background check?"

"This is a good question. I told Tracker that the more they showed me of the bottling plant, the more I felt like they were hiding something in the bottling plant. Sometimes, the absence reveals what is truly present; sometimes, the silence speaks volumes, *sí*?"

Caleb nodded thoughtfully as he slapped at a mosquito.

"Ah, time for some netting." The professor stopped and found the bag with the mosquito nets and freed one from the mild tangle for Caleb. The rest of the group appreciated the short reprieve.

"We're almost there. Over that ridge, you'll see the ocean," the professor said, while pointing ahead. Caleb fumbled with the mosquito netting. Once it was at least over his head and arms, he assessed the distance to the ridge, another half mile or more, an uphill trudge.

Perspiration poured from under Caleb's arms and down his back, mosquitos whined at his ears, the sun began breaking through the foliage in penetrating stabs. He lowered his head and followed the feet in front of him. He and the professor were near the back of the line.

"One more thing," the professor said to Caleb, but his words were interrupted.

"Professor, you better see this," one of the students called out, using a stage whisper, an ominous and low tone. The student had reached the edge of the tropical forest, but still hidden by foliage. He looked back toward the professor, but kept carefully turning his attention to the beach.

Professor López and Caleb hurried to the dune that rose above the beach. From there they could see the *Mayanagua's* and *Miskite's* village, and along the beach they saw a motorized dingy and farther out to sea they spied a modern jet boat anchored in the deeper waters. No people appeared in sight. No children playing. No women washing clothes. No men fishing.

"Get down," the professor whispered to his small party of six—himself, Caleb, Miguel and two university students. They all crouched. A huddled exchange took place. Professor whispered, "We'll go down as if nothing is out of the ordinary." He pointedly said this to the two students, who glanced with reassurance to the professor and concern to each other. "You two will stay here. Lay low," he said to Caleb and Miguel. The professor put his finger to his lips to remind them to be quiet.

Caleb and Miguel watched as the professor and the two students made their way down the sloping dune that was dressed in tall grass. Miguel turned to Caleb, saying in a whisper, "You look silly with that mosquito net on." Caleb didn't answer. He was thinking. He too, realized that something was wrong. The dingy and the motor boat didn't fit the...

"Hey, Cowboy, do you want me to tell you a story?" Without waiting, Miguel turned to look at Caleb and whispered, "So, to continue—"

Miguel's' voice abruptly stopped. His eyes widened to large circles. He held his breath. Frozen in place. His mouth open, but no words came out. The boy saw it. Caleb felt it, before he heard it.

As Caleb started to turn his head, to see what had paralyzed Miguel in mid-sentence, he felt the cold metal barrel of the pistol press against the back of his head. And then he heard the cock of the gun.

He looked at Miguel, "Was there something you wanted to tell me?"

Miguel nodded.

PART 4

THE HERE AND NOW, THEN AND
THERE OF NARRATIVE

DELTA

Mona Barthes typed a text to her brother Caleb, before turning off her phone: *Hey brother, mon frère, call me later tonight. Have been trying to reach you. Assume you are on one of your adventures. Sitting in on a presentation right now but will be home later. Love ya.*

Mona then turned off the phone and slipped it into her purse. Her advisor, Professor Delta Quinn, had already begun her presentation.

"Narrative gives birth to culture, to the meaning of life; narrative sustains us, draws us together or separates us from each other. If narrative were a character in a novel, it would be the protagonist; it would speak first and it would speak last, or at least be last spoken of in the finale. It would hold us spellbound by its charms, just as it has done for centuries. It's through narrative and in narrative that the world takes shape. Narrative says:

> Shh. Listen. I'll bring you into existence. I'll give you essence and meaning. I'll give you a past, a present, a future. A people. A climax. A conclusion. Love. Loss. Guilt. Redemption. I'll give you explanations and reasons to live. Order from chaos. Meaning from the meaningless. I'll give you beginnings. Creation stories from the *Great Buzzard* to the *Garden of Eden*. I'll give you heroes: *Gilgamesh, Lady Ikoom, Superman and Wonder Woman.* I entertain children, *Once upon a time.* I appease tyrants, *Ah, Scheherazade.* I'll chill and thrill you around the campfire. *It was a dark and stormy night*...I will claim reality as my own and history as truth; *It was once so,...il était une fois...* transfixing you with fairy tales, ghost tales, epics, sagas, and so much more. I'll teach you through parables and tease you through romances. I'll make you laugh and cry. I

give your dreams meaning and your day purpose. Most importantly, I'll *fill* your world, I'll make you who you are and who you might become. I am narrative.

The professor paused momentarily in front of the class before proceeding, "Ah, what power narrative has to enthrall us, to explain the cosmos, to create spectacle, to unnerve us, to satisfy us, entertain us, guide us, misguide us, explain us to ourselves, give us meaning. To give us a way forward and a reason to live," the professor told the students who sat mesmerized. "The first written narrative, a classic, has passed its form to contemporary times."

A student raised his hand.

"Yes?" Professor Quinn welcomed his question.

"What do you mean classic stories hold their form?" the student asked the professor who stood in the front of the classroom, beside the podium, not behind it.

"Excellent question. Think of the story of Gilgamesh. The protagonist, who is two-thirds god and one-third human, a being with might and skill, becomes King of Uruk. As king he takes the right to sleep with other men's brides and he forces his subjects to labor beyond their tolerance. The people call to the gods for help and the gods send Enkidu, the one who is wild and lives with the animals. Gilgamesh hears of Enkidu and has a temple priestess, Shamhat, seduce the Wild One, which makes Enkidu civilized. Once civilized, Enkidu is brought to Uruk and there he hears about Gilgamesh's despicable and disreputable behavior with young brides. Enkidu goes to the wedding and bars Gilgamesh from the most recently married girl's bedchamber. The two fight and in the end, although Gilgamesh wins, he is distracted from his unethical behavior by the possibilities that having a companion like Enkidu, promises. Enkidu, a man of near equal strength, and brave enough to have challenged the king, then journeys with Gilgamesh on adventures."

The students looked at the professor, waiting. At last she said, "Our first hero and side kick!"

"Ahh," they nodded.

"He is a nasty hero," one student said.

"Indeed," Delta agreed. "Selfish and self-righteous. A misogynist. Maybe we should call him the anti-hero. The protagonist, yes, but not necessarily a hero, per se."

"But not a complete anti-hero either," another student added. "Since he protects the people from Humbaba." The student seemed to be reading from his phone.

"It is difficult to develop characters that are more than two-dimensional, but Gilgamesh seems to go from bad guy to adventurer. He never fully represents what is noble and virtuous. He doesn't seem to be the stand-up man that Enkidu symbolizes by protecting the people. For those of you who have already read it, do you think Gilgamesh is concerned with his legacy more than the protection of the people when he builds the wall? If you haven't read it, I hope you look forward to reading it in my class next semester. At any rate, we can think of Gilgamesh as a more complicated character than your average hero," the professor said before moving on.

Mona listened, thinking of how people summarize others so quickly and base judgments on so little information. No one ever expected her to become a foster mother, but she always knew that part of her. Maybe others thought of her as fun, as the life of the party, but she knew that side of her was to make people smile, to bring a little laughter into the world.

"Here is another example of sustaining narrative forms," Delta Quinn was saying.

"Gilgamesh is part god, part human. Helen of Troy is the same, she had a god for a father and a mortal for a mother. Jesus has a god for a father and a human woman for his mother. And so on..." The reference to Jesus being equated with previous stories, caught a couple of students off guard. Their small collective gasp brought a sudden brief silence to the room. They had never before heard of such a sacrilegious comparison, as if Jesus were just another character in a story. It definitely gave them pause, maybe even concern.

Mona smirked. It didn't matter whether Delta believed that Jesus was the son of God or a character in the greatest story ever told, Mona knew that what Delta was doing was attempting to jar the students into critical thinking, asking important questions.

"You see what I mean?" the professor said, adding, "And having a companion, a side kick, we all know how that feels; to have a best friend or a partner in life, or at times to be without. Gilgamesh had Enkidu. Batman has Robin." The students smiled. But Delta paused ever so slightly, feeling the absence in her own life. Mona turned things around.

"Jesus had twelve side-kicks," she announced from the back of the room. The class laughed. And so did Delta. Then Delta switched stories.

"Gilgamesh is an old story, maybe one of the oldest written stories. But the stories in the "New World," as some called it, date back thousands of years, too? The most majestic Mayan murals or bas reliefs, which tell stories, date at least as far back as 100 C. E. And elegantly simple and yet surprisingly similar petroglyphs have been found carved into the surface of rocks in the Nicaraguan landscape of a far earlier period, preceding the currently known Mayan period, over 2,700 years in the past. Who were these people? And what were their stories? How did they live? Why did they die out? Was it due to drought, when crops withered and wars over food and water followed? And if so, who should tell their story? There are pockets of Maya descendants who live today and struggle to reclaim their land rights from the conquering Europeans of the past. What about ethics and narrative. Do we have the right to tell other people's story?"

"But if they're dead and gone, who else will tell it?" a student argued.

"It's something for us to discuss. And," she continued, "you can see how narrative studies crosses disciplines, including anthropology, archaeology, history, English, communication, philosophy, politics and even the physical sciences—geology, ecology, and so much more.

"And how should we define narrative?" she continued. "Narrative exists in an ephemeral, and at times, I fear, ineffable way. How can I define this concept for you when at times it gives rise to great cultures and other times encapsulates these great cultures as if they are a footnote in history or a Wikipedia entry? Stories can be grand narratives or they can be pressed into little local maxims, even into colloquialisms or clichés. Defining narrative will be tricky. Think about it," the professor said, "Narratives conjure images ranging from a bedtime story to an epic like the Battle of Troy? Or the story of Gilgamesh. Narratives are artifacts and at the same time living discourses that make us who we are.

"And which narratives should we address? Yours? Mine? Survivors of the holocaust, perhaps? Struggles of undocumented immigrants? Lost histories of refugees? Of slaves? Of sorrow? Of joy? …Of masturbation?"

At this, the professor smiled and the students laughed nervously not knowing that indeed, if they decided to register for the narrative course being offered next semester, they would come to read Blinne's article on her story and the cultural story of masturbation, as well as Ellis and Rawicki's stories of holocaust survival, Moremann and Persona Non Grata's story of undocumented immigrants, Berry's coming out story and so many more articles representing the narratives of existence—from the classic to the everyday, from artifact to a metaphor, to living expression of life.

"Well, at any rate, if we gather the stories of others or even our own stories, we must do so with tender care and accountability. After all, one day, we might be like the ancient Maya—in need of narrative telling." The professor paused.

"All right, I hope that gives you some idea of what the course will be about and I hope I have answered some of your questions about narrative."

"Will we be writing papers?"

"Probably."

"Will there be tests?

"Quite likely, reading quizzes at least."

"Okay, you have the sample syllabus and if you have any questions, my email address is on the syllabus, don't hesitate to send a message." With that said, Professor Delta Quinn began to gather her materials—packets of the readings, a syllabus that lay on the podium, and notes that she had used during the evening's guest lecture about her upcoming course.

"Professor Quinn, I have a question."

Delta looked up to find a young graduate student standing before her. The others were packing up and making their exit out of the classroom. "Sure, what is it?"

"You make narrative theory and analysis sound so overwhelming, interesting, but overwhelming, do you really think it's all that complicated?"

Delta was tired, depressed and ready to go home, but the challenge couldn't go unanswered. She kept the sound of the sigh to herself, took a deep breath and exhaled an answer. "I do," she told the student. She paused for a brief second and then continued, "Sometimes, I think of the experiences that I've lived through and I picture them as stories, stories that I carry in a knapsack on my back. And if anyone were ever to ask me, *is that knapsack light or heavy*, I'd answer, *yes, it's both. Some stories lighten the load of life; others weigh me down. But they all make me who I am.*"

The student stood quietly for a moment before saying, "I see what you mean. Thank you, Professor. Have a good night."

"You, too," Delta replied turning her gaze and her efforts toward packing her materials. She tried not to think of the story she was currently living, but she couldn't help to wonder why Caleb had stopped calling, why he hadn't returned her calls. And having Mona Barthes, Caleb's sister, sit in on the lecture only served as a reminder tonight. She and the other professor, who had invited Delta to talk about her upcoming course, exchanged ritual closings: *Thank you so much for coming. My pleasure. I'm sure a number of students will register for your course.*

"Delta," Mona said. "Wonderful presentation."

"Thanks, Mona."

"Are you interested in dinner? My house. Abigail would love to see you before she has to go to bed."

"Thanks, but not tonight. I have some papers to grade by tomorrow," she lied.

"Okay, another time," Mona offered.

"Yes, absolutely," Delta promised and thought, *just not tonight.* She was still thinking about Caleb.

Delta walked quietly down the hallway and out the door. As she left the building the icy winter air stung her lungs forcing her to gasp in little breaths. The tiny exhalations appeared like puffs of smoke. She could see her breath as she passed under the light of a street lamp. Not a student in sight. *How do they disappear so quickly, leaving the campus so quiet?* she wondered as she walked alone to her car.

It wasn't the first time Delta had been left alone to figure out the world—feeling abandoned. And it likely wouldn't be the last, she thought. *It doesn't matter whether you're young or old, it doesn't matter how many times it happens to you; it always hurts.* A teardrop spilled over the lip of Delta's eye and down her cheek, freezing halfway to her chin. *I really thought we clicked,* she thought, giving up one more tear and glad there were no students around to see her as she left the building and headed toward the parking lot. Caleb had not returned her calls. Any of them.

Another teardrop stuck to her face before she could wipe it away, as if, forever frozen in time and place. She unlocked the car's doors with a double turn of the key, stowed her bag and purse in the back, and slid into the driver's seat before slamming her fists against the steering wheel.

"Fuck that shit!" she said aloud. "Fuck *that* shit!"

She started the car, the Hummer, to be more precise. Turned on the lights against the darkness of the wintry night and drove head on into on-coming snowflakes, saying "Fuck you and you and you," to every snowflake that hit her windshield.

DISTRACTION

"I need a distraction," Delta told her friend P. J. Turner the next morning as they sipped their respectively preferred caffeinated beverages, coffee for P. J., tea for Delta. The cafeteria was nearly empty which made the wintry December day seem even colder. Ice crystals decorated the window that abutted the booth in which they were sitting. Delta wrapped her hands around the warm, ceramic mug and leaned into the steamy black tea and their conversation.

"I really fell for this guy," Delta told her friend. "He was perfect."

"And?"

"And maybe it wasn't meant to be," Delta tried to disguise her hurt.

"Destiny!?" P. J. challenged her friend while looking disappointed and annoyed.

"What?" Delta remarked defensively.

"When you say 'Maybe it wasn't meant to be,' you're letting destiny rule your life. I don't believe in such things. We make our lives." P. J.'s voice was as strong as her black coffee and held no sympathy. "Have you called him?"

"Yes."

"When? Give me the details, sister," P. J. slurped her hot coffee.

"The details aren't important. We were getting along great; and then he had to go out of town; then I had a conference. Then he was busy and then I was busy. Anyway now it's been more than three months since I've heard from him. I texted him three times last week alone. And nothing. I'm done. I'll just embarrass myself, if I don't stop now."

"Hmmm," P. J. considered the situation. "Clearly the ball is in his court. Is he the one who helped you solve the GMO seed mystery about who was poisoning farmers' crops in the area?"

"Yes."

"An investigative reporter, right?"

"Yes."

"Hmmm."

"Hmmm. What?"

"Nothing. I was just thinking that he may be given to going on adventures. New challenges. That's all."

"Oh, nice. Real nice, P. J.," Delta said sarcastically.

"What do I know? He might be a great guy. Nevertheless, he's not answering your texts. So what do you want to do?"

"I want a distraction."

"A new man?"

"No!" Delta exclaimed.

"A woman?" P. J. quipped.

This time Delta laughed aloud.

"What? You might like it, you never know," P. J. half-teased her. "Okay, so you want a distraction, it just so happens I have one for you. This is actually why I called you last night and left a message about meeting me this morning. Do you have a passport?"

"I do."

"Good. And how large are your hips?"

"Pardon me?"

"You heard me."

"They're small. Maybe 32 inches."

"Gawd! That's what I thought." P. J. had a luxurious figure—an average waist that curved into bountiful hips. She carried it beautifully and never failed to turn heads when she walked into a room. Her rich, reddish auburn curls fell over one eye more often than she liked, but she countered the unintentional Hollywood look with glasses. The archeologist was taller with broader shoulders than Delta's petite frame could muster. Delta stood about five foot four inches in heels with long, dark hair and a slender figure. Her olive-colored skin spoke of her mixed heritage—Irish, French and Cherokee; whereas, P. J.'s bi-racial background provided her with a copper-colored complexion and brown eyes.

P. J. continued, "I've got a distraction for you and all you need is a passport, money for the flight to Belize and then Managua, and small hips."

"Lay it out; I'm listening."

"Okay, I got word this week that a couple of archeologists and an anthropologist are putting a team together to study a new site in Nicaragua. The site may house the oldest stela and pictographs concerning the Lady Ikoom."

"The Lady Ikoom? Really? I just mentioned her last night in a lecture."

"Oh, fantastic. Then you know about her."

"No, not really. I just came across a mention of her as a Mayan figure and wanted to list heroines in the lecture, too. The lecture was about the power of narrative."

"So you don't know about her?"

"Not very much."

"This is so frustrating," P. J. said turning both her hands into fists and pounding the air twice before continuing. Delta watched and waited, clueless to P.J.'s frustration. P. J. reclaimed her calm.

"If only I had smaller hips. I love the stories of the Lady Ikoom and there is still so much mystery about her. Yes, she's a historical Mayan figure and little is known about her except that stela 44, found in El Peru Waka—"

"Wait, where?"

"El Peru Waka is in Northern Guatemala. So anyway, the glyphs—"

"The glyphs?"

"The hieroglyphs," P. J. explained, but Delta knew that, just needed reminding.

"Right, right. Hieroglyphs."

"So the glyphs on the monument say that it was built by Wa'oom, the son of Chak Took Ich'Aak and Lady Ikoom. Archeologists believe that Lady Ikoom commissioned it by way of her son for her late husband in order to solidify her family's power. You see at the time, there were rival powers represented by two lands—the Land of Tikal and the Land of the Snake Lords. Lady Ikoom came from the Land of the Snake Lords, whereas Chak Took Ich'Aak a.k.a. Red Spark Claw came from Tikal and he wasn't anyone terribly special. The monument tells the story of the Tikal king ruling over the land and killing Ikoom's husband, Red Spark Claw, but then Ikoom has the Tikal king murdered and builds the monument as a testament to the power of her family to rule over both lands. The Snake kingdom and the Tikal kingdom. Therefore, their son, Wa'oom has the right to rule both."

"Cool. Sounds like *Game of Thrones*," Delta concluded.

"Yes, very cool. But these lands are in Guatemala and no one has ever found any evidence of Lady Ikoom farther south. Until now! This is a fantastic find, that possible evidence of Lady Ikoom exists in Nicaragua, but the specific find can only be reached down a very narrow shaft and the researchers are putting together a team of women anthropologists, archeologists, and others who are small enough to fit down the shaft and explore the new findings. Damn my curvaceous hips!"

"It sounds very cool but I'm not an expert in this area, why would they want me? I don't know how to read the 'glyphs'; I know very little about the Mayas."

"That's not why I thought of you. Do you remember when I was at your place and you showed me your Native American pottery collection?"

"Yes, but what does that have to do with it?" Delta wondered aloud as she had no Mayan pottery in her collection, although she had seen an exquisite Mayan piece in the Smithsonian, which told the story of a hunter and his killing a deer and then offering a sacrifice to the gods for his good fortune. It encircled the vase. She particularly remembered the pictorial for death, a tiny cloud with three lines drawn from it. The docent had watched her studying it and offered the translation: "*It signifies the last breath, death.*" P. J. then interrupted Delta's drift through time and space, experiencing a different narrative.

"You told me how you became interested in collecting the pottery, how you and your grandmother had made your own pottery and had replicated the glazes of the older artifacts."

"Yes," Delta confirmed, and an image of her Cherokee grandmother entered her mind.

"Well, some of the artifacts that they've found have richly colorful details but the glazes are oxidizing when they hit the air above ground. You know what that means."

Delta did indeed know what that meant. The same thing had happened on the archeological dig in China of the famous terra cotta warriors and horses in Xi'an. The Chinese decided to stop excavating until they could find ways to keep the colors from oxidizing and thus disappearing from the statues. Delta had written an article on the topic addressing the challenges of saving cultural artifacts. P. J. had read the article and had been surprised to learn of Delta's knowledge of artifacts, glazes and pictorial narratives, something that her grandmother had taught her.

P. J. continued, "They could use someone like you to study and document the glazes and provide written details of the pictorials to go with the photographs; that is, if photographs can be taken while down in the deep chamber and without hurting the artifacts. Actually, I thought of you right away before I even knew that you were looking for a *distraction,*" she emphasized the word. "And I mentioned you and your expertise to one of the team members. So, are you interested?"

"Yes, absolutely. When do we leave?"

"Next week, when classes let out for winter break. But not *we,* just you. You would be the last to join the team. Also, the itinerary is quite full. You'll fly into Belize take a shuttle to the Mayan Rain Forest lodge to gain a little experience in cave diving—"

"Cave diving?!"

"You'll be fine," P. J. dismissed Delta's concerns and continued. "And then make a trip—"

"Wait a minute. Spelunking?!" Delta interrupted her friend again.

"Well, I wouldn't use that term with them. Spelunking is sport. Cave diving is serious business. More like speleology."

"Of course, what was I thinking?" Delta added facetiously, pretending she knew the difference between spelunking and speleology.

"Anyway, it's just in case."

"In case of what?" Delta asked, but P. J. ignored her question.

"You'll also travel across the border to Guatemala to meet an expert who will fill you in on some of the things they want you to look for regarding the pottery. He'll take you on a tour of the Mayan ruins of Tikal. It's a day trip. With others. Then back to Belize for cave-diving lessons. From Belize you'll take a flight into Managua, Nicaragua, meet a representative of the team and make your way to the archeological site."

Delta sat wide-eyed by the itinerary and stunned by the possibilities that suddenly appeared before her.

"And why isn't the Guatemalan expert going?"

"Believe me, he would if could. His hips are too wide, his shoulders too broad," P. J. reminded Delta of this requirement. "Well, yes or no? They need to know today if you'll fill the spot. The timing is perfect, right? The semester coming to a close. Your grades are turned in, right? So do you want to go?"

"Wow, when you create a distraction, you don't fool around. Okay, yes. Absolutely, yes."

CHAPTER 21

DELTA AND MONA

"All right. Do you have everything?" Mona asked Delta as they pulled up to the airport's drop off point. "Oh, I don't know why I asked that. If you don't have something you can always buy it when you get there," Mona corrected herself. "I'm just being a mother." And then with emphasis and joy, she repeated the thought, "I am a mother."

Mona Barthes, Delta's graduate advisee and good friend, had driven her to the airport without giving it a second thought. Mona was generous that way, especially with her friends. If she had any faults, it was probably that she tried to be too generous. Double and triple booking herself at times, only to cause mild anxiety when she couldn't take care of everyone. She liked Delta and they had been friends now for several years. There was no way she wouldn't take her to the airport.

Mona liked Delta enough to have had introduced Delta to her brother Caleb, a reporter for the *Chicago Tribune*, when Delta had faced a mysterious set of circumstances, months earlier. Together Caleb, Delta, Mona and others had tracked down the culprits behind a greedy corporate scheme to defraud farmers and unsuspecting customers via the sale of toxic weed chemicals and questionable GMOs. They had proven to be a good team. Mona was especially happy to see Delta and Caleb hit it off so well. But Mona also knew that the two hadn't kept in touch of late. Not being sure why, she hadn't brought it up again, but now, she couldn't help herself.

"You know, Delta, I have all the respect in the world for you. So I hope you don't mind my butting into your personal life and saying, you shouldn't give up on my brother. Not yet. And when you get to Nicaragua, perhaps you could get in touch."

Delta wasn't sure what Mona meant. She tipped her head questioningly.

"He's in Nicaragua. At least the last time I talked to him, he was. It was a while ago, but he said he was going to call you." Mona told Delta whose eyes widened.

"And you're just telling me this now?" Delta questioned as they pulled up to the curb.

"I know, I know. But I wasn't sure if I should butt in. And I haven't heard from him in weeks. Plus, I've been a little busy myself, you know," Mona reminded her.

Mona's own life had been filled with dramatic turns over the last several months. It began when she volunteered with social services as the preliminary means of collecting data for her dissertation on the sequestered stories of poverty. There she witnessed a different form of poverty than she had expected. From one family, she witnessed an emotional form of child abuse that broke her heart. Impoverished in a completely different way, the child was so starved for love that she no longer held hope in her eyes. A six-year-old named Abigail Newton, who at every turn was dismissed by her father, who had actually told her that he had hoped for a boy, that she was worthless, a failure, and didn't deserve to take up space on this earth. He told her at every turn that she couldn't do anything right—her clothes were wrong— she changed them; her hair was mussed—she combed it; her shoes scuffed, she rubbed them with her little fist; and, each time he would shake his head in disappointment at her efforts. The mother had left long ago after the father had won the custody battle to keep the girl. His abusive nature had been hidden from public view. He had painted a portrait of the mother as neglectful and himself as diligent always helping the child to improve. Only recently had bureaucrats realized the mistake that they'd made. But none would admit it aloud. Teachers (the classroom teacher, the art teacher, the music teacher) and principal alike reported the strange relationship between father and daughter whenever they saw them together and the effect on the girl. He simply didn't like her.

One social worker explained to Mona that the child was so forlorn that when she first entered school the teachers assumed she had emotional and mental challenges, but none realized the cause. Teachers noticed that when they pushed her to excel in the classroom, the child assumed defeat before ever trying. She scribbled pictures, instead of drawing; she wrote words where math scores should go and numbers where words should go; she sat instead of standing for the pledge of allegiance; she refused to speak but occasionally communicated by screaming at the most inopportune times. Any praise given to her was immediately withdrawn due to her response—she slammed her fists against a table or stabbed the desktop with scissors. Mona recognized this as true poverty. The child could not accept nor give love. Mona was the first to get the child to speak.

Mona volunteered beyond the basic social work she had been doing by offering her services to Abigail's classroom teacher. As a teacher's helper, Mona did tasks like decorating the bulletin boards, Xeroxing tests, taking the students to the lavatory and so on. She always invited little Abigail to help her and often Mona simply sat by Abigail's side in the classroom. Never expecting anything. Simply staying with her and always asking at the end of each day, "Is there anything I can do for you? Is everything okay? Are you alright?" Weeks of this finally brought a change. The little girl looked deeply into Mona's eyes one day and said, "*I'm* not right; and I'm not alright."

Mona put in effort beyond that of sympathy. She advocated for the child. She fought for her freedom from a family, a father, absent of love. One day, at the cafeteria table a teacher asked, "So let's say you prove the neglect or abuse, then what happens to the girl? The foster system has its pros and cons, you know."

Once the child was removed from her home, Mona immediately applied to be her foster parent. The bureaucratic process was a nightmare but once everything had calmed down, Mona became a mother.

One day, Mona told Delta that Abigail had finally curled up next to her on the couch and allowed Mona to read a story to her. "What story?" Delta had asked. "Does it matter?" Mona had replied. Delta smiled. Mona was right. Indeed, Delta felt as though it was Mona who could now guide *her* through life. And witty. Hadn't Mona saved the mood during the lecture by describing the Apostles as twelve side-kicks to Jesus. Delta smiled at the thought, and wished she had Mona's sense humor.

"You are going to be a great mother," Delta predicted.

Mona replied, "Great? More than great. I'm going to be one mother of a mother!"

Delta smiled. Mona's positive attitude could lean toward the hyperbolic. "Try getting in touch with Caleb," Mona suggested.

"Do you really think I should call him?" Delta asked, as Mona lifted the lid of the car trunk and pulled out Delta's suitcase for her.

"Absolutely not," Mona said. Delta's eyes widened. "Text him, don't call. Geez, sometimes you sound like you're from the Dark Ages."

"What should I write?"

"Do I have to think of everything? C'mon, you have a Ph.D."

"I don't know. I'm just not sure."

"Would there be any harm in it?" Mona asked.

"I suppose not," Delta considered.

"I mean, what's the worst that can happen?" Mona added lightly, but Delta became consumptively quiet.

"Oh my god, Delta. Reel it in, girlfriend." Mona handed over the suitcase. "My brother isn't perfect, Delta, but something about the two of you together seemed right to me," Mona added.

Delta caught on the phrase, *isn't perfect,* like a sweater snagged on a thorn from a rosebush. She had thought of Caleb as perfect. He had the qualities that make heroes who they are. He seemed to create his own epic narrative, starring in the lead role. Mona had described him as the one person who could really help Delta. Mona had made him sound like an action hero. *Maybe she's just now realizing that no one is perfect. Or that perfection isn't all it's cracked up to be. And maybe I turned him into a hero as well,* Delta thought. *But he did help me, and there was no denying that he chased bad guys, endured being knifed, was able to bring down a bi-plane by threatening the pilot and even bring the culprits to justice by working with his friends and connections from the Department of Justice.* Delta had put him on the top of Mt. Olympus and then fallen for him in the worst way.

"Perhaps, you're right," Delta said to Mona, giving her a hug before entering the terminal.

"Think about it," Mona advised. "And one more bit of parting advice," Mona said and then paused.

"Yes?" Delta turned back toward Mona.

"Don't drink the water."

Delta smiled, hugged her friend and advisee again, and then disappeared into the terminal.

MONA

Mona gripped the steering wheel a little tighter as she scanned for the right signs and entered the faster moving traffic merging onto the freeway from the airport drop-off point. Once she was in the flow she was fine. It was a long and fairly boring drive back to Lafayette, Indiana, the home of Purdue University. The land sat as flat as a deflated balloon and currently as brown as a grocery store paper bag.

Not that anyone sees grocery store paper bags much anymore, she thought. *But what will happen when they outlaw paper and plastic?* An image floated across her mind's eye of a quaint European village, somewhere in France or maybe Italy. She saw a man walking down the street with a loaf of bread under his arm and a hunk of cheese wrapped in...*wait, wrapped in what?*

She had been to both countries—Italy and France. Joining her parents, both doctors, who took vacations in Europe. Caleb had joined them on each occasion. Brother and sister had ventured about, always raising concern for their mother. Mona smiled as her thoughts drifted to another place and time, moving into and through narrative drift.

These excursions are only fun if mom is worried, Mona remembered Caleb saying to her as they headed toward a flea market in Paris, near the Arab section of the city.

And dad's the worst, isn't he? Mona had volleyed back.

Should we bother trying to make him more adventurous? Caleb had suggested and queried.

I think it's the language barrier, mon frère. Otherwise he is adventurous. Mona had said.

Agreed, mon frère. Caleb said, pretending that he didn't know what *frère* meant. And she had laughed as Caleb called her, *my brother, in French—their inside joke.* His French was terrible; actually, he struggled with any language that he tried, but his sense of humor and humility, making fun of himself, always brought a smile to Mona's face. He continued. *Dad must be absolutely beside himself by now, since I've stolen you away. You at least have a rudimentary French under your belt.* Caleb continued, *And he's probably worried about you walking around with that expensive camera hanging around your neck. Tourist, much?*

Look, look, mon frère. A group of men playing bocce ball in the neighborhood. Mona had said as she swung the camera into position. She waved a friendly hello *Bonjour* and asked permission to photograph the men as she moved closer. They laughed, embarrassed. Shooed her away. A couple of them looked angry. But she made pleading gestures. One took pity and posed dramatically and the others laughed. She clicked the camera with abandon. *Work with me,* she would say, getting them to play along. She showed them ways to pose. Caleb scanned the area as Mona played professional photographer and the men acted the part of runway models.

I'm sure 'Life' online zine will want these, mon frère. I mean, I'm almost positive.

No doubt, her brother had said as they continued toward the flea market. She waved, *au revoir* to the men playing bocce ball and called out a sincere *merci.* And then she caught up with her brother. Once there, Caleb followed her as she flitted from booth to booth. Draping colorful scarves through the air, holding up shoes and judging their size, she engaged each vendor with happy words, a broad smile of shining teeth and glimmering blue eyes. Blonde hair fell in mussy strands about her angelic face. The vendors seemed less than playful.

Mon frère, mon frère, look, perfume! Let's get a bottle for mom. She would love it, wouldn't she?

Cheap perfume, yes, of course. He teased her.

Mona picked out one with a light green label with tiny white lily of the valley flowers. She queried the vendor about the price. He ignored her and walked to the other end of the booth. She followed like a puppy who wouldn't give up. He gave her an angry look and turned away. *Americans,* he whispered under his breath. She started spraying the perfume in the air. He turned quickly, grabbed it from her, saying *"Five Euro."* Mona paid him. He put it in a bag and sent her away.

Why is he so angry? she asked her brother.

Politics. Sometimes, the French love Americans and sometimes they are angry at us.

How do you know this, mon frère?

I heard mom and dad talking about it. When America stirs things up in the Middle East, it makes the French angry.

Why?

Because if things erupt in the Middle East, the Arab countries are on France's doorstep and America is far away.

So, we're stirring things up right now?

Yes, mon frère." Again she smiled. *That's why mom and dad worry when you wander away.*

Okay, then. Let's head back, the teenaged Mona had said. Mona remembered that Caleb had nodded, just as a young man, not much more than a teenager himself, sent spit flying onto Mona's shoe. Very purposefully. Caleb jumped in front of his sister.

Let it go, mon frère.

Caleb glared at the young Frenchman. Their eyes locked on one another, a stand-off stare ensued.

It's okay, mon frère, really.

Caleb continued to hold the other man's stare as he let Mona pull him along. Mona loved her brother. He was always there for her. Always.

When they had returned to the hotel, and found their mother upset at their having left, Mona produced the bottle of perfume, the gift. And even her mother melted under Mona's charm. Caleb, however, rolled his eyes.

You're impossible, mon frère. He had said to his sister.

Really? Because I think you're wonderful, she had said to her brother.

From memories to the present, Mona smiled to herself as she continued her drive northward toward Lafayette after having dropped Delta at the airport. Now, she was excited to tell Caleb how things were going with Abigail, but he hasn't texted or returned her calls.

Why? Why? Why? She wondered. *Why hasn't Caleb been returning my calls? Or for that matter, why isn't he returning Delta's texts. He didn't usually wait so long between phone calls.* Her brain fixated on the word rather than the search for answers. *Why?*

She could hardly wait for her little girl to begin speaking. Asking, why? Others might complain about their children pestering them with, *why? why? why?* But Mona looked forward to the day that Abigail would begin speaking. She was still not talking, nearly seven years old, and no words. But the waiting would soon be over. *Patience,* the therapist had said. *Keep in mind that she was treated with contempt when she spoke, that she likely is afraid that no matter what she says, it will be wrong.*

Mona exited the freeway and drove a short distance to her friend's house. Her friend, Lisa was watching Abigail for her while Mona drove Delta to the airport. Mona's friend Lisa had done this on more than one occasion. She watched Abigail for short periods on and off for a couple of months now. All had agreed that it would be beneficial for Abigail to be with a small group of children in order to watch normal interactions. Abigail was learning how to play with others, by observing. In school, she had often been separated from the other children so that she wouldn't disturb them if she had a tantrum or began walking in circles, another habit of hers. Mona pulled into Lisa's driveway, parked the car, went up the walk and then knocked on the door.

Lisa answered. Mona could see Abigail playing with the toys in the living room. Abigail looked up, jumped up, and ran to Mona. "Mama," she said, delighted to see Mona. And the girl threw her arms around Mona's waist. Lisa watched in joyful amazement. A breakthrough, at last.

Mona embraced the girl, pressing her head to her abdomen. She stroked the girl's hair. Who knew such a simple word, such a brief exchange, could bring such joy. *Mama.* A tear rolled down Mona's cheek. She swallowed hard, and discovered that now she was the one who couldn't speak. *Mama. She called me Mama.*

ABIGAIL

Abigail couldn't explain her dreams or why she behaved as she did, but she knew that she was not like the other children. She wanted to be calm inside but couldn't make it last. She dreamt of a spool of thread unrolling in a straight line, a perfect thread, and then for no apparent reason the thread would tangle into a mass of complicated knots and messy weaves. She had told her mother, in a whisper, as she stood by her mother's side of the bed, about her dream and then asked, "Can I get in bed with you?" Her mother raised the sheet inviting the child closer and put a sleepy arm around her as the then four-year-old Abigail climbed into her parents' bed. She felt the warmth and comfort. The tangles smoothing, receding into sleep.

"No children in my bed!" the voice shook Abigail like thunder, loud and deep, low and gruff. Like a giant, fe, fi, fo, fum. There was no room for arbitration, the command was final, complete. Abigail's mother slid herself and Abigail out of bed. She pulled the bedspread onto the floor, folded it in half and whispered like a gentle wind for Abigail to sleep next to her on the floor.

When the judge asked Abigail, in private chambers and with an advocate on hand, "Did your mother ever make you sleep on the hard floor?" Abigail couldn't answer. The judge had not asked the question in a way that made sense to Abigail. He hadn't asked about the tangle nightmare; he hadn't asked about the thunder of her father's voice that made her shake; he hadn't asked about the kindness of the wind, how her mother whispered or how her mother slept next to her on the floor.

The man in the black robe put half a dozen such questions to her: "Did your mother ever make you stay under the table, hidden by a tablecloth?" Abigail felt safe there, especially if the thunder and lightning were going on at the dining room table. Her mother knew she could hear the storm of abuse above her but the tablecloth tent made

139

her feel safe. The judge did not, in Abigail's estimation, understand storms or pretend camping and the protection of tents. Once again she did not answer him. Finally, the judge asked her if her father takes good care of her. As young as she was, Abigail felt the annihilation of her mother by the judge's words. It was visceral but not translatable. Ineffable. She knew that she had to say something. Or there would be another tangle. One that she might directly cause. Tears welled in her eyes.

"My mother walks on pretend egg shells with me, we whisper like the wind."

"What?" the judge squinted. She began to explain that her father "sleeps on the edge of a cliff and if we wake him, dragons will—"

"She's too young to understand; not capable of choosing," the judge interrupted and then determined her future. The advocate nodded. Full custody was granted to the father. Abigail's tangle nightmare moved from dreams to everyday actuality.

By the time she entered kindergarten she had stopped speaking above a whisper; instead, she rarely spoke at all. She tried to behave like other children in the classroom, but would find herself turning a perfectly good line into a massive scribble that would extend from the paper to the desk and it would carry her across the room and she would scribble a tangled mess on the walls, silently screaming out while trying to whisper for the wind.

Other days, she might rock herself back and forth until the morning's end. Trickier times brought on a day of walking in a small circle for hours. The kindergarten teacher noticed her extreme perfection, not a hair out of place, not a wrinkle in her clothes, the black patent shoes were shined, in contrast to other kids' mussy hair, loose play clothes, and well-worn sneakers. Not only did this perfection stand in contrast to her class-mates attire, but in contrast to the screaming scribbles that she drew, the tangle that entrapped her.

"Where were you today?" Abigail whispered into Mona's shirt as she stood that morning at Lisa's house enveloped in Mona's hug. Mona's eyes were still filled with tears of joy as she answered.

"I took a friend to the airport."

"Who?"

"Delta. You know Delta."

"Will she come back?"

"Yes, why do you ask?"

"Did you see my other mother?"

"What?"

"You are my forest mother and my other mother is the wind mother."

"Oh, foster mother. She means that you are her foster mother," Lisa said. "Oh my gosh, she has been listening to every word we have said."

Abigail repeated, "Was my other mother at the airport?"

An overwhelming silence hung over them. Neither Mona nor Lisa knew what to say. They looked to one another without a word. It was Abigail who made sure no tangle followed.

"Never mind," she whispered. "It's okay."

CHAPTER 24

DELTA AND BELIZE

The flight to Belize gave Delta time to read through the materials she had brought along as well as the online information she could find. Having had less than a week to prepare left her with dozens of questions and more trepidation than was likely necessary. One woman had posted online not to wear expensive jewelry as you cross the border from Belize to Guatemala, not that Delta had any expensive jewelry, but the thought made her a bit uneasy. Another post said that things were a bit 'sketchy' at the border these days. These concerns were met with a multitude of others, most of which fell under the genre of placing your safety in the hands of strangers.

P. J. had informed Delta that she was on her own with regard to finding transportation from the Belize airport to the Rain Forest Lodge. With a bit of online help from Mona, she had selected a driver who promised, via an online exchange, to take her safely to her destination. Mona and Delta had been sitting in a warm café each scanning for possibilities when Mona said, "Look at this one." Mona turned the computer for Delta to see as she added, "This guy asks that you contribute school supplies for the children. See that?" she had said pointing to the line on the computer screen. "How can you go wrong with a driver who collects donations at the same time?" So, after making arrangements, Delta had crammed her suitcase with pencils, notebook paper, and crayons for the children and a large, map of the world for the teacher. Then she decided that wasn't enough and she added a stapler, staples, paper clips, and tacks. Her suitcase was small but by the time she had finished packing, it was quite heavy. She decided to have it stowed rather than carrying it on.

"And he speaks English," Mona had said.

"Everyone speaks English in Belize," Delta told Mona as they sat in the café. "It was a British colony."

"Oh."

"Actually, I just read that," Delta had confessed. Knowing that the first leg of the journey was in an English speaking country had helped to quell some of her anxiety. But she knew the same was not true of her second destination.

On the flight, after reviewing the other materials, she scanned through an English-Spanish dictionary to help with the second leg of the trip—Guatemala.

"Flight attendants, please prepare the cabin for landing."

She heard the words from the pilot over the intercom system. She began gathering her array of materials and laptop, in preparation of pushing them under the seat in front of her. The reading materials covered several genres—travel guides, history of Mayan civilization, spelunking and cave-diving, handling artifacts, ceramic patina protection, pictographs, and so on. She realized as she collected and stowed the combination of materials that she likely had such spotty knowledge and at such a surface level that she feared she would be more trouble than help to the archeological team. But academics were being encouraged to create interdisciplinary teams in order to get grants and Delta's connections to communication and her rhetoric background with a specialty in narrative and a knowledge of Native American ceramics is likely why the team accepted her, and of course, those narrow hips helped. She would join the all-female team that was comprised of an archeologist from Guatemala, an anthropologist from Ohio, a qualified diver from California, and an anthropologist-historian-museum curator from Mexico. Everyone, except Delta, had a strong background in Mayan history.

She stepped off the plane into a bright sunny day with temperatures in the 80s. The skies were clear; she shielded her eyes with one hand and followed the passenger herd into the terminal and through the customs line. Two women behind her in line, were talking about going caving. Delta couldn't help herself, she interrupted.

"You've been caving here before?"

"Oh yes. We bring a group of students every year for a quick study abroad," the one woman told her. Like Delta, the woman was only just arriving, but her face spoke of years of tan with an age spot on her cheek and permanently sun-burned nose. She must have loved other water sports as well; clearly, she had not limited her pursuits to the dark, underwater caverns.

"And the students can learn cave-diving that quickly?" Delta asked.

"No, no," the other middle-aged woman told her. "We do that on our one weekend off. The students can go into the tamer caves or go on safer tubing journeys where they can float down the cavern's rivers to see Maya artifacts. No, they won't cave-dive with us; cave-diving takes years to master."

Delta gulped slightly and pursed her lips.

"Is this your first time to Belize?" the first woman asked, changing the topic.

"Yes, I'm headed to the Rain Forest Lodge and then off to Guatemala for a trip to Tikal."

"Oh, you'll love Tikal," the second woman promised as they moved forward in line.

This casual conversation both raised Delta's concerns about cave-diving and calmed her reservations with regard to traveling through Belize and on to Guatemala. If two middle-aged teachers could handle the rigors of the rain forest and had no qualms about bringing students here, then surely she would be fine. She passed easily through customs where they checked her purse, laptop, and passport. She moved on toward the unloaded luggage that she spied across the room, no carousel; the bags were lined up on the floor, arranged with aisles between long rows of suitcases. She walked up and down the aisle searching for her bag, not there. The first glitch. She waited for more luggage to be brought in but nothing came. The crowd was dwindling.

"No luggage?" one of the teachers, whom she had met in line, asked.

"No," Delta answered.

"Go to that window." The teacher pointed to a teller's window as she wiped perspiration from her upper lip. "Good luck with your trip," she added before leaving.

Delta inquired at the window about her bag. The teller, a middle-aged man with mild wrinkles on his ochre-colored skin and black hair with touches of peppery gray, informed her that it had been lost and would be found and sent to her temporary place of residence in Belize.

"Where are you staying?"

"The Rain Forest Lodge. When do you think it will arrive?" She held little hope that it would make it there before the next leg of her trip commenced. She always packed one change of clothes in her oversized-purse. She pictured herself washing out the same t-shirt and underwear for the next few days.

"Soon, soon. By tomorrow morning at the latest. Maybe even later today."

Delta was now straggling well behind everyone else. And after a pit stop in the bathroom, she returned to find nearly all of her fellow passengers had disappeared from the terminal. She bought a bottled water and broke the sealed cap just as she heard a voice.

"Delta, Delta Quinn?" The accent was Belgian or Dutch, something completely out of place. Delta turned to see a tall, gangly man with reddish hair, fair skin and a dappling of freckles on his face. "Are you Delta Quinn?'

"I am," she said re-tightening the cap on the bottled water.

"I'm Eric, your driver. Come along then. The others are already in the van. You don't want to keep them waiting. It's hot out there."

"Yes, of course. I'm sorry. My suitcase didn't make it and I had to—"

"Oh, no worries. That happens frequently down here. They're good at getting it to you."

"But I have to leave again. Oh, and the school supplies. I brought school supplies for you but they're in the suitcase." He led the way, taking long strides and fast steps. She tried to keep up. He kept turning his head back to her and then forward again and talking.

"No worries. I'll get the supplies from you when I bring you back to the airport for your flight to Nicaragua." Glance forward. Glance back. "Glad you booked in advance; I have a busy week. Very busy." His quick steps led them into the blinding sun of Belize.

"I own a car wash, a sandwich shop, and I have the school to tend to and then, of course, the shuttle." Glance from side to side.

Stepping off the curb, "Over here." He led her to the van. She was glad to see three other passengers.

A young woman with long, wheat-colored hair and blue eyes sat in the front passenger seat. After being introduced Delta learned that both Eric and Katerina considered themselves locals as they had lived in Belize for more than fifteen years. Eric, the driver, came on holiday years ago, met a woman, and fell in love. He returned to Rotterdam, sold all of his possessions, took care of business and family matters, and returned to Belize. "Sadly," he told Delta and anyone else in the van who was listening to him, "When I returned, I couldn't find her. I never saw her again."

Katerina sighed politely. She had heard the story before.

Delta turned to Katerina, "And you, are you here on holiday?"

"No, my husband and I own a farm and like Eric I also run a school." Katerina turned her pale cheek toward the sun. Her hair streamed across her face from the wind coming through the open window. They drove along the main road, narrow but paved and smooth. The couple in the back seat were in their fifties or maybe sixties. They stared out the windows intensely and did not engage the conversation. Eric said he would drive through Hattleville, *La Democracia*, and *Belmopan* before reaching the Rain Forest Lodge. In each place he planned to make "a quick stop."

At one stop, Eric explained, "I owe this mechanic some money. I'll be right back. If you need a toilet, they're over there. He won't mind if you use it. I just say the word and he does what I want. He knows I'll put a little money in his hand later. But those guys over there," he said pointing to the group of three indigenous men standing by the building, "They hate me. So don't strike up a conversation with them. They think I'm an interloper. That I steal business from them. But look!" He nodded his head toward two run down cars. "They don't take care of their vehicles and they expect people to ride in them. My van is the best. I work hard." His voice filled with ire, which seemed to give him the bravado he needed to walk past the three men after he exited the van. The men in turn gave him a side glance of disdain as he passed.

Katerina turned to Delta, "How long are you staying?"

"A few days, then I go to Guatemala. Then back to Belize City and onto Nicaragua."

"What's happening in Nicaragua?"

"I've been invited to join an archeological dig."

"*Guardobarranco*," the man in the back said.

"Absolutely," his companion agreed. The matching overweight couple each wore beige sun hats with short brims, ready for a day of fishing perhaps. Each was dressed in a loose t-shirt with light weight cotton vests and both wore khakis and comfortable American-style shoes—canvas and plastic with thick rubber soles—Nike.

"The birds," the matronly woman added as if she had clarified the previous comments. Sweat rolled down her neck from under her permed hair.

"The *guardobarranco* is the national bird of Nicaragua," the man explained. "You shouldn't leave Nicaragua without taking in a little bird watching. Try to get to the *Montibelli* Reserve," he advised. And his companion nodded enthusiastically. "We went for our 35th anniversary," she told them. "The best trip of our lives," she said as Eric returned to the van. "We saw the *motmot*, that's another name for the *guardobarranco.* Anyway, it is the most exquisite shade of turquoise you will ever see in your life!"

Delta smiled as the bird watchers continued to describe various birds of the region. Eric and Katerina held their own discussion about the schools. Delta tried to listen in both directions.

Katerina left at the next stop, *La Democracia*. Eric got out to lift her suitcase.

"Are you okay? I don't see Tom's truck."

"I'm fine. I texted. He's on his way. You go ahead."

As they got on the road again, Eric pointed to the valley ahead, "Valley of Peace, they call it." He drove on occasionally pointing out landscapes that rose and fell in such a way as to give one the feeling of shapes that had been christened by the locals, *the sleeping giant*, and later, *the resting woman*. He drove along, slowing when he reached a one-lane bridge and again after crossing. A few houses and small businesses came into view. A man sold tacos by the side of the road. Eric slowed the van, reached into his wallet.

"Anybody want one?"

"No, thanks," the travelers were in agreement.

Eric waved his money at the man and held up one finger. The man walked over with a taco full of peppers and rice. He held out the taco. Eric took it from him and then held out the money, but as he did, he let his foot slip off the brake and the van lurched forward. The taco vender caught up with the van and reached out his hand again. This time Eric started to put the money in his hand, only to let the van lurch forward one more time. This time, anger rose into the vendor's face clearly realizing the first time had been no accident. He opened his mouth and started to speak, but Eric cut him off.

"Just kidding with you, old man. You know I always pay." Eric handed him the money and the travelers went on their way, with Eric chastising the vendor behind his back as he pulled away. "He needs to learn or someday somebody will take the taco and not pay him."

Delta thought, *What a jerk.*

The bird watchers in the back seat remained silent. Their stop was next. It'd been a little over an hour on the road, just past Jaguar's Paw. Several bed and breakfasts came into view along with small hotels. In the distance, Delta could see a luxury hotel on the hillside overlooking the river. The hotels and B & B's seemed out of place in comparison to what Delta had seen along the roadside— shanty structures, simple cement block school buildings, houses on stilts and long stretches of fields of oranges with workers of Maya descendants and Mestizos loaded down with canvas bags that hung from their shoulders and trailed beyond their feet. After unloading the bird-watchers, Eric drove again and pointed out to Delta how the trucks are filled with oranges.

"The road side is cut wide enough for a dump truck to pull off, but also deep enough that it is below the level of the farm field. See," he said pointing to the drop off loading area. "The oranges are brought from the grove to the edge of the field and poured over into the waiting truck bed. This is only a problem when the rains make the dump area too muddy for trucks. They've gotten stuck," Eric told her. "What a job getting them out then."

Farther down the road, Delta, who had been staring out the window, sat up straighter to get a better look.

"Surprised? Yes, most people are," Eric said.

"Amish?" Delta queried. "In Belize?"

"No, Mennonites," Eric corrected her.

Delta took in the scene of Mennonite men assessing a crop as Eric offered her an explanation. Broad-brimmed straw hats covered their pale skin and amber beards. They were dressed in light blue shirts and long dark trousers with suspenders to hold them up and their shirt sleeves rolled up to their elbows. Women followed, walking behind the men, their full skirts flowing nearly to the ground, stockings on their legs ended inside sensible shoes, but of course it is the little white bonnet that had first caught Delta's eye.

"The Mennonites were the secret weapon in the fight for independence from the British," Eric began.

"How so?" Delta asked.

"Well, a large group of Mennonites living in Mexico had been told by the Mexican government that they could no longer be conscientious objectors. Mexico was about to go to war against Guatemala. But in Belize things were different. The Mennonites heard that the British were able to maintain control of Belize because the indigenous people had no means of large-scale farming," he told Delta. The British controlled the ports and thus the farming equipment, everything from tractors to materials for silos, trucks for moving fruit, everything. The Mennonites knew that the Belizean people wanted to revolt but feared the British would starve them back into submission. So the Mennonites offered their services to the revolutionary forces in exchange for land and freedom to practice their religion."

"When was that?"

"1958," he told her. "It's nice. I mean that farming won the revolution for the indigenous people," Eric added. Delta began to soften her feelings for Eric until he added, "They're good people. The *Mennonites*, I mean." Delta wondered again if he held bias against the indigenous Belizeans by the way he had said that he liked the Mennonites. He interrupted her thoughts, "When I drive you back to the airport in a few days, I'll take you to their ice cream stand." Delta smiled.

Approximately, twenty-five minutes later, they arrived at Delta's destination, The Rain Forest Lodge. She gratefully removed herself from the van, stretched her legs, wiped the sweat from under her heavy, dark hair, and breathed in the fresh, albeit humid, air. They both felt awkward for a moment as they remembered she had no luggage. She had paid him in advance, she pulled out a tip and he pointed her in the direction of the main office and reminded her of her return date and time. She nodded. Eric pulled away. Delta took a moment to assess her surroundings.

She breathed deeply again and this time the fragrance of the air wafted into her nostrils bringing an olfactory beauty beyond compare. She closed her eyes. The smell of mystic and magnolia combined to create a lilac based-scent that gathered together the delicateness of the tiny white mystics, the richness of the rare *taulama magnolia* and something to which she couldn't put a name. Delta opened her eyes, looked around and discovered that the pebble-covered drive was surrounded by an herb garden. Each plant had a label card posted on a tiny stake: allspice, bay leaf, red kiss, coffee beans, and so much more. The small plants were protected by the medium-sized, colorful crotons. The four foot shrubs with the giant green, yellow and red leaves were shouldered by tall, feathery ferns which, in turn, were protected by the giant palms of the rain forest. Delta felt as if she could stand there forever.

"Please, Miss," a young man stood in front of her, a skinny teenager. "Would you like to come in and check your reservation?" He smiled at her, showing his bling, a tooth with gold inlay. She followed him. "No bag?" he inquired.

"They're supposed to deliver it later." As she entered the verandah dining area, surrounded by rain forest fauna, she felt that she had been transported to a magical and unimaginable place. She thought of the bird watchers as she took in the bright colors of the jungle and realized that hidden within the array of foliage are macaws and parrots, as well as monkeys; she smiled.

Regina, a plump woman of Maya descent, emerged from the cook house, introduced herself and presented Delta with a glass of tamarind juice—light brown liquid made from the fruit's beans with sugar and a pinch of salt poured over ice. It tasted sweet and sour, simultaneously. Delta complimented Regina's skill and followed her to the closet-sized office where Regina pulled a key from a drawer, the key was attached to a long wooden holder. The office manager handed it to Delta.

The wooden key chain was inscribed with a word: *agouti.* "Your cottage is called agouti," Regina told her. She pointed up a stone path with jungle plants on either side. Delta followed the path until she came upon a small, white cottage that was set back from the path and slightly up the hill. The cottage had a tin roof and front porch where a hammock hung lazily in the shade of the overhang.

Delta unlocked the door. The one-room cottage was colorfully decorated. Belizean blankets lay spread on the beds—reds, violets, yellows, oranges, and magentas woven together with deep forest greens. Yellow and gold curtains cast a sunset warmth over the twin beds. Two dark wooden dressers sat juxtaposed to the beds. Delta had nothing to put in them since her luggage had not arrived. The cottage had electricity and running water, but a sign on the bathroom sink reminded her that the water was not potable. She tested the shower and realized as she did so that there was no reason to have warm water in Belize—heat and humidity called for lukewarm to cool showers.

Before going to her cabin, Delta had asked about a store and Regina had told her that it gets dark early, around 5:30, and that's when the mosquitoes come out, but that she had plenty of time to walk down the hill to the store and be back for dinner if she desired. "On the other hand," Regina said, "tomorrow is Saturday. Market day."

Eventually, Delta laid on the bed with every intention of getting up shortly and walking to town, but she fell into a deep sleep and woke to the sound of a rooster even though only an hour and a half had passed making it late afternoon. She realized that she shouldn't have looked up the word *agouti* before falling asleep as she dreamt that the large rodent was sitting on the end of the bed staring at her and without speaking wanted to know what she was doing in his house.

CHAPTER 25

MOUNTAIN TO MARKET—SAN IGNACIO

On Saturday morning Delta walked down the dirt road that led to the San Ignacio market, kicking up a bit of dust with each step. She passed small, ranch-style homes of various colors and heard reggae music coming from one house, a boastful rooster cockling in front of another, and a quiet cow giving off only an occasional moo from a third yard. From the top of the hill, she took a picture of the spacious valley unfolding before her. She wound her way downhill, soaking in the sun and the view of the landscape—soft rolling hills dotted with homes. As she made her way along the winding road, she began to notice that the houses told very different stories of wealth. One, under construction on the corner of the curving road that now intersected with another road, spoke of privilege and wealth. Three stories high, this house displayed floor to ceiling cathedral windows and multiple balconies that provided a view of the valley and the city below. On the opposite side of the street, another modern architectural masterpiece sat protected behind metal fencing that was topped with barbed wire. Yet, tucked within the turns of the road, stood simpler homes with smaller windows, water cisterns outside, and dogs lounging in the dirt.

The dogs meandered about unabated by a master's leash or spiked-ground chain. And they appeared healthy, which surprised Delta. She hadn't meant to stereotype, but she couldn't help but to have images and expectations of a place she'd never before seen. She had expected to see scrawny dogs with rib cages protruding, eating from the garbage. After all, she thought, this is a poor nation. Not only did she not see the dogs eating from the garbage, she didn't see any garbage on her way to the bridge that crosses the Mopan River. The scene was idyllic. The Mopan, she later learned, meets the Macal, merging and birthing the impressive Belize River.

Walking over the bridge, provided a view of the river and the upcoming town from a distant angle, the romanticism of impressionism held firm. Pastoral stereotypes still privileged in her head would soon give way to the day-to-day realism that close-up images portray.

The residents of the Cayo district now shared their land with tourists, contemporary eco-explorers, and academics who were more interested in the past than the present. Delta could be counted among that group. The gas station and convenient mart that appeared on the corner after crossing the bridge told a tale of modern conveniences unknown to the Ancient Mayans of 600 A.D. She popped into the store and asked for a pair of sunglasses.

"Ah, the blue eyes protector," the young man behind the counter teased her. He had to bring them down from a high shelf as they were rarely requested and occasionally stolen. There were few to choose from and they were fairly expensive. But she had forgotten hers and the Belizean sun was bright against the clear blue sky. More importantly to her, her dark Cherokee hair allowed her to mingle in the crowd, her green eyes gave away her outsider status, as did her height. At almost 5'4" Delta stood a head taller than most of the Belizean women. The people of Mayan descent remained close to the earth, most women were around 4'10" with black hair and brown eyes, their skin a golden brown, their clothes colorful, feminine, their shoes sometimes spiked even though they walked the pebble-covered roads. And they did not wear sunglasses. This generalization came to light as she passed a Verizon give-away in the center of town. Local people stood waiting, lined up, a queue stretching for several blocks, for the promotional event's give away. Not a single person wore the "blue-eyes protector."

Delta by-passed the event, walking around the edge of the town square, and having already passed the large, white police station and the small resort hotel with an expansive porch, she followed those who made their way to the market. There, vendors tempted locals and tourists alike with vegetables, clothes, artwork, beans in burlap sacks, and shoes of all sizes and styles. Tarp-covered kiosks lined the way. Rows of stands formed a little city of vendors with crops and crafts. Delta entered the market with enthusiasm.

"Have a look," a sturdy, young man spoke up. "See," he said, having captured Delta's attention. "I make these myself. Mayan calendars." He held one high for her inspection. The Mayan calendar was an intricately carved circle of pictorials on a piece of slate. "Here," he handed it to Delta. She took it in her hands, which lowered unexpectedly from the weight of the stone. This pleased the vendor, who then smiled.

"It's beautiful," she told him. She took her time and looked at his other carvings. "I'll come back after I've been through the market." But she really had no intention of returning to his booth. Yes, the Mayan hand-carved calendar was tempting, but she knew it was too heavy to lug around Belize, Guatemala, and then Nicaragua. It was bound to be chipped or broken by the time she reached home. She was not a serious shopper; she didn't even plan to buy food, especially since her cottage had no kitchen and no drinkable water, although she was growing hungry. But from booth to booth she offered polite appraisals or half-hearted promises, giving hope of her return and eventual purchase to vendors who thought she might come back. Up ahead, she watched a crowd gathering around one booth. It drew her in out of curiosity, mainly due to the number of people who had converged there.

"Step up, step up," the man with the magic hands was saying as he swished the shells quickly around and over the counter. The classic pea and the shell game. "Who's next?" He kept them mesmerized by lifting the shell, showing the green pea, covering it again, and then racing the shells over and around each other on the counter top. After a moment or two of study, a man put down his money. The shells came to an abrupt stop.

"That one," the man in the crowd said firmly as he pointed to the third shell.

"Ah, a winner. A man with a keen eye." The vendor with the magic hands revealed that it was indeed the correct choice. Everyone cheered. He paid the betting man. Then the master of the pea and the shells began again. Delta wondered if the betting man was a confederate for the con man. The two did have a similar appearance, distinct from the crowd, the two were taller, with stronger features, larger noses, father and son, perhaps. Maybe everyone else wondered the same thing as bets were not coming quickly. People watched; they waited. Eventually, a young man put his money up, picked a shell and lost. Another and another took their turns. Delta watched until her growling stomach begged her to move on and as she did she heard one man in the crowd say, "the Lebanese have quick hands." At another booth, she held cloth between her fingers and considered buying the light-weight, billowing dress that she hung in one of the stalls. She inquired, the price was right, the size too small. In any event, she didn't really need it as her suitcase had arrived that morning. She moved on, leaving the market empty handed, making her way through the city streets, and sizing up the shops until she came upon a restaurant that offered the smell of fresh food, shade of indoor dining, and a place to sit.

When the banana pancakes arrived they were garnished with jicama, guava and mango slices. The bananas were sliced and embedded within the flour of the hotcakes. Delta felt saliva surge into her mouth as Mama of "Mama's restaurant" set the plate in front of her.

"My son came up with the idea," the short round woman explained, "that I should open a restaurant." While taking Delta's order, she had added that her son had also thought of the name "Mama's, he thought of that, too." Now she set the plate in front of Delta, saying "He came up with this recipe, too."

Delta saw a glimmer in Mama's eyes for her boy. "Dig in, dig in," the owner encouraged her before heading back to the kitchen. Mama was generous with her servings and her smile. She returned later and joined Delta at her table. Delta finished the last bite. Looking up, she suddenly realized that the restaurant had slowly emptied of customers.

"Oh, are you closing? I'm so sorry," Delta apologized.

"No worries. We close for a bit, do the dishes, rest and then come back to get ready for dinner." Delta made a move to rise immediately, but the woman put a hand on her shoulder.

"Sit, drink your coffee, and tell Mama why such a pretty girl is eating alone."

CHAPTER 26

GARIFUNA TO THE WARNINGS OF GUATEMALA

Later that afternoon, Delta sat on the porch of her rental cottage at the Rain Forest Lodge sipping a mixture of One Barrel Rum and a splash of berry juice that she had picked up at a grocery mart on her way back from town. There she had assessed the supplies in the store and now realized why the paper, pencils, erasures, and other school supplies were in demand. There were few groceries and even fewer school supplies at the store and what little existed was expensive. The owner-operator of the store, spoke no English, only Chinese, so Delta, who's bilingual expertise was nearly nil, couldn't get details on why it was so difficult to get school supplies to Belize. However, she had learned from Eric, the driver, that the government readily built schools, but left stocking them, running them, and hiring teachers to the nonprofit sector. Over the years, different religious missions had stepped in to manage the schools while the Chinese immigrants had excelled at grocery entrepreneurship in Belize.

Delta wiped sweat from the nape of her neck and took another sip of the rum and berry juice, an iceless drink, as she had carefully followed Mona's advice—don't drink the water. She had taken that advice to the extreme, not even looking for ice. Not that she would have found any ice. The cottage was simple, without many amenities, no coffee maker, blow dryer, or ice bucket. A comfortable bed, toilet, sink and shower were included. A chair and hammock on the front porch. *What more did anyone need in paradise?* The birds cooed above and around her; the fragrance of flowers wafted on every, nearly imperceptible, breeze. She inhaled heaven.

Her thought of the school supplies reminded her of the young students she had seen on her first day in Belize—Friday. Dressed in uniforms, they had energy even in the unrelenting heat and oppressive humidity—boys swinging school backpacks at one another; girls singing in rhythm and dancing a step or two. Delta vicariously felt that healthy, joyful release from the constraints of the Catholic or Presbyterian or Methodist school day. She had smiled then, and was smiling now. What if she could stay here, in this moment and this place, forever, she wondered.

Startled at that very moment by a sound near the edge of a tree, Delta looked to her left. There in the shrubs, a *paca*, spotted like a chipmunk, the size of a house cat, foraged for dinner. Delta watched with great interest. Its little square face and perky ears bobbed up and down in search of fallen fruit from a breadnut tree—*masapan*.

Delta realized that she too was hungry. She put her bottle of rum back in the cottage as it was nearly time for dinner on the Rain Forest Lodge patio. She locked the door of the cottage and took brisk steps down the path to the dining area. Each night the Rain Forest Lodge offered its guests a different local culinary experience—Creole, Maya, Mestizo, Lebanese and tonight, Garifuna. Delta sat alone at a table with a green tablecloth that matched the foliage that surrounded the patio. The server lit the candle on her table. The owner introduced a Garifuna family whose matriarch provided a casual but rehearsed lecture as diners awaited their dinners.

Delta learned that the Garifuna are a people of mixed races: African, Caribbean, and Arawak. Their ancestors lived through a trifecta of diaspora. The Caribs came to prominence in 1200 C.E. after conquering the Taino people—native to the area. They intermarried with the Arawak who had fled Spain's brutal assaults during the 15th and 16th centuries. And then in 1675, the Caribs/Taino/Arawaks rescued the Nigerian Mokkos who had been aboard a slave ship that crashed against the rocks. After several generations of intermarriage, the Garifuna had developed a blended culture; but, in 1862, the conquering British separated the Garifuna based on appearance: those who looked more African were sent into exile while those who looked more Amerindian were allowed to stay. The British had feared revolt by those of African heritage.

Currently, a small number of Garifuna live in Belize and other Latin American countries, the matriarch explained, and tonight an even smaller number came to the Rain Forest Lodge to teach the lodgers (from eco-travelers to newlyweds, from Mexican college students on holiday to Canadian bird watchers on an ornithology mission) about their history, their cuisine and their dances. At the lecture's conclusion, Delta, a professor who prided herself on diversity awareness, chastised herself for her total ignorance; she had never heard of the Garifuna before this evening. Sure, she knew of Afro-Caribbean cultures and people, but this particular group—Garifuna had escaped her. As a matter of fact, she had envisioned the Latin American countries as somewhat homogeneous; instead, she had met Latin and Lebanese, Garifuna and Chinese, Belgium and Mennonite, Mestizo and Mayan, all within two days of being in Belize.

The server brought Delta a bowl of *hudut*, creamy and speckled with spice. Fish floated in the savory coconut broth. Delta spun the fish with her spoon. The server set a plate of *fufu*—a pounded bread made from plantains—next to the bowl of fish stew. Suddenly, a little Garifuna girl popped up at Delta's table.

"It's very good. It's called *fufu*."

"Is it? Is it your favorite?"

"Yes, but not the fish."

"No?"

"No, I like chicken the best, but this is very good, too." The little girl disappeared as quickly as she had appeared, leaving Delta with a smile and a bowl of fish stew. She dipped her spoon in and brought the liquid to her mouth. She smiled and lifted her eyebrows. Surprisingly delicate and savory.

Delta didn't think she could eat another bite after finishing the stew and bread, yet when the dessert came, she didn't hesitate. Her fork slipped smoothly through the soft, cinnamon-flavored cassava pudding which in turn, melted in her mouth.

The dining area was dark by the time the Garifuna family began their dances. More candles were lit. Music played. Two young brothers beat out a rhythm on drums while a third shook the rattles in unison. The eldest sang. The sisters and mother danced. Some dances told stories of working in the fields, others simply expressed the joys or the hardships of life. The littlest girl, wearing a yellow cotton dress with puff sleeves and a full skirt, danced into the center with small steps and riveting hips. She confidently led the older sibling sisters. After several dances and much rhythmic clapping of the diners, the littlest girl danced her way to Delta, took her hand, and led her to the dance floor. There was no resisting the girl's charms—large brown eyes and bouncing, curly, black hair were surface level enticements indeed, but it was the way the girl dedicated herself to spreading her culture, taking Delta's hand and leading her gently but insistently onto the dance floor and into another world that captured Delta's heart.

Delta learned the steps quickly as the rhythms entered her soul and spirited her along. The little girl left her dancing with her older sisters who were also dressed in colorful clothes with bright scarves holding back free, black hair. The youngest danced from table to table until she had danced every diner to the main floor. No one was immune to the charms of the elementary school-aged, Garifuna girl. She was serious about her charge to bring fun to the group of strangers and to teach others about her culture. When it was over, Delta felt more at ease to talk with other diners as well as the Garifuna family members.

"How often do you give presentations?" she asked the mother of the troupe.

"We rotate among the hotels during the in-season as long as the children are not too busy with school."

"They were wonderful," Delta complimented. And then added, "Especially your youngest."

The mother beamed a proud smile. "She is committed." With that Delta returned to her seat.

"You did that very well. Dancing, I mean," the woman at the table next to Delta's table commented. "I'm afraid that's not my forte. Please join us," she added, having noticed that Delta was alone.

"Thank you," Delta said as she joined the woman and her companion at their table.

"Rosemary," the woman said, extending her hand. "This is my husband, Richard." Rosemary sat with a regally-draped, long-sleeved, light-weight sweater over her shoulders and a pair of glasses hung from her neck on a gold chain. Her companion, Richard, reached out his hand to Delta, adding, "Nice to meet you."

"And you. I'm Delta." Delta sat in the empty chair across from the couple. "So many stereotypes I had are dissolving," Delta said as she looked over at the Garifuna family.

"You didn't know Garifuna lived here?" Rosemary asked. Delta shook her head. "Your first time in Belize?"

"Yes."

"We're expats," Richard told her. "We live in Placentia."

"What other stereotypes are breaking?" Rosemary queried.

"I walked to town and saw such healthy dogs along the way. I guess I was expecting, well, mangier looking mutts."

The couple exchanged a knowing smile between them.

"What?" Delta insisted on being let in on the secret.

"Did you notice that the circus was just in town? Old posters, from last week?" Rosemary asked. Delta nodded; she had noticed the posters. Richard continued the explanation:

"They rounded up the scrawny dogs last week and fed them to the circus tigers."

Delta's eyes widened as did the couple's smiles. They seemed to enjoy both sharing this cultural tidbit and seeing Delta's reaction to it. When Delta didn't say anything further Rosemary changed the subject.

"We're here to direct a cave-mapping expedition. What about you?"

"Tomorrow, Tikal. The next day a crash course in caving and then onto Nicaragua to explore a new archeological site."

"You've not been caving before?" Richard asked. Delta shook her head, indicating she had never been caving. Rosemary and Richard exchanged glances again.

"You'll love Tikal," Richard said. "But caving cannot be done in a crash course."

"It's very dangerous," Rosemary inserted.

Delta explained, "I don't think I'm supposed to be able to do actual cave mapping, just be knowledgeable enough to not do anything stupid."

"Hmm. The caves around here can suddenly become very deep, very dark, and very dangerous. It's easy to lose your bearings. Sink holes can be especially dangerous. Sometimes, a lake in this area will be there one day and gone the next."

Delta didn't understand, her brow furled inquisitively and perhaps with a bit of concern. "How could a lake disappear in one day?"

"The earth is not stable here. Sometimes, an underground shift will open a hole, a shaft, and an entire surface lake will disappear overnight into a new underground cavern and that opening can cause surges in the water underground, within the caves, that is. It's truly a terrifying proposition. Sinkholes on steroids," Rosemary told her.

"The newly drained lake will appear empty the next day, like an unplugged bathtub after a bath, except you'll see fish flopping about on the old lake-bed," Richard added. "Really, something you have to see to believe."

"Underground, it's so dangerous," Rosemary continued, "that we make our divers carry three oxygen tanks." Not fully understanding the reasons nor the implications, Delta compelled them to continue.

"Tell me more," she said. Richard took up the explanation.

"When salt water eats away the limestone and causes a massive sink hole an entirely new world can be opened to a diver. Within seconds they may be sucked downward dozens of feet, discovering a whole new array of caves. Entire ancient, diluvium, Mayan cities have been discovered this way. What the divers find can be so mesmerizing that they lose track of time or the experience of the sink hole can be so discombobulating that it throws them completely off course, forcing them to turn to their back up tank. They have been known to run out of oxygen. We lost a diver that way. He had already turned to his back up supply when he was sucked farther into a cave." A short, considerate silence followed. "Now, we make our divers carry a backup for the backup."

Rosemary changed the topic. "Tikal should be less dangerous. It will also take your breath away, but that's because the views from the top of the temples are so amazing," she said with a smile.

"Ah, less dangerous maybe. But still keep a foot from the edge of the ledges if you can. One was struck by lightning because a camera crew left a lightning rod up there. Oh, but that's another story. I'm sure your guide will tell you all about it. You do have a guide, don't you?"

"And," Rosemary interrupted, "be careful crossing the border. After all, it is Guatemala."

CHAPTER 27

THE GUATEMALAN BORDER

"Now that we're all here and on our way to the great Maya ruins of Tikal, allow me to provide a few safety tips." Barlow, the guide, announced as he drove the passenger van from the Rain Forest Lodge. Delta, the fifth and final passenger to be included on the day trip, buckled her seat belt. After checking her name off the roster, Barlow stowed the clip board under the seat and turned the key in the ignition. The young man, approximately the age of Delta's undergraduate students at Purdue University, began to rattle off a list of things that could go wrong. He was raising concerns and yet also instilling confidence as he appeared to have a back-up plan for every contingency or at least a joke to set them at ease.

"The drive to Guatemala is smooth, but once we cross over the border the roads will change. I like to think of them as challenging. Fun really. Flat tires are a possibility, but we have a spare. So enjoy the rugged roads. Ah, and the border crossing," he paused in his instructions. "Before we get too far, does everyone have their passports?" The couple in the farthest back seat of the van nodded as the male tapped his jacket pocket and the female companion nodded. They appeared to be in their thirties, young with rosy cheeks and fair skin; the woman smiled. The couple directly in front of them were much older, their skin pale white, covered in freckles and brown age spots. Their girth, combined, took up all of the middle row in the van. They each had their own set of binoculars hanging around their necks. He was balding under his baseball cap and she sprouted curly, white hair from under a touristy sun hat. Delta could smell their suntan lotion via their sweat which had a hint of Rolaids or perhaps it was Tums. Delta sat in the front passenger seat of the van. The driver looked at Delta for confirmation.

"Yes, I have my passport," she assured him.

Barlow's dark hair blew back and forth across his bright eyes and the clear golden skin of his face as the breeze from the open window cooled them all. He had pulled the van out of the mountain lodge drive, made his way down the hillside and onto the two lane highway. They sped along smoothly. During the drive to the Guatemalan border, Barlow described the general itinerary for the day and provided a bit of Mayan history, including a caveat: "But I am not your Maya guide. He'll meet us on the other side of the border. We'll park the van, go through immigration, walk across the border, and then he will take us in his van, and then to Tikal. Please, be aware of your possessions during the crossing. We've had only a few incidents and we'd like to keep that number low. You may be pickpocketed if you're not paying attention to what is happening around you."

"Or kidnapped," the man in the middle seat added.

"Kidnapped?" The young woman in the back seat seemed surprised. Her accent sounded Irish to Delta, but hard to tell for sure from a one-word sentence.

"An American couple was kidnapped," the bird-watcher added.

"That was in 2014," Barlow told her. "It was resolved very quickly with negotiation," he added to reassure her. "Nothing like it has happened since. Just a little pickpocketing." Barlow continued to reassure the travelers that they were in no real danger. Both couples, as well as Delta, grew quiet.

The ride to the border took less than half an hour. Barlow parked the van.

"Stay here, please. I need to take care of something before crossing."

The passenger couples chatted amongst themselves while Barlow met another man. Delta watched as the two walked toward a *ceiba* tree several yards from the immigration building. They took a seat on the bench in the sparse shade. Barlow showed the man some money. The man reached into his pocket. Something small was exchanged. Barlow glanced up and over at his charges in the van and saw Delta studying him. She turned her glance away.

Barlow disappeared into the immigration building.

"It's getting hot," the elderly man commented, wiping sweat from his upper lip.

"You mean, hotter," the younger man added congenially as his eyes scanned the border crossing scene. Guards in camouflage uniforms held rifles. Delta changed her first impression of the young couple from Irish to Australian.

"What would you expect?" the elderly woman said with a smile, adding "After all, you are roasting on the equator."

"So we are, so we are," her male companion added.

Barlow returned and told the occupants of the van that they could now disembark and join others in the immigration line.

Several of the armed guards strolled around the outside of the immigration building where a line of people formed outside. All looking of Latin and Mestizo or Maya descent. The line outside the building moved slowly. Delta assumed the Belizeans and Guatemalans had day jobs on one side or the other of the border. Everyone in line dressed in cool cottons and simple styles. No hats. No luggage. Whereas, their little group appeared to be tourists; each one wearing a hat and sunglasses. They waited in the morning heat, currently outside, but just ready to step inside the small, white building.

"I'm already cleared for crossing the border." Barlow's voice startled Delta. She hadn't noticed him coming up behind her. He spoke quietly into her ear, "Are you paying attention to your surroundings? See that man?" Barlow nodded his head toward the Guatemalan side of the building as they stepped through the archway on the Belizean side. Delta looked past the line of people and beyond the three teller windows to her left where immigration officials checked passports and on down to the exit where a man stood leaning on the post by the door that gave way to sunshine on the Guatemalan side. She nodded.

"He was looking at you. I saw him watching you. Now, he sees me watching him, watching you. Now, you need to join the watch. Do you see?"

"Yes," Delta said with gratitude.

"And by the way, what I was doing with the old man on the bench under the tree," he said to her, "was exchanging my sim card. I need a different card for my phone while I'm in Guatemala." Delta nodded, feeling a bit awkward, even though she had held no doubts about his actions, he clearly felt she had.

After passing through immigration, she attached herself to the young couple from the van, making conversation with them, and staying to the far left of the man who had been watching her. She kept a careful eye on him and clutched the strap of her purse.

"Over here," Barlow called to his passengers as he waved. Barlow stood with Luis Dominguez, their Guatemalan tour guide. He nodded to the group, introduced himself and then provided his credentials.

"I hold a Master's degree in anthropology and am currently working with a team of forensic anthropologists to uncover the more contemporary history of the Ixil Maya people. Are you familiar with this history?" he asked the small group. All shook their heads, unaware of the Ixil Maya's history. He continued.

"During Guatemala's bloody civil war of the 1980s my father escaped to the U.S. I was born in New York City, love the Yankees." The group smiled. "Nevertheless, I left New York to work in my parents' native country—Guatemala. I'm trained in historical as well as contemporary Maya studies." All of this he told them as he ushered them into a different van. Barlow took the passenger front seat. Delta squeezed into the back seat with the elderly couple. The younger couple took the middle seat this time. Luis started the engine.

"How do you find the time to work with the forensic anthropologists and guide us?" the elderly woman in the back seat sitting next to Delta asked Luis. He answered as he drove away from the border.

"It's my duty to do both. As part of a grant that we received from the U.S. and supported by the Netherlands, for two months I work on the forensic project and for a month, I come here and act as a docent for those of you interested in ancient Maya culture and the remnants at Tikal."

"Luis, why do they split your efforts?" the husband now asked. "It doesn't seem efficient."

"A business man, eh?" Luis said before explaining. "The forensic anthropology that I do is unnerving because," he paused and swallowed hard, and then turned and looked at them, taking his eyes off the road momentarily, "because uncovering mass graves of Maya people, who were massacred, takes a toll on one's soul. This happened not so long ago. Widows sit vigil by the archeological sites. Mothers await word on whether their long missing sons have been found in this grave or not." Silence followed. "The 1980s were a bad time here," he said. "A very bad time."

Eventually, the elderly woman asked the young anthropologist, "Does walking in the ancient city of Tikal restore your sense of peace?"

"In some ways it does. I'm renewed when I share a proud history. You'll be amazed when you see the pyramid temples of Tikal and learn of the creativity and capabilities of the people."

The van had been humming along a street lined on either side with colorful stands that show-cased clothing, weavings, jewelry, food, and more. Repeating its offerings, one stand after the other, the market of goods whizzed by Delta's van window. Luis continued to talk about his country.

"The souvenirs, craft-work, and more are all for sale in Guatemala. The prices are better than in Belize," he added.

"You don't have to tell them that," Barlow quipped as he searched for a radio station with music that he liked. Luis, was not much older than Barlow. Delta guessed Barlow to be around 20 and Luis around 24 years old, maybe 25. But Luis had the air of a man and Barlow that of a boy. Their difference could be measured in the space of an experience, uncovering graves, she thought. Delta doubted that Barlow had ever had to recover human remains, he seemed so filled with teenage innocence and energy he had probably never held a skeleton bone in his hands. At least not one that represented his murdered countrymen. But Luis had done such things. Delta heard it in the weighty sound of his voice and the words he had spoken.

"I'm of Spanish and Maya descent; lived in New York, visit Belize frequently, and can assure you," Luis paused. Delta thought he was about to begin a lecture about culture, human rights advocacy, international knowledge and laws; instead, he said with a smile, "shopping in Guatemala rocks!" Everyone smiled.

The passengers seemed more at ease with Luis's jokes than his talk of political histories and massacres. He covered a range of topics as they drove. The stories that followed were of Mayan gods and goddesses and the ways of people who lived centuries ago while Barlow played hip hop on the radio between the short lectures that Luis provided. Like a well-trained team, Luis turned the radio down each time he wanted to inform his passengers of some historical nugget concerning the Maya; and each time, Barlow listened respectfully before turning the music up again at the completion of the mini-lecture; also a moment when the two friends smiled at each other. During the drive, Luis pointed out landscape features and noted that although they had just come from the highlands of Belize, these he said, turning down the music, "are the lowlands of Guatemala." Suddenly, the van jerked, throwing Barlow backward, his hand away from the radio knob. Barlow broke into a large smile and said something in Spanish to Luis that Delta couldn't make out as the van suddenly rumbled and bounced over rough, dirt roads.

"Ah, and these are the roads that we thank the Guatemalan government for keeping up so well," Luis joked over the noise of the grinding of rocks and pebbles under the now bouncing tires of the van. The asphalt road had abruptly disappeared. It seemed to Delta that they were on no road at all, but instead cutting across a dry field where a wide swath of tall grass had been driven into submission.

"This is the adventurous part," Barlow added with a smile. "And we'll get to do it two more times," he added gleefully.

The trip took about an hour and 45 minutes from crossing the border to reaching the gates of the Tikal National Park where Luis took the group on a short walk through the building that housed the model of the expansive rain forest park. "The national park is a place where it would be easy to become lost, not only because of its size, but also because of its mesmerizing beauty," he told them.

"So, stay together," Luis warned.

CHAPTER 28

TIKAL

"I know this will sound dumb at this point, but I thought the Mayans all died a long time ago. You mentioning modern Maya people threw me for a loop," the young male traveler from Australia told Luis as the group walked down a path in the park.

"Yes, this isn't uncommon to hear. I understand history books in the U.S. and Europe are lacking, even a traveler from Taiwan told me this—that all the Mayans died a long time ago. No, the great Mayan civilization was toppled, yes, but pockets of Maya, by the way, that's what we call the people—Maya, not Mayan—survived all over Latin America. There are different theories for the demise of the great Mayan civilization. The most recent is that a long drought, lasting three decades or more, brought about famine and war. The most notable war was a conquest of Tikal in the 4th century A. D. But that couldn't have been the end of it. Perhaps over time, the small surviving groups were cut off from their heritage." Luis walked and talked. The group followed and listened as they left the building and made their way along a path.

"You said that couldn't have been the end of it," Delta repeated before asking, "What do you mean?"

"Ah, you are Prof. Quinn, right?"

"Yes."

"You, of course, know that monuments in El Peru Waka were erected in 564 A.D. to honor the Lady Ikoom."

Delta nodded. Her preliminary research as well as her talk with P. J. had revealed such information.

"El Peru, what was it?" the young woman with the group asked.

"El Peru Waka, in northern Guatemala, not far from here. But let's not confuse things. Back to my talk about the modern day Maya." The group listened as they walked.

"In the 1950s a Hollywood team of documentarians came to the area where they filmed one of the isolated groups who lived in the mountains. The Hollywood producers offered to show the modern-day Mayas what their ancestors had built and so they flew one of the men and two of his wives to Tikal to see what you are seeing today. The Maya man told them he had come across such pyramid temples in the jungle and assumed that the gods had built them. He was amazed to learn that it was his fore-bearers. So pockets of Maya became isolated mostly due to the Spanish invasion. It took over two hundred years for the Spanish to defeat the Maya. And after generations of hiding, the Maya who hid in the forests eventually forgot their heritage. So the documentarians showed them Tikal."

"Are they the ones who left the lightning rod on one of the temples?" Delta asked.

Luis seemed surprised by the question. "You mean the documentarians?"

"Yes."

"Oh no, that was the Star Wars, Episode Four crew. I'll show you later," he smiled.

Delta couldn't help but to feel like a time traveler, scuttling between the new knowledge of now and the various discoveries of the past. From documentaries to science fiction movies, from ancient marvels to contemporary political tragedies, from lectures to hip hop, from temples to lightning rods, the information—

"So, you've heard of chicklet gum, yes?" Luis interrupted her thoughts.

Luis stood under a large chicle tree, the group surrounded him as he explained the origins of chewing gum. At the story's conclusion he moved down the path, pointing here and there, naming trees and flora, until he began speaking of the unending beauty of the ceiba tree with its spiny trunk and spreading branches, a sacred tree of the ancient Maya. Luis led them along to the center of Tikal, where the visitors, including Delta, suddenly stood in amazement of the ancient city which had once held a population of nearly 100,000 people. They all stopped and simply stared.

"Here, centuries ago, the elites lived in the city proper with a complex where multiple temples facing each other stood in tribute to the king and queen and to the gods, and which now reveal a splendor of their own," Luis told the group. They marveled at the sight. An open expanse of land separated these grand temples. The ball field lay to the east where ritual games were played before the nobles. The masonry of cut and quarried stone, stacked to magnificent heights, stood testament to hard working people of every caste. Architects designed, artisans configured, slaves cut and hauled the stones, masons adjusted, workers mixed and slapped mortar between the stones, and priests ascended the steps. From 500 B.C.E. to 900 C.E. the people flourished through hunting, fishing, and farming.

"This is where the upper class, the nobles, lived." Luis spread his arms to show the buildings in the heart of the city and close by. "Beyond the walls were the slaves, the farmers, the stone cutters." He pointed beyond. The group fell silent at the magnificence of the ancient buildings. Delta imagined the city flourishing. Luis encouraged them to explore on their own and to meet back at the same spot where they were currently standing, in about twenty minutes to a half hour.

"Did women hold places of prominence?" the older woman asked before the group departed.

"Yes, there were queens and upper caste women. Today, we refer to them as 'Ladies.' A young queen once ruled here. The Lady Tikal. Six years old at coronation. But more interesting was the Lady Ikoom, who I mentioned earlier, she ruled the close-by kingdom. Do you remember the name of it?"

"*El Peru' Waka,*'" Delta offered.

"Correct, professor," Luis commended her and then continued. "Around 560 A. D. the kingdom of *El Peru' Waka'* existed about 40 miles west of here. A stela of the Lady Ikoom's life was recently unveiled there. She came from the Snake Clan. Some say her life was filled with great adventures and she was so respected that her stela was rehoused within another temple in *El Peru'* some 200 years after its first testament to her. Griselda Pérez, a Guatemalan archeologist, discovered the stela. It is called stela 44. And another queen, her descendant, Lady Ka'bel was said to have been a warrior queen. She would have lived during the trying times of drought and war, which began during Ikoom's reign."

When Delta heard the name *Lady Ikoom* for the second time she drew in a breath and stood taller. She felt proud to be on the team that would bring further knowledge of Lady Ikoom's life. She wanted to know everything about her and about the Maya. "Do you know how far south Lady Ikoom traveled?" she asked.

"Interesting question. People usually ask me how far north the Maya may have traveled. There are some who believe that the Lady Ikoom had a northern outpost in Arizona. But to answer your question of how far south, things are being uncovered every day. I've heard a rumor recently that a glyph of Quetzalcoatl was found in Nicaragua. That would be the farthest south ever."

"Quetzalcoatl? The Aztec god?"

"Yes. So if the Aztecs could be there, certainly the Mayas could have been there. Since the Maya lived closer to Nicaragua than did the Aztecs. Plus, even today there is a Miskito group that lives in Nicaragua."

"Mosquito?" someone asked.

"Not that kind of mosquito. No, these are people who are of Maya heritage and inter-married with Africans, likely escaped slaves. To the north, the people have curly hair and to the south, in Nicaragua, the people have straight hair and speak a Mayan language."

Luis then shifted topics. "Now, time is short; see the ruins here; and then, I'll take you to the tallest temple in Tikal."

Delta turned slowly with much on her mind. The other members of the group headed off quickly to explore the temples. Tourists walked the grounds, snapped pictures and climbed steps to explore the interior of the buildings where allowed. Delta thought of the Lady Ikoom living during this pre-Columbian era. Surely she would have visited Tikal, a sacred city of the Maya.

Just as Delta and the others began to head off, an animal, brown and small, the size of a little dog or large squirrel, startled Delta as it skirted just in front of her on the path.

"The *coatimundus*. It sniffs out tarantulas," Luis told her. "They're harmless, but I wouldn't try to pet it."

"Tarantulas!" Delta hadn't given the wildlife much thought as she had been so focused on the Mayan history and the Mesoamerican architecture. Luis only smiled and added, "Honestly, I wouldn't try to pet either one. But my friend, Barlow, here, he likes to let the tarantulas crawl in his palm and up his arm." The group that had begun to disperse, but was still within ear shot, stopped and turned toward the guide.

The young woman with them made a squeamish face and recoiled at the thought.

"It's true," Barlow said.

"I'd like to see that," the elder man dared Barlow.

"Perhaps you will," Barlow accepted the challenge.

Everyone smiled before the group members dispersed in different directions to explore the city temples, houses, steles and more. Each person with a companion, Delta noticed. Luis and Barlow, the older couple, and the younger couple. Delta suddenly missed having a friend or lover with whom to share this excursion, the sights, the history, the smells, the sounds. She thought of Caleb—how adventurous he is, how he'd likely be the first to climb the steps or hold a tarantula, how his brown hair curled loosely on his forehead, how bright his smile is when he greets anyone, how he smelled, and the taste of his kiss.

"It tasted bitter," the voice behind her said. She turned. It was a docent, leading and lecturing to another group of tourists. "The Mayas discovered the cocoa bean. Some people think it was the Aztecs but they came later. The Mayas turned the bean into a drink, likely around 900 A.D. It was bitter and even spicy with chili peppers added to the drink. Before that people chewed the beans," the docent droned on. Delta quickly turned her body and her thoughts toward the Mayan architecture. She walked toward the temples.

Later, the members of Delta's entourage regrouped. Following Luis and Barlow, they walked miles through the jungle along mildly-manicured paths that gave way to huge canopies of jungle trees. Some appeared to be outgrowths covering large hills. Luis stopped at one such outcropping and stood in front of a jungle-covered hill that rose steeply toward the sky. The group fanned out around him, ready to learn. Luis cocked his head and said, "Hear that?" They listened to a steady humming buzz. "Spider wasps," Luis said without explaining further. "Do you want to see?"

"Sounds like something out of *The Hunger Games*," the young man said.

Luis nodded, "Well, want to see?"

Some nodded; others were hesitant. Luis encouraged them with a smile and then led them off the path until they came to stand under a looming kapok tree, its roots taller than Delta. The roots spread wide like buttresses supporting a cathedral's looming arches and dome. The tree's circumference would have taken the entire group holding outstretched hands with one another to encircle it. They looked high into the branches. The intense buzzing came from a huge nest.

"Let's not disturb them," Luis suggested quietly.

"Agreed," the older man whispered.

As they stepped carefully over and between jutting roots, making their way back to the trail, Luis told them that wasps eat the tiniest insects from the mortar holding the temple stones together. "In doing so, they crack and damage the mortar."

"What keeps the buildings from collapsing?" someone asked.

"The bats!" Luis told them. It took a moment, before everyone understood that bats eat the wasps. "Even today you'll find little bat dung piles under the cornices' of the temples." Once solidly back on the official trail, Luis took a moment to regroup, checking to make sure everyone was there. He stood again in front of the tall hill engulfed and entangled in tropical foliage, where they had stood before heading off the path. Trees grew up the side of the hill, large rocks protruded and vines hung from trees.

"What is behind me?" he then asked of them. The tourists looked more closely at the hillside. Some thought they were searching for another wasps' nests or spider monkeys, but it was Delta who first spotted the door, an archway covered in thick vines and nearly hidden by the trees.

"A door!" she cried out with amazement. Luis smiled and said, "Good. What else?"

"Oh my gosh! It's not a hill at all, is it? It's a temple!"

"That's right. There are still thousands of structures to be uncovered."

The group stood and stared with amazement. Delta felt the joy of discovery.

"Why haven't they been uncovered?" the older man asked, excitement in his voice, as he seconded Delta's thrill of discovery.

"It's expensive."

"Couldn't you get volunteers from universities, maybe from other countries? I'm sure archaeology and anthropology students would love to help with such excavation."

"It's been tried. They turned out to be less than respectful of the sites and even helped themselves to artifacts. So, now only Guatemalans are permitted to work on excavations," Luis explained.

The tourists became silent, each perhaps in their own way reflecting on the greed of the outsiders; and reflecting on themselves as representative of those outsiders. No more was said on the subject. But Delta also considered the way the older man had assumed that he could solve the problem of excavation for the people of this 'developing' country as if they were not bright enough to have thought of such an idea.

Under a heavy silence, they walked deeper into the jungle. Within minutes a horrendous sound brought them to a standstill and broke the somber mood. Delta listened, trying to name the sound that she had never before heard. It seemed as if mythical and monstrous jaguars were amassing in the jungle ahead and their growls were echoing off the temples. Loud and ferocious. Delta stood still and whispered without realizing that she was saying it aloud, "It sounds as if the jaws of hell have opened."

"Howler monkeys," Luis announced with a smile. "But they do sound *espeluznante.*"

Delta looked at him and cocked her head, as she didn't understand the meaning of the word.

"Horrible and unholy," Luis translated his description of the cries of the howler monkeys.

"My favorite!" Barlow exclaimed with delight as he darted down the path to see if he could spot the howler monkeys swinging in the trees above.

"C'mon! C'mon," he called to the group. He veered off the path and everyone followed quickly after looking to Luis for permission; Luis nodded. They all raced like school children following Barlow's lead. Barlow imitated the fierce howling sound as he ran down the path, every now again stopping, cupping a hand behind his ear to tell where the howler monkey cries were coming from and waiting to see if they would answer his calls. The howler monkeys cried back asserting their territorial privilege and scaring off predators. "Here, here," Barlow yelled looking up and pointing to the troupe of monkeys. As each person breathlessly caught up, they looked high into the ceiba trees. Soon they were pulling out their smart phones and snapping photos.

"There's one."

"Oh, and another."

"Look a mother with a baby!"

"Where?"

"There, see?"

And then one monkey swung from branch to branch.

"Oh, look, look."

They watched, enthralled by the energetic primates. Luis had to pull the small group away with enticements that they needed to leave if they wanted to visit the tallest temple of Tikal. "And just because the howler monkeys are adorable to watch, is no reason not to be careful. Keep an eye out for actual jaguars and don't forget to glance both up and down. Up for snakes curled in branches and down for snakes and spiders making their way around tree roots. We will leave the path and take a short cut to the temple, so heed my precautions."

Winding their way forward, they held thick foliage aside for one another, stepped over massive root systems, and ducked under heavy branches of forest green, eventually arriving at another park path, an official and paved path. As each member of the group emerged from the thick foliage, they straightened their previously stooped necks backward and looked up, they beheld Temple IV. It rose grandly forth from earth to sky.

The massive temple, which Luis told them had been built around 740 A.D., marked the rule of *Yik'in Chan K'awiil*, the 27th king of the Tikal dynasty. The pyramid was built as a series of platforms. As Luis described it, the group members visually consumed it.

"It's as long as a football field," the young man said of the length of the wide base with narrow stairs that led to the first platform. A shrine had been restored at the first level. Luis described details in meters and converted to feet, as well.

"It's 144 ft. wide and the walls are 39 ft. thick. The stones are massive," Luis said with pride. They could see that the next set of narrow steps led to another platform and so on until the pyramid reached a ledge and above it a limestone summit.

"Can we climb it?" the younger man from the group queried with anticipation.

"Yes, but not here. Follow me," Luis said, turning to take them to the visitors' stairs. Luis and Barlow led them to a side of the pyramid where a wooden scaffolding of multiple staircases ascended the side of the pyramid.

"This will take you to the top of the ancient Mayan temple. I'll wait here for you." And with that Luis and Barlow made their way to a bench and each pulled out their cell phones. No one else backed out of taking the climb to the top, even the elderly couple moved forward, but each held at least mild trepidation for the wooden stairs. Delta could see it in their faces and the way they each took hold of the railing and shook it gently to see how sturdy it handled. Delta took the first flight of twenty steps with ease, even the second flight wasn't too taxing, but on the third flight, she looked for a spot to rest for a moment only to discover the platform side rails had come loose and several had broken away. She breathed deeply and then started up the next flight. The older couple rested at every landing. The younger couple moved quickly, racing for the top. Their lithe and lean bodies breezed up the stairs. Delta didn't rest again until she reached the summit. Ten flights in all of twenty steps each, placed them almost at the top of the pyramid.

Delta stepped from the wooden staircase to the pyramid's uppermost ledge, only a capstone towered above and behind her. She edged her way along the very narrow limestone cornice brushing her palm against the wall for balance until she had reached the center of the temple ledge. There she stood at the highest peak possible to view Tikal. Nothing between her and the world below, no guard rails, no safety features. She beheld an awe-inspiring, sense of pure, unadulterated, unencumbered connection with sky and earth. It took her breath away and gave back *cielo y el paraíso*. Heaven and paradise.

Lush rain forest unfolded below and stretched for miles and miles. But it was the celestial sky that hypnotized Delta.

The sky no longer seemed to be above her. Rather it was all around her. The few pure white clouds appeared at eye level. She existed as a part of the sky. Reaching out her fingertips, she felt she could have touched the clouds. She took a deep meditative breath and looked over the expansive jungle below that unfolded in shades of green—luxuriant, rolling, deep-forest-greens, emerald greens, sparkling greens, iridescent greens where blues speckled forth here and there from winding rivers and tiny waterfalls. The land rolled on into a bright and glorious eternity. Only one other manmade object met her view—another temple of the Mayan kings and queens. Delta felt overwhelmed with an awe that allowed a single thought to pass through her mind—*if I had been asked to throw myself from the temple as a sacrifice to the gods, I would have done so with pleasure. I would have leapt into the bright blue sky touching the clouds as I free fell to the rich green paradise below.*

"Would you take a picture of us?" the young man asked in that delightful Australian accent, interrupting Delta's moment.

"Of course," she said, reaching out for his camera. As he and his girlfriend turned their backs to the sky, drawing in close to each other for the Kodak moment, the limestone ledge cracked. The girlfriend gasped and teetered. He looked down. The ledge made another cracking sound and then a chunk of limestone slipped from under foot and went hurtling 215 feet downward.

The scream that followed could be heard for miles.

TEMPLE IV

The scream echoed through the valley. Even the howler monkeys stood silent in response to the cry. In fact, the scream from the young woman who grabbed her boyfriend's pant leg as she slipped backward and downward from the precipice could most certainly be heard at the bottom of the pyramid where Luis and Barlow had been joking and laughing about something they later called inconsequential. But it was when the boyfriend instinctively reached forward for something to grab onto and found only Delta's arm, reaching out to him, that the scene pointed toward multiple tragedy. The couple's double weight dragged Delta downward, quickly. She scratched her fingernails into the limestone precipice, digging into the mortar. The young man also grabbed at the limestone with his free hand; his downward motion flipped Delta forward, sideways and then head first. All three dangling near death. Yet, Delta saw something as her head was pulled toward eternity. She yelled to the girl.

"Get your footing! There's a small ledge. Feel for it with your foot. It's right underneath you."

The girl gasped with relief as she felt the stone, just centimeters under her tiptoes, now within reach. In another second, her feet sat flat on the stone ledge. She moved carefully to her left, making room for her boyfriend while pulling his pant leg toward stability. And then he too felt the safety under his feet. He released his grip on Delta.

Delta swung herself back up to be fully situated on the ledge above them. Her heart raced. The veins in her temples throbbed. Her arms continued to burn. How had his weight not pulled her over the ledge head first? She was only now realizing that someone had grabbed her. The birdwatcher.

"Are you okay?"

"Yes, Oh my god, yes. Thank you," Delta said to the man.

"Are you two okay?" Delta called to the couple, now standing safely on the ledge below.

"Yes," the young man said.

"Yeah, me too," his girlfriend answered.

"There's no way to the staircase from the ledge that they're on," the birdwatcher's wife added quietly and with concern.

"They'll have to climb back up," her husband added. Delta called out to them, "I think you are about to become temple climbers. I see indents for a handhold and then a foot grip just above you. Don't look; just reach for it."

"I can help," the birdwatcher said. The young woman had found the handhold and then a step for her foot. She climbed upward. Her boyfriend, giving her leg support and a boost, gave aid. The girl secured her foot upward and then one more step before reaching for Delta. The older man, the birdwatcher, took a low stance, squatting, and secured Delta by the waist, who in turn offered her hand to the young woman.

At first, the older man needed only to lean back to bring Delta and the girl toward him. Then he reached around Delta and helped to pull the girl onto the ledge. Delta aided him, pulling the young woman's upper body onto the narrow ledge. Delta grabbed the waistband of the girl's jeans, yanking her legs upward and sideways swinging her onto the slightly wider part of the ledge. They all heaved a sigh of relief.

It was easier getting the young man onto the ledge. When his hands reached the precipice, he pulled him himself upward as if he were getting out of a swimming pool. Palms flat on the surface of the ledge. Delta and the birdwatcher steadied the young man's arms as he lifted himself upward. Once high enough, he landed one knee on the ledge and then the other. He needed little help.

None of them remembered the climb back down the wooden steps that zigzagged with each flight back to the floor of the jungle. But they would never forget the relieved expressions on Luis' and Barlow's face when they reached the bottom. Nor would they ever forget the moments when they had nearly expressed their last breath at the top of Temple IV. Later that evening, they all stopped for dinner, relived the harrowing experience, and how they had saved each other. At the border, they thanked Luis before heading back to Belize.

At the end of the long and spectacularly adventurous day, they rode in the van with Barlow driving them toward their respective hotels in Belize. Both younger and older couples were exhausted and each napped. The young woman slept with her head on her boyfriend's shoulder. The extra beer that Barlow bought for them had helped them relax. Barlow and Delta didn't drink at dinner. Now on the ride back, Delta sat in the front passenger seat. Barlow drove the van. A light rain fell.

"Quite a day," Barlow said turning on the wipers.

"A story to tell my students when I get back."

"You're a teacher?"

"A professor," she answered.

"Ah, yes, I remember Luis called you professor. I think Luis will become a professor someday."

"And what about you?"

"I like what I do," he said. "What would you guess their occupations?" Barlow asked, nodding his head toward the back, referring to the passengers behind them and casually steering the conversation away from himself. Delta played along.

"The young man, a computer salesman, who was eager to get out of the office. He probably doesn't get enough sunshine and he rock climbs and cycles to stay in shape." Barlow smiled at her answer. The sun was setting; the rain came down harder. Delta noticed the one lane bridge approaching.

"And his girlfriend?" Barlow queried.

Delta turned to look at the young woman. "I think she—"

Her words were cut short. They heard a bang. The van swerved to the left and then to right so suddenly on the slippery pavement of the bridge that Delta could barely see what was happening. The rain blurred her vision. The van spun dramatically. The tires squealed. Everyone was flung to the left, to the right, and then to the left again, before the van banged into the guard rail and flipped on its side dangling from the one lane bridge over the rocky stream below.

CHAPTER 29

All went quiet. All became motionless, except for the tires of the overturned van which slowly came to a halt. Only the rain made a noise.

PART 5

AN INTERLUDE: THE LADY IKOOM

CHAPTER 30

IKOOM AND *CHEN KU*

Ikoom had survived the night in the *Deep Well*. Her mother had nourished her with a bitter and spicy tasting cocoa and chili drink, black and steaming. Ikoom sipped from the cup each morning during her recovery. Any thoughts of Ku'tl that entered her mind were quickly pushed away. Her life depended on this. The gods would not forgive a second betrayal. She knew that she needed to prepare herself physically and mentally to endure the challenges that lay ahead. First, a series of rituals needed to be performed, beginning at the place of sacrifice, the *Chen Ku*. Then a stay on the *Island of Women* would test her endurance, resourcefulness, and bravery. Finally, if she survived, she would travel into the *Chasm* to find the beginning and the end of *All*.

When the time came, Ikoom journeyed on foot through the rain forest, accompanied by two priests and eight warriors who protected her during this arduous trek to *Chichen Itza*. Months of travel allowed for purity through extended prayer. At night she assessed the length of time their travels had taken by the light and size of the moon. The priests, like Ikoom, also watched the position of the stars and the path of the moon. The priests were on her side; they wanted her to reach the island during the day and the time of month when the nights would be lit by the fullness of the moon. This would increase her chances of survival. They brought provisions along with bags of turquoise and jade for the gods—the four *Chaacs*, which would be offered as a sacrifice at the *Deep Water Hole* before taking Ikoom to the *Island of Women* by square bottom boat.

When they arrived at the road to *Chichen Itza*, the priest pointed forward and stepped out of Ikoom's way. Ikoom, with head held high, took long strides as she led the ritual party down the *Sacbe*—the holy white road—that led to the sacred ritual site. They followed.

Once at the grotto, the priests and warriors fanned out around her in a semi-circle. They all felt the presence of the spirits in this holy place. The grotto, where large rocks encircled a deep water-filled sinkhole that reflected the blue of the sky, held the spirits of many Maya who had given their lives. Waterlilies floated on the surface, especially at the edges of the deep water, like silent tribute to the dead. The call of birds echoed in the air, like the sound of the ancestors speaking from their watery grave.

Ikoom stopped, turned and faced the priests, palms up, prepared to be painted blue. The two priests mixed the pigment with holy water. Each man had used pestle and a large mortar to crush the indigo with palygorskite clay before pouring the mixture into larger bowls, and then they placed the bowls onto a stone in the center of a fire of *palo santo* wood that a warrior had built. Its incense filled the air. Ikoom closed her eyes and breathed in the wisps of fragrant smoke. When she looked again at the fire, she discovered the pigment was changing color under the heat of the flames, eventually becoming a blue hue of Mayan nobility. She prayed. The flames disappeared into quiet embers and the smoke trailed like silver wisps in the air.

Each priest wrapped his hands in palmetto leaves and removed the heated bowls from the fire. They then scooped the warm paint onto their fingers and with holy words slipping from their lips, they slathered the blue pigment onto Ikoom's body. Her forehead, her cheeks, her neck, her shoulders, her arms and so on. Finally, they put the bowls down and took up small leather bags. Each priest extracted gifts for the gods. One showed her turquoise stones and told her that these are for later. The other priest pulled out a smooth piece of jade that had been sharpened into the shape of a spearhead. He handed it to Ikoom. She held it in her left palm. The priest unsheathed a knife.

He handed the knife to Ikoom. Its blade glimmered in the sun as she turned it over, considering it. She took a deep breath, raised the knife high into the air and pointed it at the piece of jade in her palm. The priest and warriors watched, without a word. Then the priest nodded to Ikoom who knew what she must do.

Ikoom spoke words of praise and honor for the Chaacs. And then suddenly, with all her strength, she thrust the knife downward into the jade, cutting a chunk of the gem, chipping it, hurlting a small portion of it and stabbing the center of her palm in the process. Without a cry, only her eyes told of the pain. Ikoom turned and took a step closer to the deep water. She cupped the jade in her bleeding palm and then held it over the deep waterhole of the gods. Blood droplets fell into the water. She opened her palm and removed the smaller piece of jade. Then she released the larger jade stone, dropping it into the water with the following words:

> Only blood can release tears!
> Chaac! I have brought you a sacrifice.
> Accept this gift.
> Chaac! I ask for your protection as I journey to the *Island of Women.*
> Chaac! Give us rain.

Ikoom would not throw herself into the well. Others had. Male and female, young and old. Humans had sacrificed their lives at the *Chen Ku.* These sacrifices were from the people and of the people. When enemies were captured their leader would have been sacrificed on the precipice of the temple pyramid, the heart cut from the body, the body thrown down the steps of the pyramid temple. Decapitation was also a possibility for the enemy. The enemy was made into a sight for those who had lost loved ones in battle. The enemy might even have been disemboweled on the playing field in front of a crowd, thus reenacting the battle and the victory. In any of the cases, his skin would have been stripped from his body and a warrior or priest would have donned the enemy's skin and performed a heroic dance in the sacrificial victim's honor; he who would have died slowly, perhaps bravely, to appease the needs of gods, as well as the needs of the people. And to create fear in surviving enemies. These ways of death were kind in comparison to Death by Arrows—the slowest form of sacrificial death. Death by Arrows called for the warriors to shoot all around the restrained victim's heart until the heart could beat no longer. These are all ways for enemies to die, but enemies would not have been thrown into the *Chen Ku—the unending water.* This was a place of gifts from the people, of the people, who came far and wide to worship and pray for rich rains and healthy harvests. Objects could also be substituted as long as they had value. These sacrifices were always cut, chipped or broken to symbolize blood-letting. To symbolize the sacrifice of life. But some actual blood was always required. And those who gave their lives or their blood at *Chen Ku* did so in the same way that Ikoom did, rendered blue and self-mutilated, voluntarily. Now, finished with the ritual, she bravely led her own procession to the boats that would carry her, and this party of priests and warriors, to the *Island of Women*.

CHAPTER 31

IKOOM AND THE *ISLAND OF WOMEN*

Fear curled in Ikoom's stomach as the boat, rowed by warriors, came into view of the *Island of Women*, so named because the women who ventured there never returned. But it was not this thought that made Ikoom's stomach rise into her throat, rather it was the view of the land mass arising from the sea, the island's earth, the beach, appeared alive. It writhed and moved. How would she ever get her footing on such unholy ground, she wondered? The land did not stand still. The black and tan soil formed itself into coils and wound itself around itself, curling in on itself like the snake that eats its own tail and there were thousands of them. *This bizarre ground can only be a trick of the gods that—*

Wait, she thought. *That is what I'm seeing. This is no trick of the gods. The mangrove is covered in black and tan snakes.* Ikoom remembered seeing a man who had been bitten, not by a coral snake, but by a yellow jaw snake whose venom digests the prey before the snake ever tries to eat it. Bitten on the ankle, the victim had limped back to the city where he endured a painful death; first watching his own leg decompose. It turned pale blue from lack of blood and oxygen, and then strips of flesh fell away revealing even paler, bloodless muscle, until there was nothing but bone. Ikoom shrunk at the memory.

Ikoom realized that the rowers were headed straight for the snake-covered mangrove. She looked to the right of it and to the left. On one side, the mangrove of trees became even more entangled with branches that glittered green and gold under the late afternoon sun. Apparently a safer place to dock if one didn't know about the poisonous golden dart frogs that lived in such trees. In the opposite direction a rockier beach appeared.

"Wait!" she called out. The priests turned their heads.

"This is not where Chaac told me to land."

"This is the *Island of Women*," one priest told her calmly.

"No, Chaac came to me and told me to disembark on the rock, not on the writhing swampland."

"Rock? There is no rock," the priest told her.

"Go south," she told them. "Turn south toward the southern end of the island. That is where Chaac wants me to meet Ixchel!"

The rowers looked to the priest. But Ikoom bellowed in a commanding voice, "Go where I direct you! I have spoken with the Chaac!" She pointed toward the southern side of the island. The rowers obeyed her order and turned the boat southward.

As they rounded the tip of the island's southeastern curve, the men could see that the shore was too rocky. The oars slowed under their concern.

"There are too many rocks and the coral reef will break the boat apart," the priest argued.

"No, you must do this. Chaac commands it. This is where Ixchel will meet me and give instructions."

Under the spell of the strong-willed girl, the priest allowed the rowers to continue; but, they brought the boat in just close enough to the island rocks that Ikoom could be lowered over the side of the boat into the crystal clear water. There, standing waist deep in the sea, Ikoom held the small piece of jade against the wound on her palm that now stung from the salt water. She looked down to find fish circling her toes and she looked up and across the sea, spotting dolphins in the distance. A sea turtle swam close by her. *This is where Ixchel lives. No wonder the other women died; they never found Ixchel's entrance to the island. I will survive the Island of Women!*

Ikoom held out her other hand as one of the rowers passed her a bag with food and bits of flint and obsidian, as well as a canteen of water. She strung each cross-wise over her shoulder and around her neck. Then she held out her empty hand to a particular priest, the one who had not given her any jade earlier at *Chen Ku,* but had promised turquoise stones instead.

"What are you asking for?"

"I am asking for a gift to give Ixchel." Washed by the sea, her once blue-painted palm, returned to its golden brown flesh color.

Outstretched and waiting, her empty hand and demanding eyes spoke volumes to the priest. He had not given her a gift yet, and currently seemed slow to satisfy the request. Ikoom waited. Everyone looked to the priest. Ikoom would not retract her request. She waited defiantly. Silently. Eventually, the old priest handed over the small purse of turquoise stones. Ikoom received it graciously. "I was chosen at birth. I will make your sacrifice worthwhile. I will learn from Ixchel how we can get Chaac to give us rain."

The priest nodded. "Seven days. In seven days, if we see your fire, we will return for you. Meet us here at dawn."

"Here, at this point," she said pointing to the rocks, "I will build a fire in seven days." Ikoom wouldn't be forced to meet them in the snake-infested mangrove, a home to mosquitoes, and deadly frogs and poisonous fish. Other dangers might loom there, as well; she could only imagine.

Ikoom turned her back on the party of warriors and priests. She waded through the water to a rocky outcropping, pulled herself up and eventually stood alone on a ledge. She watched the boat, which had already turned away from the *Island of Women* and toward the land of the Maya, disappear into the distance.

LESSON ONE FROM THE *ISLAND OF WOMEN*

Ikoom inhaled deeply, breathing the salty air and filling her lungs with oxygen and fortitude. She turned her back to the sea and introduced herself to the *Island of Women.*

"I am Ikoom," she said. "Ixchel, I am here! Tell me, what are the secrets of the Chaac?"

No reply came forth. Ikoom hadn't expected one, not yet. Gods and goddesses are busy. She also knew that Ixchel wouldn't show herself until she had proven her worth in some way. *But how?* she wondered. And even before meeting the desires of Ixchel, Ikoom knew that she needed to address her most basic needs—water, food, and shelter. In that order, as she had been given enough water for perhaps, one or two days, if she was conservative, and enough food for three or four days, if she stretched it, and she needed a shelter from the intense sun and from the harsh sea winds. But she couldn't simply sleep under the trees on an island like this one for fear a poisonous snake might become her evening companion or a dart frog might climb in bed with her. Ikoom put the thought of poisonous reptiles and amphibians out of her mind for now as she knew that water was her primary concern. She rationed a small sip from the flask that hung around her neck as she was already parched from the hard work of wading through the water and the trek up the rocky hill. Sipping the water and tipping her head back, the sky unfolded above her and this act reminded her that she should thank the gods for what she did have. So, she prayed to Chaac of the east, of the north, of the west, and of the south, facing each direction in turn.

Ikoom assessed her surroundings. The eastern coastline of the island, rocky and barren of much vegetation, might offer the easier path as long as she stayed out of the reach of the salty waves that beat against the shore's crusty landscape. She could take a northeastern path until she was farther along and then she could turn inland in search of fresh water and food. Long white beaches appeared on the western side of the island but there also appeared thick mangroves before them. Ikoom chose the barren sandier and rockier path to begin her journey.

She walked in silence for a long time, thinking about her mission. But her lofty thoughts left her as she noticed the sky disappearing under a canopy of foliage; that's when she also realized that the sun was setting and jungle growing thicker in vegetation. It would be night soon. Still, she had not come upon fresh water or food.

The white teardrops of the chicklet tree offered her a bit of sustenance beyond what was in her bag—corn meal bread, but it wouldn't be enough. She ate a little, but worried as she had found no stream, either. Without rain, the paths were dry and didn't reveal tracks of animals, which might have shown her the way. Ikoom couldn't know for sure if the gentle deer or the ferocious jaguar roamed the island jungle, but she also couldn't find where they drank fresh water. *The animals can be my friends as well as my enemies*, she thought. She needed to find their prints.

Once she was deep enough into the island forest, Ikoom selected a sturdy *ceiba* tree as the base for her shelter. The roots were tall and the trunk wide. She had looked up, scanned for snakes and tree-frogs and having found none, she dragged a dead log from nearby and then several branches to build a roof. She pulled dead tree limbs and large prongs of leaves to create a nest for herself. As darkness fell, Ikoom climbed into the shelter and fell asleep.

She awoke in partial darkness from a growing hunger in her belly and a tremendous thirst. She felt around for her flask and then drank more water than she intended. She poked a hole in the leaf-covered roof and saw the nearly full moon above her. She opened the food bag and discovered that her mother had made the 13 layer *janlikool* for her, but Ikoom knew this masa-based food was meant not for her alone; it was also meant to be shared with Ixchel and with Chaac. When she saw it, it reminded her to pray to the goddess for guidance concerning how to approach the Chaac-Who-Cries. Ikoom's stomach cramped with hunger and growled, but she put the food away. Eventually, she slept again.

Ixchel appeared to Ikoom in a dream. A goddess-woman who had once been young revealed herself as wizened and wrinkled. Ikoom left this dream, image by image, as the sun forced her eyelids to blink quickly and meet the morning. Fortunately, her hunger had retreated. But her thirst had not. She drank from the flask, the water now more than half gone. She thanked the goddess for the morning light and beseeched her help in finding food and water.

Ikoom climbed out of her self-made nest and stretched under the canopy of the ceiba tree. She would now follow the sun toward the center of the island, in search of water. As she walked, she prayed to Ixchel. This helped her to remain focused on her duties. At first she prayed aloud but in a soft whisper, like wind from the ocean breeze, but the deeper into the island's jungle she went, the less she felt the wind of the sea and the more her throat became parched, and so she prayed silently. *Silent prayers*, she worried, *might not be heard*. Eventually, Ikoom felt the sun beat straight down upon the crown of her head, as she reached a clearing. Her lips and throat were dry. Her skin prickled from the numerous tiny scratches that covered her arms, which had been scraped by thorny brush. Her legs were tired. She stopped for only a moment, took a deep breath.

Move on, she thought she heard a voice say. And so she did until she came upon another clearing.

Ah, sparkling like diamonds, Ikoom finally saw, through the branches of trees and shrubs, the water of the lagoon that lay ahead of her. She quickened her pace. Upon reaching the fresh water, she thanked Ixchel for leading the way. She knelt by the water, cupped it into her hands and drank thirstily. Then joyfully she took up her flask, finished the last drop of what she had and refilled it. She left her bag of food and gems and obsidian on the branch of a tree. Then, she dropped her skirt and dove into the water. Refreshing. The water cooled her whole body and soothed her scratches.

Ikoom now knew the way to water. But her hunger went unabated. She lay on the ground near the water's edge staring up at the trees that surrounded her. None seemed to bear fruit. But one was a ceiba, and so she could build a strong nesting home for herself again this evening. Today, she would search for the *spote and callaloo* leaves, and *jicama*. Her mouth watered at the mere thought of these foods. None were in sight. If she couldn't find these she decided she would have to make her way back to the eastern side of the island where she might be able to find the fruit, she thought of the sweet prickly pear with hope. At this moment Ikoom was tempted, so tempted to eat the food meant for the gods that she nearly wept. She forced back her tears, sat up and wrapped her skirt about herself. She then gathered her supplies and headed off in search of food.

By evening, Ikoom had returned with *callaloo* leaves, of which she had munched on sufficiently during the afternoon to quell her hunger. Although she still longed for *spote*, she had found none. But she had found an agouti's stash of nuts and she now returned to her new nesting area by the lagoon to crush their shells and make a meal of them with *jicama* root that she had dug with her own strong fingernails from the earth. The *jicama* was small, insuring its sweet taste, but unfortunately promising that her hunger would return by morning. She gnawed on it, scraping it against her teeth. That was when she decided a spear could be a useful tool if she encountered a predator and a blow gun might come in handy for hunting. She focused her efforts first on fashioning a spear.

That night Ikoom slept well. And Ixchel paid her another visit. But once again, the goddess said nothing, leaving the girl without wisdom or knowledge of how to make Chaac cry.

On the third night, Ikoom ate well. She had gathered more *callaloo* leaves and traced her steps back to the sandier shores where she picked prickly pear and later cut away the spiny skin of the fruit with the jagged side of her piece of jade. The rich, sweet pulp pleased her lips and tongue.

On the fourth day, she found *soursop* or *guanábana* and took only what she needed. *Cho cho* hung from trees to the north and Ikoom whittled a stick with her sharp piece of jade, determined to spear fish the next day. That night she curled up in her nest under the grand canopy of the *ceiba* tree, quite content except for not having spoken with Ixchel. However, she awoke with a start!

Painful pricks jolted her up so fast that she struck her head against the branches that formed the roof of her nest. Under the light of the moon, she saw them—rats! Their claws digging into her skin as they ran across her now twitching legs. She withheld a scream but gasped for air. She hated rats! She could see their beady eyes, these nocturnal nightmares. She hustled out of the nest. *They must have been after my food. I should have taken the prickly pear and sousop scraps far from my nest.* She leapt farther from the tree, the moon shone brightly on the water. She quickly scooped up the scraps and ran past the lagoon waters toward the western side of the island; occasionally, leaving a trail of tiny scraps along the way; the brazen rats followed.

Ikoom ran faster, panting, and holding tight to the satchel of food and scraps until she broke through the thick foliage. She stopped. Inhaled deeply, stood tall and then expelled her breath, heaving the remaining food into the mass of snakes. The rats' eyes followed the food as it arced through the air. They ran after it.

The commotion stirred the snakes who had just started to bed down. The intrusion of the rats that followed the food brought the snakes into full assault. Ikoom jumped back after throwing the food into the den of vipers. She watched as the rats fell under attack of the hissing and biting venomous reptiles.

Ikoom breathed easier. She stood silent for a moment watching one enemy kill and devour the other. Behind her, the sun whispered across the eastern sky. She turned to meet the morning. Exhausted, she made her way back to the lagoon where she drank the cool water, packed her food and hung it from a high branch, and climbed back into her nook in the giant tree. She fell into a deep sleep.

"You cannot always lead one enemy into the jaws of another, but it is one good strategy," Ixchel said. And then the goddess added, "Prepare to meet Chaac."

Ikoom awoke with Ixchel's words in her head. *You cannot always lead one enemy into the jaws of another.* She had seen Ixchel quite clearly in her dream. Standing above her, with Mayan headdress and a sun-shaped necklace, earrings that dangled down like the wrinkles at the corner of Ixchel's mouth. The goddess lacked emotion. She was merely stating a fact. A fact that Ikoom should consider carefully.

"Prepare to meet Chaac!" the revered goddess had said. Something in her tone gave Ikoom a sense of foreboding. She stirred quietly, somewhere between sleep and wakefulness. As she gained footing in the land of awareness, she realized the sun had more than dawned overhead. Mid-morning. She reached for her bags and carefully hooked each one over her neck and shoulder. Then Ikoom took up her spear and climbed down and then crawled out of the roots of the ceiba.

Momentarily on all fours, Ikoom turned herself around, ready to stand up and meet the challenges of the day, but instead, after turning, she froze. There, in front of her appeared the waiting stare of a crocodile. Paralyzed with fear, Ikoom couldn't think, couldn't move, couldn't scream. The croc remained still.

CHAPTER 33

LESSON TWO FROM THE *ISLAND OF WOMEN*

Barely ten feet away, the crocodile studied Ikoom; and Ikoom studied the croc. They now stared at one another. Neither moving.

Being on all fours, having just climbed down and out of her nest, made Ikoom even more vulnerable. She knew this. Petrified, a paralysis nearly consumed her. She wasn't sure what the croc would do once she stood, but it had to be done. Fear had to be forced away. There was only life or death.

She stood. The croc leapt through the air. Instantly, Ikoom threw her spear forward into the crocodile's eye and then without looking back, she ran through the jungle toward the sea of dawn and as she ran, Ixchel carried on a conversation with the girl:

"Is that how you plan to meet Chaac? By throwing a spear into his eye?"

"It was a crocodile!"

"Guarding the water that you want," Ixchel pointed out.

"It would have killed me!"

"How do you know Chaac won't kill you?"

"I don't know," Ikoom said as she bounded, nearly out of breath. Panting. Her heart still racing.

"Does Chaac want to kill me?"

"You want to make him cry, don't you?"

"Not by hurting him."

"How else?" Ixchel asked her.

"I don't know. Tell me," she pleaded as she continued to sprint. Leaves slapped her in the face; roots tried to trip her.

"If Chaac were that crocodile, did you show him respect or fear?"

"Both," Ikoom insisted.

"How so?" Ixchel demanded an explanation.

"I stood. I met his stare. I respected and feared his strength. I didn't cower. I drove the spear into him because he is stronger than me and then I ran."

"Because you are mortal," Ixchel noted. "You are mortal and Chaac is immortal. You were wise to throw the spear at the crocodile," Ixchel conceded, "but don't throw a spear at Chaac. He's not your enemy. You must make him your friend. He'll live forever. And he has a long memory."

Ikoom was beginning to lose her strength. She hoped the crocodile wasn't behind her. Her steps slowed as she brushed vegetation out of her way and loped forward toward the sea.

"Ixchel, help me."

"I have helped you. I have taught you another lesson. What have you learned?"

"Know that I must always respect my enemy, but also be prepared to take my enemy's life. And consider that Chaac may want to kill me or may want to befriend me. I cannot know the will of the gods. And—"

"And what?" Ixchel queried.

"And never camp too close to the water's edge where crocodiles live."

Ixchel smiled, "I like you, Ikoom. I'll share my secrets with you. Secrets from the *Island of Women*. Go to the rocky ledge where you first entered the *Island of Women*. There, you'll build an altar for me. And while you carry the stones for the altar, I'll instruct you in the lessons that you'll need for the rest of your life, no matter how short or long that might be," Ixchel told the girl. "From the lessons, you'll derive a means to make Chaac cry."

Ikoom gladly followed Ixchel's orders for she suddenly felt under her protection and even if the goddess had hinted at a short life, Ikoom knew that she would live long enough to meet the Chaac and perhaps save her people. She did worry that three days wasn't enough time to build an altar and that she only had a small flask of water and no food, but Ixchel must've heard her thoughts.

"My thoughts will quench your thirst and work will nourish you."

Ikoom continued her trek through the jungle, reached the eastern sea, walked to the rocky south edge of the island and climbed the summit. There, she lay on the ledge, too weak to move a muscle. All energy abated, Ikoom fell into a dead sleep.

CHAPTER 34

LESSON THREE FROM THE *ISLAND OF WOMEN*

She awoke with a powerful thirst, but worried about how long she'd slept; so, she ignored her needs. Instead, Ikoom began the hard work of carrying stones from a nearby grove to the flat ledge that overlooked the sea. But in the midst of her moving the rocks, Ixchel appeared to her.

"I've chosen the rock that should act as the altar top. Come see." Ixchel led the girl downhill toward a sandy patch of land where a large, flat piece of smooth, dark slate lay under the shade of an evergreen palm tree. As wide as Ikoom was tall, the slate shimmered in the sun with shadows cast at its edges from beach grass, salt grass, and sweet grass, which sprouted around the proposed altar rock. Ikoom knew how heavy slate could be. She hesitated before approaching the stone slab and studied it more closely. She attempted to lift it, but the weight was intolerable, moving it inconceivable. She managed to raise it only a few inches before dropping it back in place.

"How can I possibly…" Ikoom turned to ask Ixchel, or rather *tell* Ixchel of the impossibility of the task, but Ixchel was gone. Ikoom realized that she couldn't waste time. *If this is what Ixchel wants, then I must find a way.* She tightened her muscles, pursed her lips, thought for a moment, and then headed into the jungle. Ikoom scoured the tropical forest until she found a long limb of a redwood tree, strong and beautiful, laying on the ground. The limb was burned on one end, *lightning must have severed it from the trunk,* she thought. She pulled and dragged the limb back to the slate where she considered how to wedge it under the altar rock. She knew that she couldn't simply lift the rock and slide the limb underneath; she would have to find another way.

Ikoom tried digging the sand out from underneath, but it continually collapsed back in on itself. It was too dry and feathery.

This is exactly how my throat feels, she thought. *Parched. I need water. That's it!*

Trusting in Ixchel's promise to take care of her, Ikoom opened her flask and drank the last of her fresh water. With renewed energy she ran to the ocean and filled the container with salt water. She returned pouring the water on the sand. After repeating this task several times, Ikoom was able to dig a hole under the slate, opposite the tall and sturdy palm tree. She then took the redwood branch and inserted one end of it under the slate. She used it as a lever. It took all her weight to raise the slate, which she then let topple against the near-by palm tree. It stood like a table on its edge, ready to be rolled to the summit. But before doing that she needed to finish building the base and she was running out of time. She had only one day left to build the base and raise the altar. She'd never finish in time, if she carried each rock separately.

Discouraged, she sat down, hung her head, and let tears fill her eyes. With hazy vision from her own tears, she noticed the sand and grasses by her feet in a blended blur. And then it came to her. The sturdy rhizome root and tall grasses provide material for weaving. *Yes! Yes!* Ikoom wiped her tears and ripped the tangled roots from the ground, gathering the loose palm leaves that lay all around. She began weaving a strong mat. By noon, the sky was filled with tropical blue and Ikoom's mat was filled with small to medium sized rocks to be dragged to the summit and layered like a brick mason's sturdy foundation as a base for Ixchel's altar.

By sunset, the two table bases stood erect and Ikoom had rolled the table top to the summit, leaned it as close as possible to the short leg bases, and used her own body as a counter weight to tip the slate into place. It landed with a resounding thud, like thunder. Exhausted, she now lay nearly lifeless on top of the altar. Her energy spent, only a strand of hair blew across her face and against her will.

Ikoom awoke with the bright sun on her face and a fear of failure in her heart. Yes, she had built the altar but the sun was rising and she hadn't built a signal fire for the priests. And worse yet, she didn't know how to make Chaac cry. She feared she would die now, before learning all the mysteries and being able to save her people. In addition, because her thirst was beyond quenching, her hunger beyond pain, and her muscles in a state of exhaustion, she felt that she was too weak to move. *I will die on Ixchel's altar, and maybe,* she thought, *this is what Ixchel wants.* Alone, abandoned and barely alive, Ikoom decided to give herself up to the goddess. She had been presumptuous to think she could survive the *Island of Women*, she thought.

"Ikoom, what have you learned?" Ikoom heard Ixchel's voice echo through her mind. Ikoom was too tired to answer. Instead, she sighed heavily through blistered and parched lips.

"Ikoom, get up." Ikoom felt too weak to move.

"Ikoom, it's time for food, water, and a fire."

Ikoom still lay on the altar top, not answering Ixchel. Not moving. She had no water. She had no food. She had no fire. She could barely open her swollen eyelids to see the sun inching its way higher into the sky. Ikoom thought of her family, of Kut'l, of the people she loved and whom she thought she would never see again. She thought of her own mother who had nourished her and given her food for herself and for the gods. She didn't know how long she had slept but was sure she had missed the day that the priests and protectors would return for her.

"Ikoom, must I tell you everything. Get up! Take the flint from your pouch and place the grass mat on the altar with the obsidian you brought. Build a fire on my altar and burn the incense in my honor. Leave the food and the gems for me. Then walk to the beach, there I've placed a gift for you."

Ikoom dragged herself off the altar and followed the goddess's commands. She placed the mat on the altar, she extracted the flint and struck it against another rock, a small piece of pyrite that she always carried with the flint. Several strikes later, Ikoom had a tiny fire; the mat began to burn. Ikoom became so excited that she forgot her hunger and thirst and made her way to beach to gather more grass, twigs and branches to secure a bigger flame. Before not too long, Ikoom watched a healthy blaze rising from Ixchel's altar and a fragrance of incense filled the air. Ikoom placed the gems on the altar, and then she returned to the beach one more time to gather more wood. There she heard Ixchel's voice again.

"Ikoom, here is a gift," Ixchel said. But Ikoom looked around and saw nothing.

"Look again," Ixchel told the girl. This time when she looked, she realized that the lavender and saw palmetto were dripping with dew, the rosemary plants sparkled and the beach grasses glistened. Ikoom dragged herself closer to the plants and licked the flower petals and cupped the larger leaves and poured the dew into her mouth. She moved down the beach drinking in her fill until at last her thirst was quenched, but her hunger continued and she fell among the various grasses face down, too weak to go in search of sustenance.

"Roll over, Ikoom," Ixchel's voice told her. With great effort, Ikoom rolled over onto her back. She opened her eyes and looked up. She found herself under a sapodilla tree. The sun's rays highlighted the leaves and danced on the tan and reddish-brown-dappled fruit.

Her joy was indescribable. The *sapote, zapote,* hung from branches above her. She reached out her hand upward, but weakness caused her arm to fall back to earth. Her fingertips hit something wet. She turned her head. Ripe pieces of the fruit lay on the ground within easy reach, some split open, some still in-tact, the fruit glistening in the sun. Tears welled in her eyes. Ikoom's mouth watered. *Zapote, my favorite!* She lifted one to her mouth, broke the skin with a bite and felt the juice squirt into her mouth, covering her tongue and trickling over her lips as her teeth sunk deeper into the pulp and meat of the sweet fruit—a nectar and sustenance of the gods.

"Oh! Thank you, Ixchel. Thank you." She ate with her eyes closed, savoring every bite until she had had her fill and regained her strength.

After making her way back to the altar, Ikoom tended the fire and prayed to the goddess. With her hunger and thirst satisfied, her thoughts turned to her original mission, she sat near the altar and wondered whether she would live out her days on the *Island of Women* or whether Ixchel would send her back to her people. Most importantly, she wondered if Ixchel would teach her how to make the great Chaac cry.

"Oh child, what I've taught you is that *you* can discover how to make Chaac cry. *You* are clever and strong; yet, you know humility is important, too. Honor the gods and goddesses and use *your* talents wisely; trust yourself. Just as your mother has nourished you, you will live to nourish children of your own."

Ikoom smiled and once again sunk her teeth into a *zapote,* which she had carried to the altar area. Stronger and filled with hope, she sat up and looked out to sea. Suddenly, she stood, spotting something on the horizon. She lifted a hand to her forehead minimizing the glare on the waves. It appeared to be a Mayan boat. It came closer, bobbing up and down with the motion of the waves and moving forward with the steady rhythm of the oars. Ikoom could now see that the boat carried two priests and six protectors rowing toward the *Island of Women,* toward her, toward Ixchel's altar, toward the flames from the fire that she had built. Ikoom's eyes filled with tears of joy.

PART 6

WATER—AZTECA CORPORATION

ROBERT MADERA

"Rain! Let's make it rain," Robert Madera announced with energy to the surprise of his executive team members. They glanced at each other unsure of how to respond.

"California needs rain! Yes. True. But let's make it rain the other way!" Madera said sprinkling his fingers as if he were throwing money into the air and watching it float chaotically back to earth. The board members now relaxed their shoulders and let wide smiles cross their faces. Their light laughter and nods to one another seemed to pat each other on the back.

"Well, ladies and gentlemen, stage one of Agua Managua Nicaragua is under way!" The handsome, thirty-nine years-old, Robert Madera engaged them with a gleaming smile. "I'm pleased by the reports." His tone of voice projected pride in his team; yet, the announcement from Madera, owner of Azteca Corporation, was met with surprise by some and mixed approval among his executive employees—Vice President of Marketing and Advertising, Renée Chavon, Chief Financial Officer, Ted Benson, Vice President of Production, Carl Johnson, Chief Distribution Officer, Larry Ketterer, Licensing and Global Contracts Specialist, Gail Kurts, Vice President of Human Resources, Marcus Reed, Vice President of Resource, Research and Development, Tommy Lee and of course, the newly named President of Azteca, Robert Madera's brother-in-law, Mannie Morales. They sat around the mahogany table in comfortable leather chairs politely applauding the announcement, some smiling, but some with pursed lips.

None of them held quite the same passion for the project as did Madera. Madera knew this. They all had been quite happy specializing in Spanish and South American wines. *Why water?* They had silently questioned. Concerns arose considering the proposition from every angle, asserting that the profit margins would be too low considering the competition, the artistry of the product is too plain, distribution too difficult, advertising Nicaraguan water politically suspect, dealing with the legalities of the Latin American country just plain crazy, and so on. But Madera had been determined and designated assignments to each of them several months earlier. He had lavished them with his enthusiastic praise via compliments of their talents and they were beginning to adjust to the idea, some were even beginning to like it. Their reports had been given to Madera, privately and he had made each of them feel special. He had studied them and their reports, and now despite their earlier naysaying, he could tell that most of them were on board with the project and those who were not on board yet, were at least listening in a politely skeptical manner. He could see what surprised them most was his comment that *stage one of Agua Managua Nicaragua is under way.* He hadn't told them that he had enacted anything, but he knew he would win them all over by the end of the day.

Madera understood their concerns. He knew that he had assembled a group of smart and talented people to work for him who were clever but cautious; he also knew that only one of them was as clever and as smart as himself. The rest lacked that certain something, that critical edge to manipulate and maneuver as if it were all a chess game. Pawns to be sacrificed; queens to be exploited. Plus, for the most part, they were too comfortable, too satisfied. They simply weren't hungry enough, he thought. And they were too trusting. The only one he held out hope for was Renée Chavon; she seemed to have a spark that might ignite a firestorm of creativity someday. And she held the potential to see, truly see, what's going on. That also made her dangerous. He would keep a careful eye on her.

"Alright then, I'll bring you up to speed," Madera told them as he sat down at the head of the conference table. He ran a hand through his thick dark hair, then leaned forward.

"Stage one of Agua Managua Nicaragua included locating an appropriate location to tap into fresh spring water, developing a relationship with local beverage suppliers, assessing legal concerns, studying the various possibilities of undertaking the project, exploring employee hiring and development, exploring distribution issues that might arise, judging competition, and assessing marketability,"

Madera reminded them all. "Today, we're ready to hear the reports and consider further action. Let's start with feasibility of the plan in terms of access to our raw product—water." Madera turned to Vice-President of Resource, Research and Development Tommy Lee. Lee, a medium-sized man with brown hair and glasses, nodded to Madera and then began to provide details as he gathered his stack of reports.

"Initial studies of the water samples from just outside Managua that were sent to us were given to an independent lab for testing run by a well-respected professor who teaches at the university. The results," Lee said as he slid copies of the analysis around the table to the other executives, "safe levels of lead and fluoride exist and no additional contaminants were found that would cause harm to humans. You'll find that on page two." Everyone turned the cover page over and then flipped to page two.

"The water courses through a rocky region of the country, not far from a volcano, quartz is abundant and the rocks filter the water to a more than acceptable level of purification. You can see the levels of pyrite and sulfur are minimal although they do exist, but according to blind taste tests from focus groups that we conducted with Renée's help, we discovered the water has impeccable taste and has picked up no rotten egg odor."

Madera smiled at the simplification of malodorous sulfur being translated to lay language, quite simply, rotten eggs; and rotten eggs stink. But not his water. It smelled and tasted as pure as any mountain spring. He then turned to Chief Distribution Officer, Larry Ketterer. "The water itself is excellent. That is, the product is pure. But Larry has a less enthusiastic report on distribution issues. Nevertheless, let's hear from production." Larry set his report down.

Vice President of Production, Carl Johnson, leaned forward, "Production in Nicaragua would require building a bottling plant in an area that sits just at the edge of an urban infrastructure that gives way to a very, and I do mean *very*, rural area. We go from poor city slums with impoverished infrastructure to rural, practically uninhabitable areas of the rain forest. Downstream there is farmland and coffee plantations. It is possible that roads near the plant could be washed out during heavy rains, but we should see smooth sailing as we get closer to the airport or to the seaports."

"So, we could consider offering to put in a road in exchange for land rights," Madera inserted. The lawyer, Gail Kurts, scribbled a note. Johnson continued his report.

"As for the building of the plant, the plant itself, well, a bottling plant for water wouldn't be nearly as complex as a bottling plant for wine. I mean, we deal with wine coming from huge stainless steel storage containers to fragile glass bottles; whereas, when it comes to water I have one word for you—plastics." He smiled hoping they would get the reference to the movie, *The Graduate*. A few of them smiled, mostly the older members of the team. He moved on. "Plastic! It's cheap, lightweight, durable, clear—"

"Is the transparency of the container important to you?" Madera interrupted.

"Hmm, I hadn't thought much about the transparency. Just assumed..." He thought about it, putting a hand on his goatee-covered chin and rubbing it before continuing. "Perhaps, the transparency doesn't matter in terms of production, but it saves money as it does come most cheaply in clear form and with respect to water there might be a psychological component that people want to see the clear water."

"That's my territory," Renée smiled. Carl conceded with a nod; he moved on. She tried to conceal her excitement. Renée was anxious to give her report.

"The bottling plant can be built directly on the site of the spring. The building can be minimal as the weather is generally mild, hot, but not given to as many hurricanes as it's not on the east coast of Nicaragua. We need a conveyor belt, pumps, generator, capping machine, glue labeling machine, etc. It's all in the report. Overall it wouldn't be an expensive structure or production operation. Packaging and trucking the product require the bottles and cardboard boxes but both can be supplied fairly cheaply. Overall, the whole affair is lighter, cheaper and easier than bottling wine. Far more cost effective than I had earlier thought," Carl Johnson provided his opinion and his colleagues nodded in agreement.

"Plastic is good, but I'm considering some different packaging possibilities." They all paused and looked to Madera to finish his thought on alternative packaging. He responded, "Just playing with a

couple of ideas. Go on; go on. Renée can tell us more about it later."
She smiled. Madera turned his attention back to Carl.

"That's all really. If you turn to page four of the report you can
see a cost comparison for production for bottling water versus bottling
wine. It looks like a winning proposition," Carl concluded.

"Larry has a different take on distribution," Madera added
turning the floor over to his Distribution Vice-President, Larry Ketterer.
Ketterer a man of great bulk with a pocked-mark face and the eyes of
an owl, who had a great deal of experience in distribution appreciated
that his minority report was being heard.

"I understand where Carl is coming from in terms of cheaper
production costs. And the profit margin is incredible, but distribution
depends on where we want to move the product to. Nicaragua has port
cities on the west coast and we can easily bring the product by ship along
the coast and up into the States. We'd have easy distribution in Mexico
along the way, but if we want to distribute across Nicaragua, going east,
where the water is most needed by indigenous groups, then we run into
problems. The infrastructure is nearly nonexistent. Some areas heading
east are so isolated that they move essentials like medicine by mule.
They have no port cities on the east coast, the ocean depth is simply
too shallow for anything but motorboats or primitive rafts. They don't
have airports on the east coast and even if they did it's too costly to fly
the product. So we would likely be restricted to a west coast operation,
which could cost us an enormous amount in the long run."

"But once we get it to California couldn't we ship all across the
U.S. by truck?" Madera's brother-in-law, Mannie, asked.

"We could but then we'd have to be aware that we'll face stiff
competition if we try to target the U.S. market. Honestly, I think the
U.S. market may be saturated. People are drowning in bottled water
choices. No pun intended," Larry Ketterer told them with a smile.

"Larry, now you're *tapping* into my territory. Pun intended,"
Renée said with a smile. "I've got the marketing figures, my friends.
And you'll be amazed."

"Go ahead, Renée. Fill us in," Madera told her. She stood and
started sliding her report across the table to each, faster than a Las
Vegas dealer.

"No, no, wait a minute. Let's get the broader scope first, if you don't mind," Madera changed the order.

"Oh no, no. I don't mind at all," Renée lied, taking her seat. The young woman was biting at the bit to share her information. False starts frustrated her.

"Ted, as Chief Financial wizard, would you give us the big picture."

"Sure," Ted passed out his stapled stack of spreadsheets with a bullet point summary and the executives set Renée's report with the glossy cover aside as they took up Ted's analysis and projection.

"The water industry is a multi-billion-dollar business," Ted said, pushing his glasses up his nose only to have them slide down again. "We can divide the water market into two groups: those who focus on water privatization by way of large scale water sanitation systems and those who bottle water for sale. Of the first category the major players are Vivendi and Suez. Others have tried their hand at it—Enron and Bechtel come to mind, but they had unsuccessful attempts. For Bechtel there was the Bolivian nightmare that you all know about. And Enron, well, we all know that story, too. Suez, on the other hand, has been quite successful at negotiating large scale municipal contracts. They've also had a number of bribery suits brought against them."

Everyone nodded. Several shrugged lightly as if giving bribes were an expected and accepted part of doing business these days.

"The second category, more pertinent to us, is the bottlers; they include Coke, Pepsi, Nestlé, and a few others. Nestlé, for the most part, is drawing from local spring water. Pepsi and Coke have been bottling tap water, distilling it, and selling within the U.S. Other companies or those mentioned in some places, are simply bottling tap water, not bothering to distill it first. There is a growing resistance against those companies that are bottling tap water and reselling it as *pure*." Ted drew little quote marks in the air as he said the word, pure. He continued.

"People are catching onto the game. They need to do something there. In the meantime, the bottlers have teamed with the privatizers and together they are creating a coalition, lobbying the IMF and the

World Bank to create laws on their behalf. Combining the two, we're talking about a $500 billion industry with bottled water accounting for around $70 billion a year. The profit margin on bottled water is higher than oil." Everyone either nodded or widened their eyes at the profit margin. "So while the profits could be extremely handsome, we'll have to become strong political players. In addition, not all of the players are terribly ethical, so we risk being lumped in with them. Depending on whether you assess their behaviors as maniacal geniuses or clever bastards or just plain assholes is up to you. I'm just pointing out the facts."

"My favorite story is," and Ted simultaneously smiled and shook his head as he told the following, "about the bottling company who promised to provide 150 new jobs to a suburb of Detroit, if given free utilities, reprieve from municipal and state taxes for five years, and city financial assistance in building the plant…," he paused. "Get this. They bottled the tap water which they didn't pay for because they had free utilities in the building that they only partially paid for and that they didn't pay taxes on for five years at which time they closed shop and moved to another city that begged them to come." Ted chortled, snorted, and shook his head in disbelief. "People bought it— hook, line, and sinker. And it was all perfectly legal. Perfectly, legal!"

"I'll tell you how they do it," Renée said. Everyone turned to their stack of reports and fished out Renée's graphically superior design. "Marketing and advertising." She flipped the report to page one.

"Just a second," Madera said to Renée. "Ted, what do you see as the most serious drawback."

"I think one of the other bottlers will put a great deal of effort into trying to shut us down."

"How would they do it?"

"They'd likely try to tie us up in court somehow."

"Land rights, likely," Gail inserted.

"Could they completely shut us down?"

"It's Nicaragua. Anything could happen. But I would say, no. More likely, they'll just try to discourage us by bringing things to court. We can find ways to stall as well though. It just becomes a headache. As long we have all our ducks in row and they don't manage to get some kind of 'Cease and Desist' order, we should be okay."

"Could we slow down a 'Cease and Desist'?" Madera asked.

"Sure, we would ignore it and file a counter suit. But would it be worth it? It would be expensive," Gail questioned and informed them.

"Well, let's find out. Renée, what do you have to tell us?" Madera asked turning to Renée who responded enthusiastically.

"Absolutely. This timing is perfect. That's also why the bottling companies won't be happy with us moving into their territory. The main players have huge budgets for advertising and they've been doing it for years, which is actually a benefit for us. People seem to think they need bottled water and that their own tap water is inferior. In the U.S. the Flint, Michigan story has only helped to bolster that demand for bottled water as people aren't sure they can trust their own city management. And from California to Latin America, the drought is getting worse. In Nicaragua the water rationing is becoming more common. Managua especially because the water is being polluted at an increasing rate as the government let's more industry dump toxic waste in the lakes. From Flint to Managua people don't trust their governments and in turn their water. We could certainly build on these insecurities and advertise doubt and fear. And we'll need to do so since some companies are starting to promote tap water again."

"Which companies? Who would do that?" Mannie asked.

"Oh, not the water bottling companies. No. It's the manufactures of water coolers, water fountains, and water bottles for businesses. *Hydrate*, for one." They looked at her quizzically. She continued. "*Hydrate* is a long standing firm with a solid reputation. They're launching campaigns that city water is safe and then installing water fountains with new features for filling water bottles, the kind that people carry around with them. Their advertising right now is mostly in the trade journals. But the eco thing will get the average person on board. They're locking in contracts with corporations, universities, public high schools, government buildings, hospitals, and so on."

She flipped the cover page and turning to Madera, said, "Do you want me to bring up the PowerPoint?"

"Sure."

Renée clicked the buttons on her laptop. Heads turned to the screen on the wall in the conference room. "Bottled water is priced at approximately 1,000 times that of tap water in the U.S. and it's advertised as pure, whether it is or isn't doesn't seem to matter too much yet. People are still buying like crazy. They're demonstrating an addiction to bottled water. Oral fixation for many of them. We have to make sure they don't start refilling from the taps. Also they're not only addicted or fixated on drinking it, but also carrying it. That's good for us. They're addicted to having it with them all the time, like their phones. Plus, the more they carry it, the more *they* advertise it. As long as we have our logo on the container, well… Carriers. Like a pandemic. They spread the word." She smiled at the thought of people being advertising carriers like a disease. "It's fantastic! It's ultimate in the branding world. Like when the clothing industry talked the public into displaying their brands. Branding became all the rage. With water, half the work is done for us. What we need is a very catchy brand. We are currently considering two: one draws directly from our wine label—Azteca; the second, could be created around the Mayan god theme—Chaac, the rain god," she said as she clicked to the next slide bringing up an image of the powerfully handsome Chaac in full regalia—the rain god wore golden armor and a headdress in the shape of a crocodile." The executives nodded with approval.

"This is great!" Larry added before Renée continued. She quickly pointed to the counter argument before anyone could beat her to the creative punch.

"Chaac is great, as Larry says, really cool, but if we stick with Azteca, we increase advertising that name as well. Meaning we can put Azteca's name on every water bottle. Plus, since much of the hard work has been done for us; that is, the water bottling companies have been spending about $95 million a year over the last 10–15 years to create this pseudo-addiction to water, ad-induced-addiction, I call it. Anyway, we can ride their coattails on the water addiction that they've created and we can indirectly advertise our wine without worrying about age restrictions the way we have to with an alcoholic beverage. Azteca could be on everything from toys to t-shirts that kids wear to school if its advertising water instead of wine. Eventually, kids will grow up and be loyal brand consumers who will buy our wine, too."

"That all sounds good," Gail Kurts interrupted, "but we're talking about Nicaragua. Nicaragua could be a legal nightmare for us. First, there are international trade regulations to discern. CAFTA and NAFTA have been helpful, but Nicaragua is a world of its own. There would be international, national and local laws to adhere to with which we're unfamiliar. We can't purchase land without a partner and even then the scams are plentiful in places like Nicaragua and Belize, where the land you think you have bought turns out is already under dispute in the courts with respect to ownership. The American consulate deals with these kinds of issues on a regular basis. So just obtaining mineral rights or utilities won't be easy. And like I mentioned before, the other companies who've already staked out territory in Nicaragua could make things very difficult for us."

Vice President of Human Resources, Marcus Reed interrupted, adding, "And although workers' salaries are low, the government requires a minimum wage and a yearly bonus in December that's equal to at least one month's salary for all workers. On the upside for us, the unemployment level is high, the minimum wage quite low, very low, so it should be easy to find workers and keep them. Labor is *really* cheap."

"Let's go back to the legal hurdles. Gail?" Madera redirected.

"Well, the initial hurdle is the highest. In order for an American company to do business in Nicaragua, they must have a Nicaraguan business partner. If you can find the right partner, the rest of your worries will disappear. The wrong business partner could make life difficult. We would want someone with influence, but not too leftist. Someone who can relate to the workers, but is also not opposed to making a healthy profit for him or herself; someone who has connections with both bureaucrats and wrench-turners. This means we need someone who is a Sandinista, but not without a capitalist bent. So if they turn off the electricity, we have someone who can either grease the palm of a politician or get somebody in the trenches willing to break some rules to turn the electricity back on. We need someone who understands the workings of the political scene, both the apparent and the backroom sort of thing. Someone who won't tow the party line completely, who can be persuaded by a little extra money, if you know what I mean."

"Gail, you surprise me. Are we stepping beyond the legal?" Madera teased her. She smiled in return.

"I'm just saying his salary or bonuses might have to be larger or more frequent."

"Are you serious about the electricity or is that a hypothetical?" Mannie Morales asked.

"I'm wondering if she's serious about the bribe," Larry joked. Everyone laughed.

Gail straightened her well-fitted suit jacket and crossed her legs. "not a bribe; a higher salary." She turned her attention to Mannie, glancing into his eyes and then quickly averting her gaze as she spoke on. Madera noticed both the glance and Gail's reluctance to look Mannie in the eye. Madera shifted his studied gaze from Gail to Mannie with the slightest turn of his head to assess whether his brother-in-law could be having an affair with his in-house attorney. It was certainly possible. He wouldn't put it past Mannie.

"Yes, electricity and water are rationed by the government," Gail confirmed.

"I see. Well, you've certainly done your homework well," Mannie responded.

Madera realized then that Mannie didn't care about the electricity. It had been the first time Mannie had shown much interest during the meeting and it was to hear Gail speak, to get her attention, to play with her, fluster her, and then demonstrate his authority by giving her a little pat on back—*Well, you've certainly done your homework well.* Madera had named his brother-in-law President of the company while he, himself, remained sole owner and CEO. Titles are ambiguous things, they can be used in very selective ways, and Madera knew how to use them. On the other hand, Madera didn't want to jump to unjust conclusions. Mannie may have been the only one who hadn't done his homework concerning the basics of Nicaragua. To his brother-in-law's defense, Madera reminded himself that he hadn't given him an assignment. Mannie was more of a figure head who could stand in for Madera at local wine-tasting dinners or employee funerals. Madera hated that sort of thing and he wasn't terribly fond of his brother-in-law, but Mannie's handsome Latin look had helped to seal the deal on more than one occasion, even though he was a sixth generation American mixed pup—Spanish, Portuguese, French, and a smidgeon of British blood. Madera feared his brother-in-law was even part Mexican. Madera was given to the old school ethnic divide which considered the Spanish well-bred Europeans and the Mexicans low class, mixed bloods. But Mannie also supplied votes when Madera wanted something to look like a democratic decision among his executive committee.

"She's serious, Mannie. The country suffers from rolling brown outs during the day and black outs at night. The hospitals have generators as do wealthy home owners. Businesses don't run at night unless they have their own generators. Third shift is pretty much out of the question, unless we want to consider large generators," Larry explained. Renée took up the thread of conversation and explained further.

"And this is one of the reasons that the people of Nicaragua don't have running water. The pumping stations get shut down. People have to fill and store bottles of water for lean times. Our bottled water could be more than the artificial need it is in the U.S.," Renée said. "It could provide clean water to those who really need it." As she said this, she knew she sounded like she was giving them a syrupy PSA. She knew they'd never buy it. There were no sappy liberals in this room. She changed her tone and topic, calling their attention to her report.

The executives of Azteca Corporation dug her report out of their piles, since she had switched to PowerPoint none of them had lifted a finger to explore her paper report. Now, they did so and rediscovered the glossy cover image, a graphic of a tipped water bottle releasing its contents like an exquisite waterfall, pristine and blue with silver and white highlights.

She could hardly wait to tell them her marketing and advertising ideas.

CHAPTER 36

MADERA MEETS WITH JACKSON

Robert Madera entered the brightly lit California restaurant with his sunglasses reflecting the interior of the room. The sun-drenched dining area appeared a bleached brightness with white walls, chrome tables and chairs, and mirrored backdrops which held the white iciness of a winter day in the north, except where the over-sized paintings with rich reds, warm golds and deep browns, which one might find in a De Chirico painting, gave warmth back to the otherwise crisp, clean California-style. Madera took off his sunglasses with one hand. His gaze swept the room in search of Jackson T. Jackson, Attorney-at-Large.

Jackson had arrived first. He knew his place in this relationship or at least how to play his role, he wouldn't keep the owner of Azteca wines waiting. He stood to welcome Robert Madera with outstretched palm.

"Robert, so good to see you again." They shook hands. Three pumps. Nice and firm.

Jackson offered Madera a seat. Madera took his place at the table. Neither man wanted to sit with his back to the door. Jackson had wisely chosen a table that sat sideways, giving each of them the angle they preferred.

"I was just about to order. Can I get you a wine? An Azteca, I presume?"

"Of course," Madera smiled, adding "Chilean Pinot."

Jackson waived the server over to the table and placed the drink order. The server attempted to hand them menus, but Jackson added, "Just the drinks."

"And a water for me, as well" Madera said. The server left the table without another word, just a nod.

"How have the meetings been going?" Jackson asked Madera.

"Too smooth to describe, my friend. All I can think of is having celebration sex when I get home."

"Good to hear. Good to hear." Jackson laughed and now had sexual images running through his own head. Images of Madera's wife. He reached for his water glass, wishing he had something stronger.

Madera noticed the sparkling water, thinking, as Jackson reached for his glass, *like nothing and everything.* As soon as the server returned with a glass of water for Madera he took his own glass and had a long cool sip; he held it in his mouth for a second or two, as if it were wine. He hadn't realized how thirsty he was until he felt the water in his mouth. The dry hot day had left him parched. He followed the cool sip with a long, greedy glug. "A hot one," Madera said after finishing the water. Jackson nodded.

"Do we need to change the contracts at all?" Jackson queried, reaching for his briefcase.

"I don't think so." Madera added, "but let me see them again to be on the safe side."

"Certainly," Jackson replied. "Let's make sure everything is exactly as you want it."

The server arrived with two glasses of Chilean Pinot. Madera noticed the glasses and found them interesting. The stems were solid white, the bodies of the glass, clear and filled three-fourths of the way with the red pinot noir. He made a mental note of the combined opaqueness coupled with transparency.

"To glory and profit," Jackson saluted his client by raising his glass. Madera raised his as well and nodded in response.

Jackson retrieved the contracts from his briefcase and slid his wine aside. He had the pen ready, a black pen with gold trim, which he laid next to the contract. The pen practically begged to be picked up.

Jackson turned the contracts for Madera to see.

"I'm hesitant about becoming a smuggler, Jackson." Although Madera's voice was low and seemed sincere, he wasn't really hesitant about becoming a smuggler, what really concerned him was whether he was getting into bed with the right partners.

"Then don't," Jackson said, surprising Madera.

"What do you mean?"

"The federal laws allow you to bring in gold currency—coins, bullion—duty free, but you are expected to declare it."

"But this won't be coins."

"True enough. The contract assures that the minerals are yours. You're simply returning what is yours to the States; it belongs to you. We already negotiated the land rights with the water and mineral rights. Well, yours and your new partner, FourOre and whatever you give your Nicaraguan partner, but he's a different story. You're exporting it out of Nicaragua and importing into the U.S."

"What if the Nicaraguans find out?"

"Again the contract has been signed. They have given you the land, water, and mineral rights for the duration of your partnership with Alejandro. The gold is yours. They just don't know that there is gold on the land. No law says that you have to declare the finding. They won't like it of course if they find out, but they won't be able to stop you. At least not legally. The only thing you must find a way to do is to declare that you have it without the Nicaraguans finding out that you have it. Declare and you won't be smuggling."

"Yes, that's the part I haven't figured out yet."

"You will. You're not a smuggler, my friend. Smugglers are low-life characters who don't want to work; you on the other hand, have worked hard and entered into a brilliant business collaboration with FourOre. Smugglers are criminals; they do an injustice to society. They bring drugs and guns. They do not contribute to the American way. You bring water and gold. You're not a smuggler, more like a good capitalist pirate." This last comment made Madera laugh.

Changing the subject slightly, he said, "Which brings us to FourOre. Have they agreed to my stipulations?"

"Yes. It wasn't easy, but they have agreed."

"In writing?"

"Yes," Jackson flipped a few pages ahead and showed Madera the statements."

"They've signed?"

"Yes," and here Jackson glanced at the pen waiting to be taken up by Madera.

"They'll supply the mining equipment, the expertise and much of the drilling, while I supply distribution and protection?"

"Yes," Jackson affirmed.

"To be under my control?"

"Yes." Jackson flipped to the next page showing Madera by pointing to the paragraph.

"Okay, then."

"All right, then. Let me summarize before you sign. First, you'll be incorporated under the name of Agua Managua, defined primarily as a water bottling operation. You will have partnership of this business with Alejandro Martínez and will adhere to Nicaraguan laws regarding hiring and treatment of employees." Here Jackson flipped back to the beginning of the contract, specifically page two and pointed to several paragraphs in a contiguous order. "You'll maintain all mineral, land, and water rights for the duration of your use of the property," Jackson pointed to the paragraphs on pages three and four of the contract. You may hire two U.S. American citizens for your management team. Do you still want them to be Mannie, listed as Interim-Acting CEO and Director of Manufacturing and Bottling, and Renée Chavon for Vice-President of Marketing, Packaging and Advertising?"

"Yes, but neither of them knows it yet."

"Not a concern to me," Jackson didn't want to know more than he had to know. Jackson went over additional simple details, flipping pages, double checking what they had agreed upon earlier. Madera was thinking, brainstorming, and something was beginning to take shape.

He was glad that he had chosen Mannie as the front man. And whatever ideas he, Madera developed, he would put into Mannie's head. Renée would think her orders were coming from Mannie. That way if anything went wrong Mannie would take the blame. Of course, Madera didn't want anything to go wrong, but he also knew this was a tricky operation.

"Just sign here," Jackson was saying to him. And without his knowledge of how the pen had entered his hand, Madera pressed against the point of pen to the black line on the ever so white paper.

"Wait," he said. Madera looked at Jackson. "What if I want to send Gail Kurts instead of Renée Chavon?"

"We can change that. FourOre won't care who you send down. But isn't she your global contracts specialist? That could get her asking questions."

"I know but she is also an expert in labor laws. I think she could handle H.R., International labor, and local political issues etc., if we run into problems."

"But I will still be your lawyer, right?"

"Oh, absolutely. Absolutely. Don't get paranoid, Jackson."

"I'm thinking of the December payments and such."

"The what?"

"You see what I mean. Gail is the one who told me about the mandatory Christmas bonus that must be paid to workers." Madera lied well. It was actually Marcus Reed who had told him. But the way Mannie had looked at Gail, gave Madera an idea.

"Oh, I didn't know."

Jackson changed the name and title on the contract. Madera initialed it. Jackson flipped the pages showing Madera the final signature line. The witness line remained blank.

Madera signed the first contract to be presented to his Nicaraguan partner and government officials.

"Let me see FourOre's contract," Madera said.

Jackson pulled FourOre's contract out of his briefcase. He began going over it with Madera. FourOre would provide expertise and extraction of "the product" from the location; Madera would provide distribution to Nicaraguan ports and north including San Diego. In San Diego, Madera would deposit one third of "the raw mineral product" extracted from Nicaragua into the hands of the owners of FourOre. The rest would belong to him. This contract was not the kind that anyone would take to court. This contract was a means of protecting each partner from the other, neither would double-cross the other if each could hold the other responsible. Furthermore, Madera felt he held the better hand even though FourOre found the gold. Madera was taking the risk. He had guaranteed protection of "the product" within Nicaragua and in any and all other countries to which "the product" is exported until delivered to FourOre. He would have the "security" on his side. Retired Blackwater operatives would have his back.

"What about Alejandro? Could he make claim on it?"

"No, his contract stipulates that he receives half the revenue of bottled water sold in Nicaragua. He doesn't even actually have any claim over the water or "the product" that you export. Perhaps, he could argue that he has ownership of half the ore in the ground, but you'll be leaving at least half of it behind, right?"

"Yes, FourOre says that only about half of the vein is easily extractable."

"FourOre has one *recommendation* for you."

"What's that?"

"They want you to find a way to bring the "protection" in without causing concern to the locals."

"Not a problem. The locals will be begging for security operatives," Madera predicted with certainty and a sly smile. He opened his mouth as if to share when Jackson interrupted him.

"Again, not my concern how you do it," Jackson said raising his empty hands. "I'm just passing along their message. They've faced the locals in the past, you know. And," Jackson added, "they don't want anything to go wrong."

Madera didn't expect anything to go wrong. He felt good. The contracts were in order. His plan detailed to the nth degree. Jackson was pointing his index finger to a spot on the paper saying, "...and sign here, and here," flipping the page, "and here."

Jackson took one set of contracts, folded them and put them into a white envelope. He handed them to Madera. "These are for your records." The attorney then opened his briefcase and returned the other set of contracts to where they had come from. "The pen is for you," Jackson added with a smile. Madera put the envelope as well as the pen into his inside jacket pocket. He then withdrew an envelope and handed it to Jackson, saying, "And this is for you."

Jackson raised his wine glass again, "To glory and profit! You bring noble pirates back from the grave."

Madera raised his glass in response. He had much on his mind.

"Bringing the wealth and possibilities of capitalism to impoverished parts of the world. Jobs for the poor. Water for the thirsty. A noble quest, indeed." Jackson reiterated and raised his glass a tad higher, repeating the toast, "To noble pirates."

"To noble pirates!" Madera agreed.

VALERIA'S GOLD EARRING

Madera's wife had been the inspiration. He recalled a day when he'd been lying in bed on pearl-colored, 2000 thread-count sheets, with his wife, Valeria, who preferred high quality cotton to slippery satin sheets, when the initial idea came to him. They lay in the after-exhaustion of having made love, her head on his bare chest, blondish-hair (highlights and lowlights, conceived and created at an exclusive salon on Rodeo Drive) streaming across his bare chest. He stroked stray strands away from her face and over and around her ear, exposing the gold earring. A delicate earring. It shimmered with a crusting of diamonds down the loops' center with etched gold on the sides. *Discover the gold. Agua Managua. The gold standard in sparkling spring water. From Azteca.* His memory triggered his future strategy; his daydream of Valeria gave him the plan for how to declare the gold, so that he wouldn't be a smuggler.

Over the next couple of weeks, Robert Madera moved ahead. He had assigned tasks, coordinated meetings, and made secret pacts. His team had all attended the first round of reports on Agua Managua, and none of them had any idea that Madera had acquired Alejandro as a partner, signed contracts, and even begun building a warehouse, a plant, and a road. Only Jackson Jackson and the miners knew the double duty that the heavy equipment was serving. Madera had moved ahead with everything, *everything.* The only unresolved issues had to do with moving the product and declaring the contents, how to export water, and the gold. But that day, when he looked at Valeria's earring it all came together. Madera committed to the idea that water is gold and winning is everything. Declaring is simple, obvious. Gold 'n Water.

Now, once again he called his team together. They awaited his words as they sat in their usual places around the conference table.

"I will be flying to Managua to meet with our Nicaraguan partner this week. The bottling plant has gone up quickly. I want to check on the arrival of the glass bottles from Mexico and the plastic bottles from the plant near Ventura. Madera had been busy, locking in deals with bottle manufacturers, printing companies, distributors, and more. The team couldn't believe how fast he had been able to bring it all together. Always impressive, Madera left them with the impression that they could never achieve his level of business savvy. And likely, they couldn't. Of course, he never let on that he had worked out deals with these manufacturers' weeks ago after he'd had his moment of inspiration based on Valeria's earrings. He just needed to say the word and the shipments would begin arriving. In the flurry of activity Madera had assigned various additional jobs to each of them.

"This time Renée is up first."

Excitedly, Renée smiled, clicked a PowerPoint onto the screen and began her presentation.

"Robert decided to pursue several lines, one of sparkling water that brilliantly connects us to our wine label and three more waters that segue the product to different audiences. He wants the sparkling water on shelves in time for New Year's Eve. He selected a general theme to tie them together—

Renée clicked; the slide appeared.

"*Discover the gold! Agua Managua. The Gold 'n Water of the Gods. The gold standard in sparkling, spring water. A gift from Azteca.*" A wine-shaped bottle appeared with a label. An image of a waterfall of diamonds poured over a golden rock encrusted cliff. *Gold 'n Water* was printed on the label—gold letters on black background. The rest of the theme was printed on the back with a story of the bottlers and their history in fine wines. The bottles would be dark, like champagne or wine bottles. Renée moved to the next slide.

Agua Managua. An Ancient Promise. Spring Water. A Gold 'n Gift from the Gods. Certified pure spring water. From Azteca. This one would be carried in clear, plastic bottles with a label that used the same concept of the diamond waterfall spilling over a gold encrusted ledge. In the background on the label was a cave with shimmering stalactites and stalagmites indicating an underground source for the water and at the very farthest spot of the cave, a tiny, tiny drawing of a golden Aztec sun-god circle could be seen.

She clicked again:

Fire Water! A Volcano of Gold 'n Molten Lava Water in your Mouth. We dare you! From Azteca.

"This one is so fricking cool! I love it. It'll be flavored with hot peppers and eventually sold in varying degrees of heat. The hottest, will attract young male drinkers who'll mix it with tequila or drink it straight up. The heat will range from medium to extremely hot chili peppers. And the back label will add that we don't mess around with mild, we jump right into the heat." She clicked to show them the label and the container. Chaac appeared in full regalia, powerful and menacing on the bottle, volcano in the background, but as she started to click again.

"I thought he was a Mayan rain god?'

"He is. Your point?"

"Nothing. Never mind."

"Do you have anything for young women?"

"Today, it's *Flawless Agua Managua. Spring Water. Pure and Flawless. For a golden, crystal clear complexion.*"

"Won't Beyoncé sue us?"

"She doesn't own 'flawless.'"

"Are you sure about that?" Gail asked.

"Well, if she does, we'll apologize and move onto the latest in-thing."

"Or get her to be the spokesperson."

"Right! Oh, that's good, really good. I'll get on it."

"Renée, let Gail check on the legalities first," Madera said. And then turning to Gail, his in-house council, he added "Could you do that?"

"Of course."

"But I'm not sold on Beyoncé," he said with a bit of a frown. Everyone knew when to be quiet, they just didn't always know why. Clearly Madera didn't want anyone as high profile as Beyoncé, too much attention could bring too much scrutiny. He couldn't afford to let something like that jeopardize the operation. But why he didn't want Beyoncé would have to remain a mystery.

"Shall I?" Renée wondered if she should proceed.

"Yes, yes," Madera encouraged.

"Okay then, here is the other version we're considering— *¡Desperado!*" She clicked and the slide showed the face of Chaac on a circular canteen with a strap which was long enough to cross over the shoulder. It had a worn, bronzed look as if the gold had been weathered and tarnished. She clicked again. A poster showed an image reminiscent of Clint Eastwood—a silhouette of a man in a hat and long coat with his canteen to the side."

"Nice, but won't this one cost more?"

"It will."

"And they'll refill it from the tap," Larry said with some concern.

"We're working on that."

"Hey, maybe you could get them to refill it with the Fire Water."

"Sounds good. We'll look into marketing for that."

Madera liked the smiles on their faces. He was looking forward to Renée's next slide and seeing his team's response.

"And..." Renée held them in suspense momentarily. "Our children's line." She clicked and up popped an image of a silver balloon with gold trim and a colorful image in the center. The image was Chaac, the great Mayan rain god diminished to a cartoon character on the face of a water balloon. The words *Make It Rain! Mylar Mayan Rain Balloon! A Gift of Gold 'n Water from Azteca.* Renée beamed with pride.

"Lord on Earth, nothing like creating loyal customers from birth," Ted declared with excitement and an incredulous shake of his head. "This is so good, so very, very good."

"Renée, you're brilliant. From birth. Like giving water to a baby. How 'bout baby bottles?"

"Or water rattles?"

"That you could drink from, of course," Renée added.

"Well, all in good time," Madera brought them back from their manic brainstorming. "Let's hear from Ted on finances."

As Ted went over the figures and profit margin projections and how various phases of the venture and product lines might unfold, Robert Madera's thoughts drifted toward the covert plans to which no one sitting at that conference table was or would be aware. After everything was in place, warehouse and factory complete, the workers hired, the spring water being bottled, he would create a situation that only he could master-mind in order to get the workers themselves to invite in the security team. Madera let a smile slip across his lips. He would get the plant up and running, befriend Alejandro, their Nicaraguan partner, and he would befriend the workers as if they were his own family. Then he would send Mannie to the plant to oversee things. Then Madera would return in November to hand-deliver the one-month salary bonus to the workers. He would ensure that after he made the hand off to Mannie, who would place the bonus money in the company safe, it would turn up missing the very next day. Everyone would be under suspicion—workers, Mannie, Alejandro, everybody except for himself, of course. Workers, who would mistrust each other, doubt Mannie and Alejandro, would demand recompense. And then Madera would promise to see justice done and would offer to pay for the most highly trained security force in the world to protect his second attempt to provide their bonuses. FourOre would extract the gold from an underground vein with the help of the retired Blackwater operatives. The crushed gold pebbles would be hidden in the Mylar *Chaac* balloons and the *desperado* canteens and the sparkling water in the dark-colored wine bottles. The special shipments' distribution would take place in late December and early to mid-January and would be sent to a warehouse in L.A. There, the specially-marked water containers would be "processed" with Madera, himself, over-seeing the separation of the gold and water. At $2000.00 an ounce they stood to make a fortune worth millions, maybe even billions. FourOre had found the gold vein, Jackson Jackson, the attorney for FourOre had found Robert Madera. Madera had found the way to bring the gold out. He didn't care what FourOre did with their share, but he would quickly melt his raw gold and have it formed into jewelry—gold earrings, for example, for quick distribution. He would take the lion's share, as he was taking the most risk.

He now recalled Valeria and the afternoon that they had made love. He remembered her blonde hair on his chest, her sparkling diamond and 24 carat gold earring. Madera smiled. He would take the water and the gold. *Yes,* he thought, *I'm a pirate.* He liked the image. *Maybe, I'll double the workers' bonus. A noble pirate.* Madera smiled again.

"Okay, team, let's get to work!"

CHAPTER 38

MADERA AND CHAMBERS

Robert Madera's plan had taken shape quickly. Alejandro turned out to be the perfect Nicaraguan partner. His ties to the local community as well as the Nicaraguan congress had come in handy and his friendly demeanor at the plant made him a solid, even if unsuspecting, ally. Water purity tests were conducted by Professor López at Alejandro's request. Paperwork was filed with the municipality (no charge), and the warehouse and plant erected within weeks, after obtaining the feasibility certificate ($500), the okay on environmental issues. Yes, Madera of course wanted running water, but chose compost toilets instead of a sewage system, arguing it was even more environmentally friendly. The water was for sanitation purposes, washing hands, and keeping the place clean. He wasn't going to steal the municipal water. He didn't have to rely on municipal water, the natural spring would supply the water for his plant and his product. Electrical permit from DISMORTE (no charge), design approval ($1,000), project approval ($3,000 cash), electrical fire safety permit, ($1,500), final building permit plus 1.1% tax on entire project cost ($5,000), inspection fee ($4.00 per square foot), additional fire inspection (no charge), water connection ($10.00), inspection from the Ministry of Labor (no charge), Occupational and Hygiene inspection (no charge), and finally registration with the Real Estate Appraisal Board (no charge). Alejandro had been paying in US currency even when the lower costs of NIO money could have covered the cost and saved him a few dollars. He did so without asking for change. Alejandro was working toward a bonus for himself if all could be achieved, including the building construction and hiring of workers by October; for that Madera had promised a healthy bonus. Madera watched as the plan took shape at amazing speed. He realized then that Jackson Jackson, who found Alejandro, must have worked with Alejandro on other joint American Nicaraguan ventures.

In October, Mannie had been sent to the plant to be the U.S. face of the operation's joint partnership. By November, Agua Managua Azteca had about fifty employees at the Nicaraguan bottling and distribution center and even though the workers had only been working for a month, they would indeed expect their bonuses for the Feast of the Immaculate Conception prior to Christmas. And this is why it was so important to Madera to be up and running by October. Now, as Madera sat on the plane, he thought about his next, very calculated and trickiest, move.

He must plant the seed of an idea in his Nicaraguan business partner's mind. Madera needed to be subtle but convincing for the plan to be effective. Madera had thought it through carefully, so that it could not possibly backfire on him, unless Alejandro kept the information to himself. And that, he thought, goes against human nature.

Madera listened in his first-class seat as the pilot announced that the plane was beginning its descent. The owner of Azteca enterprises pictured the owner of FourOre descending into the *cave of good fortune*. At least that was how Carl Chambers had described it.

Chambers was a weathered looking man who had met with Madera during the onset of the venture. Madera remembered how grizzly Chambers had appeared on that first day that they met. Chambers was big, strong, and wrinkled from years of outdoor work. His tanned skinned sagged a little around his jowls and crinkled deeply at the corner of his eyes. His once-brown hair was streaked with blonde and grey sprouts, especially at the temples. He had combed the rivers and searched the land from Arizona to Nicaragua for gold deposits most of his life, he had explained to Madera. Mostly he had made enough to live on, and since his wants were few, he had been nearly overwhelmed by his discovery of the *cave of good fortune*. Madera knew he had little to worry about from Chambers. He sized him up quickly. Chambers was the kind of man who would lose his fortune quickly without realizing that he did so just so he could return to the life he loved—prospecting. Madera could understand it. He had to agree that more than half the joy of life came in *the search, the prospecting, the chase, the game*. Whatever you called it, Madera thought, that is how a man proves to himself his mettle, and satisfies his cravings for success. That kind of man would always have to chase his fortune again and again and win it over and over. He knew Chambers fit this model, not so unlike himself. As his flight descended closer to the Managua airport, Madera recalled, in more detail, his past meeting with Chambers:

"It's a high-grade deposit," Chambers had told Jackson and Madera when they met in person.

"How did you find it?" Robert Madera remembered asking.

"I'd been looking on land in Nicaragua for a couple of months before I found the river. I dredged for about a week or two at the edge before followin' the windin' streambed farther uphill. First, I found higher deposits of iron ore rocks in the small stream. Yer know, yer getting' close when yer find iron ore. I could 'a dredged there for weeks, but instead took that there path that I spotted, yer know. Somethin' 'bout that river just spoke to me. Like it was singing, *follow me.* So's I went up river farther. Sure enough farther upstream, I found *placer* gold where most would least expect it." Chambers eyes widened to indicate his own surprise. Yet behind the surprise was a look of pride. "Placer gold suggests a mother lode is nearby," he explained to Madera.

"How's that?" Madera queried.

"First, yer might find pay-streaks, where microscopic gold dust has accumulated in cracks and crevices of the rocky streambed. Gold's weight keeps it low and it takes solid floods to move it along," Chambers explained. Madera nodded his understanding and Chambers continued. "So instead, it builds up in certain places. Finding such *places* indicates the possibility of a mother lode. So I followed the stream to its source." Chamber's eyes widened as he narrowed in on the story. He leaned forward, "I found six or seven very small springs, bubbling up from the earth and spilling forward until they joined together into a sort a delta." He used his hand to demonstrate the bubbling springs. "Yer know what I mean? So, I stepped into the spot where the spring water merged and then outa nowhere, it sucked me right down."

Chambers then made a slurping sound with great force, before continuing in his animated telling of the adventure. "Knee high in my hip high boots! Yes, siree, yer know, I almost lost my boot to that quicksand." With a second slurping sound, Chambers explained that, "I managed to pull my foot back out. I truly feared the quicksand would make it impossible to retrieve any gold in the area. Bu not so. Anyway, I walked on, skirting the sand and springs, when all of a sudden, it happened!" Chambers did more than pause, he waited for Madera to beg for more story. Madera didn't want to but he needed this man's good will so he let him think he took the conversational bait.

"What happened?" Madera asked as if he didn't have a clue and was sitting on the edge of his seat, although Jackson Jackson had told him the whole story earlier. Robert Madera had insisted on hearing it from the source.

"I fell, literally, fell into the *cave of good fortune.* I fell into a hole."

"Go on, go on" Madera pleaded.

"And that hole was about waist deep. The floor of the hole felt solid, slippery but solid. And no quicksand. I had a feeling that it was more than a hole, that it might be the entrance to a cave. So I climbed back out. Got my equipment, tied off a rope and went in for a look. I had to crawl about six to seven feet on a downward slope, before this little hallway of a cave, turned into a mammoth with stalactites and stalagmites. Incredible! I held up my flashlight. Yer should've seen the lights sparkle on those icicles. And there it was before me. In all its glory!" He paused, then leaned in again and with penetrating old eyes he said to Madera, "Right there in the center of the cave stood a column of rock, and it was marbled with gold." Chambers sat back as if taking in the moment over again. Madera could envision it.

"There might be even more. There might be deeper water, as well. We would need scuba gear. But the thing is, if we take the gold from the column, it will be a one-time thing. The cave could collapse in on itself once the gold is removed. Yer know what I mean?"

"How do we get it out of the rock?" Madera wanted to know.

"We can use an old-fashioned hydraulic mining technique. We can use the water from the spring itself to create a water system of hoses and troughs and sluices. The hoses will have to have the strength of firehoses. They take a couple of men at least to handle 'em. The force breaks down the rock around the gold, releasing the gold."

"And collapsing the column in the process," Madera added.

"Yes, but we can build in supports before we do it. On either side and behind where the hoses will be aimed."

"Still, it'll destroy the spring, right?"

"Possibly."

"So this is a one-time deal," Madera added.

"This is a once in a lifetime deal."

"How much gold?"

"Hard to say, specifically."

"Estimate."

"If the gold is mostly on the surface of the column, 10–20 million dollars; if it goes all the way through the column, we're looking at billions."

"What are the risks?"

"Multiple. Hydraulic mining is like fracking; the excess water could destroy local farmland. It could trigger a small quake, but not likely because we won't be there that long. That's why it's basically illegal in much of the U.S. Companies are doing it for a longer period and on a larger scale than what we're thinking. We'll be done quickly. And it would have to be done during heavy rains if we want to conceal the project. Then the gold will have to be crushed into smaller pieces for us to get it out of the country. We could do it with one massive hammer and crankshaft but we'd need to be able to explain the noise. Louder than a freight train. But then again, it'll be down in the cave, which is a-good-ways from the city. Finally, we could use mercury to chemically bring out the final product. So we'd need to get rid of the mercury somehow."

"How?" Madera wanted answers.

"We could find an isolated spot to dump it. You know bury it in canisters."

Madera was still recalling this when the flight attendant asked Madera to check his seatbelt. The pilot announced. "Flight attendants take your seats for landing." The Boeing descended at a steep incline. Madera remembered his favorite part of Chambers' story—sliding down the hole and looking up with his flashlight shining, to find a column of marbled gold surrounded by sparkling stalagmites and stalactites.

Madera had insisted on seeing it for himself before proceeding with the partnership with Chambers (a.k.a. owner of *FourOre*).

Madera had flown to Nicaragua with Chambers, made his way along the streams and beyond the quicksand, and had slid down the hole behind Chambers, just the two of them. Once underground, Chambers had led the way until they reached the spot in the cavernous tunnel where they could stand upright. Chambers shone the flashlight. A majestic column appeared. No words. Just exhilaration. The glory of gold. *The cave of good fortune* was not an old man's imagination; it's real, Madera had concluded.

Madera had a piece tested. Chambers was right. Highest grade gold on the planet!

Now, nearly everything was in place to remove the gold. Madera jerked forward as the wheels of the plane touched down on the tarmac of the Augusto C. Sandino International Airport in Managua.

PART 7

THE LADY IKOOM AND
THE LABYRINTH OF DOOM

CHAPTER 39

LABYRINTH OF DOOM

Ikoom had returned from the *Island of Women* to a welcome full of feasting. After she'd been laden with flowers and dressed in fresh clothes, she'd been given her fill of food. She rested for nearly seven days. And then a ball game was played in her honor. Dances were performed late into the night. The joy and excitement eventually brought exhaustion for all involved, but especially for Ikoom. She slept that night more deeply than ever before and she dreamt the dreams of The Deep. She dreamt of Ixchel and Chaac. She knew that she would meet them again.

One week later, Ikoom was taken to the mouth of a mammoth cave. The mouth of the cave stretched wide, like a snake's unhinged jaw and a river flowed through it. There she stepped into a canoe with a priest and his assistants. The canoe flowed down the river, directed by the paddles, beyond the mouth and down the throat of the cave as if it were a small animal being swallowed by a viper. Torches lit the way. And she could see ledges on either side of the river, where the cave walls offered a place for someone to walk along the way. She could also see the skeletons of victims along the ledges of the cavernous watercourse. Skulls. Arm bones. Phalanges stripped bare to the mineral leaving bony fingers holding jade. Gems sparkled, treasures left with the victims for the gods. Ikoom had known that she would be left alive at a sacred place in the cave. After all, her charge was to speak with Chaac. The priests had given her a preview of what was to come. Then took her back for another day of feasting and celebration in her honor.

Her preview became her reality. The second time, however, the priest left her on the ledge. Again, like when left at the *Island of Women*, she was granted a flask of water, some food and a few jewels. She was also given a torch. She watched as the priest and rowers returned to the light. She knew that she couldn't follow the priest back out again. Her only choice was to move forward, deeper into the cave, along the ledges, above the water, down its throat and through its passageways. She entrusted herself to Ixchel and began her journey. After a long while, Ikoom had no sense of time. She lit the cave passageways with the light of her torch. She carried a small sack of fuel and flints, but she knew she would soon be enveloped in total darkness. It'd be difficult to keep her tinder from getting wet. Holding the flint tightly, she traversed dry ledges as well as ankle deep curves of water in the caves. She took nourishment only occasionally and slept often, conserving energy and staving off loneliness and fear.

After a time, Ikoom couldn't tell morning from night. She knew only waking and falling into sleep and waking again. She stopped thinking of the people above ground and thought only of Chaac. "Chaac!" she called out as she felt her way along an immeasurably narrow ledge, her tiptoes alone hugged the tapering rock and skirted the edge, her fingertips felt for crevices to grip, her torch unlit and tied with her arrows and set within the quiver on her back, her flint and food secured at her waist. Days, maybe weeks passed. "Chaac!" she prayed. "I can't go on."

She let the heel of her foot down, she couldn't go on even if it meant falling into dark waters below. She accepted the labyrinth as her doom. She was ready to die. Determination disappeared. Resistance evaporated. She let go.

To her surprise, her heel met solid slate. She didn't fall, but instead stood on the floor of a wider ledge. With each additional step the ledge became broader until she found herself in a place wide enough to provide space to build a fire and create a berth for sleep. Tiny cracks in the ceiling of this cave allowed in slim shafts of light. At this discovery, Ikoom cried tears of relief and of joy. Perhaps, the Sun Chaac had taken pity on her, even if the Rain Chaac would not.

Ikoom made a tiny fire, ate some nuts and dried berries, and thanked all four Chaacs. She slept on the cold floor of the cave. When she awoke she began her dark journey again. Renewed. Committed to her charge.

She started to talk to Chaac on a regular basis as she walked. And he answered her every query.

"Do you know why I've come, Chaac?"

"Of course."

"Tell me, please," she said.

"You want me to release my tears, to rain on the lands of fire and water."

"And will you?"

"How can I, I have no more tears."

"Tell me what happened," she pleaded as she walked through another passageway.

Chaac inhaled and then exhaled. Ikoom felt it like a great warm wind with a chill at the end.

"I seduced my sister-in-law," he said. Silence followed.

"Did you love her?"

"Does it matter?"

"I'm young; I don't know much about these things," Ikoom kept him talking.

Chaac began, "I have three brothers. We're all called Chaac. I am Chaac, God of Rain. One brother, in particular was my favorite— Chaac, God of the Sun. Together, we hunted with lightning spears, fished with nets made of trees, and wrestled on the earth, making the ground shake and quake, we swallowed stars and belched them into volcanoes which rose up and spit back. We laughed. Our laughter rumbled like thunder making me cry with joy.

"One day, my brother met Moon. He fell in love with Moon. She stole his heart, his time and attention. He forgot about me. I understood because she was so beautiful and mysterious, but I missed my brother and I must admit I wanted his wife. So I set out to seduce her.

"Chaac, perhaps we could talk to Sun."

"No! Sun has reconciled with his wife, Moon, and they have an agreed existence in the sky. Neither will have anything to do with me. I have cried the last of my tears. I accept my dismal fate."

"Chaac, open a small hole in the cave and take a peek. See if Sun is watching you, wondering, how is my brother doing?" Ikoom suggested.

"Do you think he has forgiven me?"

"There is only one way to know for sure," Ikoom suggested. Chaac became silent as he thought. Ikoom continued to carefully place one foot in front of the other down slippery inclines and up rocky cave paths, sometimes having to duck low under overhangs and climb around stalagmites. She glanced up as she heard the dripping of water hit the stalagmite. Above her, a speck of light shone through. A small dot of sunshine drew her forward and upward.

"Wait here, Chaac. I'll check." Ikoom went ahead and even though her torch had gone out, she could see by the speck of light that grew in size as she climbed higher. At last, she could see an opening large enough for her to pass through. She seized the opportunity and squeezed her way upward into the full light of day.

Ecstatic, a squinting Ikoom drank in the sunshine and the warm air. Once acclimated, she skipped down the hillside and bounded from tree to tree in search of fruit, berries, nuts and seeds. She found fresh water and drank her fill. She searched for fuel for her torch. And at the end of the day, she lay down in a bed of flowers with her face to the sun. "Sun, you must forgive your brother, Chaac." She watched Sun slip away without a word in warm glowing colors from the family of ambers, set against an amethyst sky. Ikoom fell asleep.

"Ikoom!" The voice belonged to Ixchel. "I didn't send you to Chaac so that you could trick him into releasing you. Do your duty."

Ikoom awoke with a start. She knew that Ixchel's message spoke the truth. But she also knew that Chaac didn't belong in these catacombs. She returned to the cave, but continued to trick Chaac by telling him that Sun said they should check with him again in a few days. Every few days Ikoom was able to surface, gather supplies and then return again to be Chaac's companion. She wandered the passageways for months exiting as often as possible under this pretext. Searching for different means to make Chaac return to the sky, Chaac didn't want to show his face to either Sun or Moon. "I'm ashamed," he told Ikoom.

Ikoom began to lose her way, both within the labyrinth of The Deep and on the face of the earth. Each time she surfaced she was farther from her homeland. Each time she stepped on land it was drier, more parched. The winding of the caves had taken her east and west, north and south. Circling and turning in various directions.

At one point, when Ikoom surfaced to gather supplies she thought of Ku'tl. She had come across a basin of clay which reminded her of his vase that she had observed so long ago. She let her hands take up the clay. She felt it slide between her fingers. She began to roll worm-like strips and wind them around a base slab. In very little time at all, she had made a vase, and she had gathered the pigments and painted the story of a hunter who shoots a deer with his arrow and drapes the beast over his shoulder with the last breath of air expelled from its mouth—three little lines coming from a cloud. But Ikoom added something to the story on the vase—she painted a water bowl, as though it were tipped, dropping its last drop of water, which fell from the lip of the bowl. She took the vase back with her into The Deep.

One day from within the labyrinth, with a shaft of light shining upon the vase, Ikoom began to cry.

"Why are you crying?" Chaac asked her.

"The vase."

"Get rid of it then."

"I can't. It brings me joy and sorrow. It reminds me of home, family, and of Kut'l, which warms my heart; but, it also makes me miss my family, my home, and Kut'l. I'm lonely, Chaac. I want to go home."

"You made a promise to me that you would never speak to Ku'tl again."

"I'll keep my promise."

"Then go. I'll not stop you."

With that Chaac released the girl from her commitment to him by opening a hole in the cave once more, but she stopped and turned around.

"Chaac,"

"What?"

"Return to the sky. Share the heavens with Sun and Moon."

"Go."

Ikoom turned again to leave, but once again she hesitated.

"Chaac," she said with a quiver in her tone. He had become her friend, "I'll miss you. I'll worry about you."

"Go!"

Ikoom had a long treacherous journey to her homeland. On her way, she had prayed every day for the Sun Chaac to see his way to forgive the Rain Chaac. But it was Moon, who had been staying far, far away from Sun, who proposed a plan. She came to Ikoom in a dream and told the girl that she loved both Chaacs and she proposed that she would come to each of the Chaacs on separate occasions, at different times of the month. She told Ikoom that she would slip away when the Chaacs slept, and when each Chaac was alone they would cry. And when Moon was without either of them, she too would weep. *We'll cry when we're lonely and we'll cry when we're filled with joy. Rains—strong and powerful or soft and gentle, grief, guilt, or joy. The rain will come. When the right time comes, I'll slip out of the sky and meet Chaac in The Deep and I'll bring him back to the sky. Your loyalty and dedication to your people and to Chaac will be rewarded. You gave me this idea when you cried both tears of loneliness and tears of joy. Go home now, and all this will come to pass.* When Ikoom awoke from the dream, she realized that the Sun and the Moon and the Rain loved each other. She realized that tears of joy and tears of sorrow would most certainly follow.

Many years had passed since she had left her home to meet Chaac, first in the well and then in the cave, after the Island of Women. When Ikoom walked back into Tikal she was no longer a girl, she was a woman. There had been mountains and valleys to cross. Deep forests to traverse. Trials to be overcome, but every step of the journey she felt as though Sun and Rain and Moon were watching over her. Yet, in all that time not a single rain drop fell. The ground remained hard, the plants shriveled by the dry river beds.

Once home, she filled herself with the power of the pyramids, she stretched up her arms to the sky to thank Moon and just as Moon had promised, rain began to fall. The people came running to see the rain as they smelled the muskiness of it in the air and heard the droplets hit the dry dirt. Gigantic drops that turned into splashes. And at the center of it all, they saw Ikoom. Her face lifted to the sky, her arms out, her palms up, as she turned in a circle, letting rain drops dance across her eye lids and down her face. The people broke into songs of praise. They played flutes and danced into the night. Most importantly, none would ever forget the image at dusk on that evening, the Sun appeared in the western sky and the Moon rose to the north east. Between them, Chaac filled the distant northern sky with lightning and tears of joy so that a rainbow arced across the heavens. Chaac had been forgiven, tears of jubilation fell upon the land. Ikoom had made the great god cry again.

PART 8

MADERA'S PLAN

CHAPTER 40

MADERA ARRIVES

Robert Madera's plane landed at Augusto C. Sandino International Airport early in the day. The sun shone brightly; the humidity lower than usual, the pilot had reported just prior to the passengers disembarking. Madera found his brother-in-law Mannie and his Nicaraguan partner Alejandro waiting for him just beyond customs clearance. Madera offered each of them a smile and brotherly embrace.

"Ah, so good to see you, Alejandro," Madera said as he gave him a friendly embrace.

"And Mannie," he hugged his brother-in-law lightly. "You've both come to the airport. Who is minding the shop?" They walked and talked as they made their way out of the airport.

"Gail has everything under control."

Madera recalled his suspicions that the two might be having an affair. "You look good, Mannie. Getting a lot of exercise?"

"I do my best."

Madera directed Mannie to drive directly to the water bottling plant.

"Don't you want to stop at the hotel first?"

"No, I want the workers' bonus money in our safe." Madera carried one bundle of cash inside a bulging envelope within his inside jacket pocket, and the rest in the pockets of the money vest he wore. He tapped it thoughtfully. He chose not to let it out of his sight even for a few seconds. At the airport in Los Angeles, on his way to Nicaragua, his TSA pre-approval allowed him through the x-ray machine without taking off his shoes or his jacket. And the cut of his suit, the expense of his wrist watch, the white of his newly pressed suit, and the silk tie spoke volumes of his wealth and position. The guards waved him on through. Carrying the money in his jacket pocket meant he had to endure wearing an extra layer of clothes under the heat of the equatorial sun. Even on the plane, he kept the money close to his heart. Not until they reached Mannie's car, did Madera remove the jacket. He took the front passenger seat and laid it over his lap. Mannie drove; Alejandro Martínez took his place in the back seat.

"So how are things coming along?" Madera asked as if he didn't already know. He directed his question to Mannie.

"Gail's been a godsend. She understands all the Nicaraguan rules of employment. After you hired the first ten workers, she did the rest of the hiring with Alejandro." Mannie nodded to Alejandro in the back seat. "She has all the benefits worked out, the paperwork is all in order. And Chambers, the man you hired to help with production and distribution, he's been quite helpful. Quite the character, too," Mannie reported. Madera smiled in agreement.

"So you brought the workers' bonus with you?" Alejandro questioned.

"Yes."

"How were the transaction fees?"

"Horrible. I decided to pay them in U.S. dollars. I read that they can get a good exchange rate from, let's say, less than formal banks."

Alejandro smiled. "That's probably true. They won't mind being paid in U.S. currency as long as it will equal one month's salary Nicaraguan."

They drove up the simple asphalt road which Madera had paid for and turned into the parking area for Agua Managua Azteca. As they stepped out of the car, Madera glanced first at the warehouse and then quickly switched his gaze to the bottling plant. Car doors slammed shut; Madera took in the sight of the bottling plant. *Not much of a building to speak of,* he thought. It'd been built quickly, a wood frame supported prefab walls that sat under an inexpensive corrugated tin roof. The second building, the warehouse in the back, was not much sturdier. Madera had mandated the warehouse building be built on skids which were supported by stilts. That is, the warehouse was a raised building, raised to the level of the trucks. Madera informed them that this would make loading easier, less expensive, less labor intensive. He'd seen somewhat similar designs in the Latin American countries that loaded tons of tropical fruit for international distribution.

In addition, Madera had noticed the rural homes on previous trips to Belize and Guatemala, where the houses are built on stilts. Such raised structures provide outdoor living space for residents and outdoor storage for businesses that is shaded, giving relief from the heat, and the stilts keep things inside dry in the rainy season. Madera turned and gazed intently at the warehouse. He had directed Chambers to line the outside parameter of the warehouse building with a light corrugated tin which he said could be removed to catch the breeze again after the rainy season. For now, it hid the tunnel excavation and excess dirt as well as machinery that had been brought in before a single employee was hired, before Mannie and Alejandro had stepped foot on the land or in the plant. What took place at the warehouse, especially underneath the warehouse, was completely out of view, and controlled by Chambers, who reported directly to Madera. Bottled water was moved from the plant to the warehouse by forklift, but only Chambers' crew unloaded it and stacked it in the warehouse.

What didn't make sense is that Madera had insisted that the warehouse be in the back and the bottling plant and office be in front. Mannie had pointed out that if efficiency were the goal shouldn't the distribution point be closer to the road. His question was dismissed by Madera and quickly explained away—*Image is still important. The people will see the office, the logo, the place where we've given Nicaraguans jobs.*

"Would you like the tour?" Alejandro asked. "Though not much has changed since your last visit."

"Not yet, let's put the money in the safe first."

"By all means," Alejandro said and Mannie led the way.

They entered the bottling plant. A simple pipe line fed spring water into bottles that were then moved along a conveyor belt for cappers and labelers. The bottles moved down the line and another worker slid them onto skids. A forklift driver would eventually move the full skid to the warehouse for storage until a complete load was ready for distribution across the country and beyond. A simple enough operation. With Mannie in the lead, they headed directly toward the office. Like a politician running for office, Madera stopped along the way to shake hands and embrace workers who straddled the conveyor belt, each with their respective jobs on the line—filling water bottles, capping, labeling, lifting and boxing.

Madera had learned more names of the workers on each of his trips, he'd asked about their health and their families. Now, as he walked along the line, he shook hands or embraced a worker with questions about how the family is doing. One man queried in return:

"How long will you be staying this time, *Señor* Madera?"

"Long enough to have dinner with your family," he added with a smile.

The man laughed. They all loved Madera.

"At least long enough to personally give you your bonus," Madera added with even more sincerity, patting his jacket pocket, after giving the man a hug.

Madera entered the office, pulled the package of money from his vest and breast coat pockets, and handed it to Mannie, who set it on top of the small, floor safe. The safe was about twenty inches high, fifteen inches wide, and just as deep. The fire proof safe weighed about 250 pounds, just enough to be a deterrent to thieves and this was one of the reasons why the office in the bottling plant had to have a solid floor and couldn't be built on stilts like the warehouse, Madera had earlier explained this to his executive team. Mannie squatted in front of the safe, spun the combination of the lock, forward, back, forward—click, click, click. He swung the door open.

"Hey, Mannie, we should invite Gail to join us for lunch," Madera suggested.

"Yeah, sure."

"Go ahead, we'll get this. Alejandro, let's put all the money in one envelope."

Madera took the envelope and Mannie's place in front of the safe. "Oh, wait a minute," he said. He stood up from bended knee and looked around. "There's something else that I want to put in here. I'll be right back." Madera handed the envelope to Alejandro to hang onto. Several minutes later, Madera returned with a small box in his hand.

"I'd left this in the car," he said to Alejandro when he returned. Madera held up a small bag. Then he reached in and retrieved a tiny black box. "I picked these up at the airport for Valeria." He opened

254

the box and showed Alejandro the new pair of gleaming gold earrings that he'd purchased for his wife on the U.S. side, in the Los Angeles airport. "I couldn't resist."

"She'll love them," Alejandro said, admiring the earrings. Madera squatted again and placed the earrings in the office safe. He held out his hand to Alejandro who then placed the envelope of U.S. currency in Madera's waiting palm. Madera slid it into the safe, shut the door and spun the combination.

"Okay, off to lunch."

"Oh, wait. Let's invite Chambers, too. Will you get him? Then meet us by the car."

QUESTIONS

Madera recounted the events of the past three days, from the beginning, for Detective Gonzalez, who held out no hope of recovering the stolen money. The detective's face held a hint of disbelief that the owner had been so naïve as to carry cash, store it in a small safe, where so many had access to it. The detective went through the motions.

"So, you put the gift for your wife in first, you say?"

"Yes, I put the earrings in the safe and then Alejandro handed me the package of bills and I put that in the safe. I'm positive I shut the door to the safe."

"He did; I saw him," Alejandro confirmed.

"And who all knows the combination besides yourself, *Señor* Madera?"

"Well, yes, myself, my brother-in-law Mannie and my partner Alejandro."

"And Gail," Alejandro added. Turning and looking at Gail, who also answered the Detective's questions.

"I was—"

"Gail was with me when we, I mean Robert, put the money in the safe," Mannie interrupted Gail, providing her alibi.

"What about Chambers?" Alejandro ventured.

"What about him?"

"Does he have access to the safe?"

"No, Gail writes all the checks for local deliveries. Chambers doesn't have to pay anybody."

"That's correct," Gail assured the detective.

"Detective, none of us would have taken the bonus money. We don't need it," Madera told him calmly.

"So you are accusing one of your workers?" the detective surmised and slyly queried.

"I'm not accusing anybody. You're the detective."

"Yes, that's true. So if I dusted the envelope for prints, whose would be on it?"

"Mine and Mannie's" Robert Madera concluded.

"And Alejandro's," the detective added.

"Yes, yes," Madera agreed.

"Any other prints would be the thief's prints?"

"Yes, I suppose so," Madera said.

"Do you think there would be prints?" Mannie asked.

"Why wouldn't there be prints? If someone has stolen the money from the envelope, then there should be prints on the empty envelope that was left behind," the detective reasoned.

"They could have worn gloves," Madera suggested.

"Gloves? This is Nicaragua. Where would anybody even find gloves?"

"So you'll test the envelope for prints?"

"Again, this is Nicaragua. Testing for prints means sending it to a lab and that could take months, possibly years, and it would be costly."

"Then why did you bring it up?"

"I'm just doing my job. Getting a full report. All the facts. Well, anyway, that should do it. Don't hold out any hope," he concluded dismally.

"With all due respect, Detective, I hope you don't mind if I bring a small security team in to watch over the payroll from now until Christmas," Madera's voice didn't indicate due respect at all as he made this suggestion. It rather leaked disappointment in the detective's lack of interest and hope.

"As you wish. I'm not the one who was supposed to be guarding your money in the first place, why would I care?" The detective complied and countered, before asking another question. "So, you'll still pay the bonus to the workers?"

"Of course, it's my duty. I'll fly back to L.A. and withdraw the money."

"Why not just a write them a check?"

Madera hesitated, "Transaction fees are quite high these days and besides this way I can bring a couple of security guards back with me."

"Hmm," the detective reopened his notebook, jotted a few more notes, and then wished a good afternoon to the owners and present executives of Azteca Corporation before taking his leave. But when he reached the door, he turned around once again.

"How much was the total again?" The detective flipped back to the first page of his notes.

"It was the monthly pay—$700.00, plus the bonus pay—another $700 for all forty-seven employees. That's a grand total of $65,800. Replacing that is now going to cost me $131,600." Madera was beginning to sound angry and frustrated.

"You're good with numbers," the detective concluded.

"I'm good with a lot of things."

"Hmm," the detective flipped his notebook shut again and nodded a good day to them again. Then he paused again.

"Hmm. $700.00 a month. Isn't that about $172.00 per week? Let's see, what's that, $4.30 an hour?"

Madera nodded. The detective cocked his head thoughtfully. "That's high pay for Nicaraguans."

"It's hard work," Madera replied.

"Yes, of course," the detective said and once again bid them a good afternoon. He paused again, before asking another question.

"The airport, how did you walk through the airport with so much money?"

"I wore a travel vest."

"Of course. But I meant isn't it illegal to travel with so much cash

"Not in the States," Madera answered.

"And Nicaragua?"

"I declared the money. Employee pay."

"It must have been hot," the detective added.

"Hot?" Madera looked confused.

"The vest. It must have been hot to wear such a vest."

"Not bad. They make very light-weight, pick-pocket-proof vests these days."

"But you also kept one bulging envelope in your jacket pocket. Weren't your nervous?"

"I needed to have one handy."

"Detective, Robert Madera is a generous man. He tips people. He needs ready access to some of the money," Alejandro jumped into the conversation.

"I see. Well, good day."

After the detective left, the four of them stood in the office. Alejandro spoke first.

"It's hopeless, you know. Our police are far better than what you will find in Belize or Guatemala, but still they have few resources."

"I think they are about to have bigger problems on their hands," Madera said.

"What do you mean?" Mannie asked.

"I heard that a certain company is going to try to privatize the water here."

"What? Really? Who? They should know better. Nicaragua will be ready for them," Alejandro assured whoever would listen.

"The people won't stand for it," Gail predicted having read the literature and history.

"What are you talking about?" Mannie injected. Madera leaned against the desk in the office and explained.

"Someone, I won't say who, came to me in L.A. when they found out we had opened a water bottling facility here. And they said, just as a heads up, we're looking at taking over the water system. We'll offer clean, reliable water for decent prices. We have connections in Congress and we have money from the World Bank. It's a country of six million people. We won't charge much, but water won't be free either. And they won't need bottled water."

"No, the people won't let it happen," Alejandro declared, seconding his earlier comment. Gail nodded in agreement.

"But they could have clean water on a regular basis," Mannie said. "I've been living here; I know what it's like. Water on, water off. You never know when,"

"It doesn't matter. They all know what happened in Bolivia. These companies have outlawed the use of rain water in other places. They've charged farmers for irrigation water and peasants for their drinking water. No, no, this will never get past the people of Nicaragua. They're too smart," Alejandro stated. "They're wise to these kinds of capitalist schemes."

"Maybe so, maybe, you're right," Madera told Alejandro. "Maybe you're right. But I was told this in confidence. So we must keep it between us."

PART 9

PIRATES

CHAPTER 42

GUN POINT

Caleb felt the cold steel of the gun barrel against the back of his head. He faced Miguel. The boy's eyes blinked back fear. Caleb tried to reassure Miguel with a slight nod of his head and a nearly imperceptible smile.

"*¡Muéves!* Move! Let's go," the man with the gun commanded.

Miguel and Caleb stood. They walked toward the small village. Caleb started to lift the mosquito netting over his head.

"*¿Qué hace aqui?*" the man with the gun demanded to know.

"What did he say?" Caleb asked Miguel.

"He wants to know what you're doing," Miguel told Caleb.

"I'm taking off the mosquito net. I don't need it near the ocean, tell him," Caleb directed his comment to Miguel.

Miguel translated: "He thinks he looks silly. He is a brave man. If you are going to shoot him, he doesn't want to die looking like an idiot. Let him take it off," Miguel said in Spanish.

The gunman waved permission with his Glock 19. Caleb took off the netting. He considered throwing it over the man, but the man's gun was simply too close. Miguel could get hurt and he could get equally entangled. Plus, he had a feeling this guy wasn't alone. Another gunman might be holding the professor and the graduate students captive in the village. They were nowhere in sight. Caleb decided to wait. He rolled the netting and tied it around his waist. His military training took over. Keep everything; anything might become a weapon later. He scanned the area as they walked toward the beach, noted the motorboat anchored farther out to sea, the small dingy on shore, footprints in the wet sand. The gunmen hadn't been here long, he determined. Two sets of footprints. No one else in sight. The man with the gun seemed nervous, not in command. An unplanned landing, Caleb thought, which was followed by the unexpected arrival of the professor and his team.

They moved in the general direction of the small structure. Caleb noticed that outside the building a rack of stored plastic bottles, half-full of water, lay on their sides in the sun. He recognized the system as a means to sterilize water using the sun's UV-rays. He had learned about it when he and Sofía had attended Prof. López's lecture. Not much else in the way of resources, he thought. Nothing much that could help him outmaneuver a man with a gun pointed at the back of his head. Caleb didn't see the professor. *Where is the professor,* he wondered? *Inside? Being held at gun point also?*

The man with the gun pushed Caleb up the steps and into the community center. There sat Professor López, his assistants, two women, two toddlers and a baby. The mother modestly nursed the infant. Miguel and Caleb sat down on the floor next to the professor.

"What do they want?" Caleb asked the professor.

"*¡Cállate!* Shut up! I'll do the talking," said one gunman. The man turned his head and began speaking in a low voice to his compadre. Caleb could make out parts of it, *Americano, problema,... la pesca,* …, but not enough to make sense out of it.

The professor interrupted. Speaking in Spanish, he said, "These are poor people. They have nothing for you. What do you want of them?"

But the gunman once again turned away and spoke only with his companion. Caleb realized that they needed something, but what?

"Let the women go," the professor suggested. "They need to feed their children." This time he spoke in English. "You have us."

"We can't, the husband has something of ours. We don't want any trouble from you."

"I can see that."

The two talked again in hushed tones. This time they were saying something about *chico,* and here they glanced at Miguel, and then something about *la pesca,* …

"What does the husband have?" the professor asked.

"I think you can guess?"

"A white package?"

"*Sí.*"

"How did he get it?"

"None of your concern."

"If it washed up on shore, he'll think it is from the grace of God, from the spirit world. He'll not give it up easily. Let us go find him," the professor said of himself and his assistants. "We know this part of the jungle."

"How do I know you'll come back?"

"I'm responsible for these two," he said nodding toward Miguel and Caleb.

"The American looks like trouble," the man said in Spanish.

"No, no. He's nobody. Just a reporter." The professor also spoke in Spanish.

"A reporter? He should tell our story."

"That's a good idea. Tell him your story, while we find the husband and the white package. You speak enough English, yes? If not, the boy can translate," the professor suggested.

Everyone looked at Caleb.

"Do they want to kidnap me?" Caleb asked in a low tone.

"No, just say, yes. They want you to tell their story. And don't let Miguel out of your sight."

"Why?"

"If they kidnap anybody, it'll be Miguel."

"Miguel?"

"Yes," the professor whispered. "I overheard them. If we don't come back with the white package, they'll take Miguel and sell him."

"Sell him?!"

"Forced labor is not unheard of by such pirates. They sell boys to fishermen to catch lobsters and other seafood or for slave labor in cocoa fields."

"Enough talking!"

One of the two men looked a bit twitchy, *an addict, perhaps*, Caleb thought.

"Sure, sure. I'll tell your story." Caleb began to reach into his duffel bag that had been over his shoulder.

"Slowly," the man cautioned.

"I have a recorder and a note pad," Caleb assured them. Miguel translated. Caleb realized then that Miguel knew exactly how much he had to fear. "Your story. I want to know everything," he said, adding, "Miguel, tell them." Miguel translated Caleb's assurances.

"So we'll go; we'll find the white package. I think I know where they would've gone with it," the professor told them.

"Yes, okay." The taller man waved them out with his gun.

The professor and his assistants gathered their things. One gunman advised them, "Be back within two days, or we will change our plan."

"And the women and children?"

"Okay, fine. They can leave."

The professor helped a woman to her feet and ushered her along with the others outside and toward safety. Caleb and Miguel settled in for a two-day stay.

"Any food in your bag?" the gunman asked.

Miguel translated. Caleb reached into his bag and produced power bars to share.

"We have a story," one of the men said as he unwrapped the protein bar. And each sentence in the exchange was translated by Miguel for Caleb, and from Caleb to the gunmen.

"About being pirates?" Caleb asked.

"Not all smugglers are bad."

"How did you come to be a smuggler?"

"Some of us were good boys once, like this one." He nodded in Miguel's direction. Miguel continued to translate. Caleb asked questions, drawing the story out, beginning when the pirate was just a boy; he took careful notes.

"I was young, only nine almost ten, when a man came up to me on the street."

"Did you know him?"

"No, he was a stranger. He said that he could hire me for much money. I told my parents that I had found a job."

"What did they say?"

"They were so happy. We would be able to buy food."

"How old are you now?"

"Seventeen." Caleb scribbled notes quickly and then noted the pirates age.

"So those men put you into forced labor at the age of ten? And when you escaped how old were you?"

"Fourteen, maybe fifteen. Time is tricky on the sea. And even trickier when you are in bondage." Caleb jotted down number fourteen as he thought that is the same age as Miguel right now. So many questions. These pirates are young; he had guessed their age much older from their weathered skin.

"But you didn't return to your family?"

"No, I was too ashamed."

"Ashamed of what?"

"My own stupidity. My addiction."

"So you didn't get to go to school?"

"School?" both men laughed wryly. "School, humph, School of the Slaves, maybe." The words mentally moved Caleb from captive to reporter. *School of the Slaves*, he thought, *perfect title for an article about these two young men, teenagers, really. Now addicts from the life they had led.*

"No, there is no school for slaves," the taller teen said in a serious tone.

"What did you do?"

"I worked on the fishing boats. Hauling up large catches of fish. They gave us coca leaves instead of food. We worked all day and half the night. So far out to sea that there was no land in sight."

"It confuses you," said the other. "Eternity is everything and it is nothing, it is everywhere and absolutely nowhere. There is only madness in that existence, if not for the other boys and the cocaine. Cocaine makes you work, work without thinking, or hoping."

"And yet, you would consider doing that to someone else?" Caleb asked.

"We do not want to be monsters, simply survivors."

Caleb listened and questioned and wrote long into the night. The pirates took turns sleeping; they took turns telling their respective stories.

"How did you escape..." Caleb asked, but no translation followed.

Miguel had fallen asleep.

CAPTIVE AND CAPTOR, MORE THAN ONE STORY

"We were kidnapped by smugglers!" Miguel yelled with excitement.

"How did you escape?" Sofía asked with evident concern and current relief showing on her face.

"No, not escape. They let us go," Miguel told his mother. "Sometimes the word is more powerful than the sword. Right, Cowboy." Miguel quickly corrected himself, adding, "I'll never call you 'Cowboy' again. Hey, Hunter S. Thompson, tell my mother what happened next."

They stood in the doorway. She had come running when she heard Miguel calling to her as he ran toward the house from the street. She had thrown her arms around her son, hugging him to her, and simultaneously looked up to meet Caleb's eyes and offer him a smile, as well.

"He's Hunter S. Thompson and I'm Gonzo."

Caleb smiled, shaking his head, always surprised by Miguel's witty comments and cultural acumen. *Where does he get it from?* Caleb wondered, *this 1970s knowledge.*

"Tell her. Tell my mother what happened." Miguel was like an excited pup. Caleb remained quiet soaking in Sofía's smile and warm eyes. When Caleb didn't speak, Miguel launched into the explanation, "After spending two days taking notes on their story, Hunter S. Thompson and his trusty translator and protector, that's me, Gonzo, explained to them that they couldn't hurt anybody. If they hurt anyone of us, they would become the bad guys in the story. Protagonists are the good guys. But they said, they still wanted their white package. You see the locals had found their white package—"

"What is a white package?" Sofía asked.

"Oh my mother is so innocent. Cocaine or heroin or something like that," the boy explained. Sofía nodded and Miguel continued.

"So Hunter, here, promised to pay them for their story because Professor López was not back yet with the husbands or the white package."

"The husbands?"

"The pirates were holding two women and their children."

"So how did you get away? Are the women and children safe?"

"The professor had an idea. He told the smugglers that he and his students would go and find the husbands and the white package and while they were gone Caleb would take notes to write their story for the newspapers. But when the professor and his students didn't come back, Caleb Barthes, the famous reporter from the *Chicago Tribune* hatched a plan to negotiate our freedom. He promised he would pay them for their story. So the smugglers gave Hunter an email address of a family member in Columbia; he sent a small amount of money to their bank account and promised to send more; and that bought everybody's freedom, including Professor López and his graduate students.

"But I thought they hadn't come back."

"They hadn't, but the pirates were satisfied. We made our way back into the jungle where we found Professor López and the students." Miguel gulped a sigh of relief before adding, "Such a negotiator, this one." Miguel looked up to Caleb with pride. "*¡Vivir para contarla!* We live to tell the tale!"

The reference to Gabríel Garcia Márquez was not lost on either of the adults. They both smiled and Sofía hugged her son again.

"And I have a story to tell," Caleb told Sofía. "Maybe, not the one I came for, but a good story, an important story. People need to know what's happening to these kids."

"What kids?"

"Oh, the smugglers, they were just young teenagers when they had been forced into slave labor on fishing vessels, as young as Miguel. Their story. I mean I'll write their story for the newspapers. Albeit our story was pretty exciting too, right?" Caleb said this to Miguel who high-fived his adventurous friend.

"I'll never let you out of my sight again!" Sofía said grabbing hold of Miguel and embracing her son again. She showered him with kisses. "Smugglers!" She shook her head at the thought of it and kissed Miguel again on the top of his head.

"*Mamá, mamá,* too much, you embarrass me."

"Fine, fine," she said ruffling his hair.

She led the way into the house, but paused at the threshold of the door.

"Things haven't been so dull here either. I'm glad you're both safe. But now, we've other worries. Uncle Guillermo is here."

Caleb and Miguel followed Sofía to the courtyard of the house where they discovered Guillermo talking with a dozen or more people. Mostly men, a few women, standing around in groups of two or three, having multiple and overlapping conversations that sounded like the rain forest abuzz with insects.

"What's going on?" Caleb asked.

Guillermo started to tell him what had been happening in their absence over the last two weeks and others interjected details. Detective González was the last to speak.

"There were problems at the plant," Guillermo told Caleb as he approached and offered a hug.

"The water bottling plant?" Caleb asked. There was no need for Guillermo to introduce Caleb, as his neighbors, friends, and family knew about the U.S. American reporter—news travels fast when strangers come to town. Nevertheless, Guillermo reintroduced him and as he turned to do so, he remembered that Detective González might not know about Caleb. Plus, a few farmers had come to the meeting, saying they had something to discuss, as well. "This is Caleb Barthes. He writes for the *Chicago Tribune.* An investigative reporter." With one exception, everyone nodded as they knew that investigative reporters were on the side of the people. The exception—Detective González who remained skeptical. Gonzáles stood off to the side with a small notebook in hand. He jotted something in his notebook. Caleb glanced at him.

"This is Detective González," Guillermo told Caleb as he walked toward the detective, bringing Caleb closer, as well. Caleb extended his hand and the two men shook without a word. They turned their attention to Guillermo.

"The owner, Robert Madera, brought the payroll plus the yearly bonus. He's a very good man, I've met him, I know. He asks about our families and cares about the workers. He's not like some American CEOs." The people surrounding Guillermo nodded again.

"*Sí*, some Americans run their companies as if the workers are strangers, or worse yet, slaves. They exploit them for profit. It's far worse of course in places like Columbia and Guatemala. We don't stand for that sort of thing here in Nicaragua. We won't be abused," another one of Miguel's uncles retorted.

"*Sí*, we're wise to that kind of trickery, but Madera seems genuine," a different man said.

"I work there, too" a woman spoke up. "And I have had good relations with both bosses."

"How many bosses are there?" Caleb queried.

"Two," one man said

"Three," another worker said at the same time.

"Two or three?" Caleb sought clarity for his notes sake.

Guillermo explained, "Every partnership with an American company requires a Nicaraguan sponsor. So the company is owned by Azteca of California, but is partnered with Alejandro Martínez. Robert Madera owns Azteca, but his brother-in-law is the CEO of the water bottling plant."

"What's his name?" Caleb wanted to know.

"Mannie Morales."

"He's not bad to the workers, but he is not an especially good man," one man said.

"Why do you say that?" Caleb asked.

"He spends a lot of time with his American assistant, Gail Kurts and leaves his wife in the United States."

"How did you know he has a wife," one of the workers asked the man who was speaking.

"I know. I heard him call home one day and ask her about the kids and said he was sorry that the job in Nicaragua was taking so long. Soon after he left with the other woman and didn't come back all afternoon."

"So, he's having an affair, that doesn't make him a thief," the other man interjected.

"Thief?" Caleb wanted more information and the workers didn't mind sharing.

Guillermo continued, "Like I was saying Madera brought the payroll and the bonuses in cash in time for the Feast of the Immaculate Conception and within two days the money turned up missing."

"Who had access to it?" Caleb asked. A question that had crossed Detective González's mind more than once.

"The bosses. None of us has the combination. But I think Mannie Morales stole the money."

"Why?"

"To get money to spend on his mistress."

"You don't even know for sure that he has a mistress," another said.

"What about Alejandro?"

"There is another man," Detective González interrupted.

"Who's that?"

"Don't forget Chambers."

"The handyman?" Guillermo chirped. "I thought you ruled him out."

"I haven't ruled out anyone for sure yet."

"Again I ask, what about Alejandro?"

"No, Alejandro says we have bigger things to worry about than our bonuses."

"Like what?"

"He says he heard that a private company is trying to take over the national water supply."

"We can't let that happen."

"We need to march on the National Assembly."

"Sofía, we need you to lead us."

"Yes, absolutely," another insisted.

"*Sí, sí.* We need Sofía." They all talked of her importance. One after another pleaded with her to lead the march. Spanish was flying in all directions; Miguel was having trouble keeping up the translations for Caleb. Caleb stepped out of the excitement and stood next to the detective. He leaned closer and asked, "Why Sofía?"

"You don't know?" speaking in English, Detective González seemed surprised. Caleb shook his head. "She is the widow of Marco Rodríguez, the famous poet and activist who helped to hold the Sandinista's together. And as a child, she lost her smile to the Contras, surely you know of that," the detective said. Caleb nodded. He knew how she had lost her teeth; he knew nothing of how she lost her husband or who he was. "That's why the people were shocked that she let an American into her home. Then we found out that you are an investigative journalist, the people who uncover and expose American greed, so we trusted that Sofía knew what she was doing."

The detective continued to tell the story of Sofía's husband's death. But Caleb's attention wandered, he imagined Sofía in the arms of another man. He felt the folded paper in his pocket, the poem. He thought Sofía had written it for him. Now he wondered, had she written it for her former husband, Marco Rodríguez? It suddenly came to him that perhaps she hadn't written it all, maybe Rodríguez had written it to her and it had fallen into his hands quite by accident.

"I thought you knew more. What do you know about Madera?"

"Nothing," Caleb shook off his distant thoughts about the poem, and told him again, "Nothing." Then he regained his focus and turned to the detective, "What do *you* know?"

"I know that I don't trust him."

"Don't trust who?" someone commented after overhearing the detective.

"I don't trust Madera."

"Why not?"

"He had as much access to the money as his brother-in-law," the detective inserted.

"Why would he steal his own money? Plus, he paid twice-fold and gave us two weeks off."

"Exactly my point," the detective moved to center stage. "He has access to the money, he brought in armed security to protect the second payroll and then closed the plant for two weeks. Who does that? What's he up to?"

"No, you're distracting us from the more important concern. If another company is trying to privatize the water, we could have another Bolivia on our hands. The Bolivians warned us to stay ever vigilant on this matter."

"Sofía," the man continued, "They'll make it illegal to collect rain water and they'll charge the poor people outrageous sums of money." Miguel made his way to Caleb's side to translate.

"This coming from the mouth of a farmer," the detective added. Caleb understood the translation that Miguel provided but not the implication,

"What's that supposed to mean?" the farmer voiced his resentment.

"It means that you may have more than the poor on your mind. Being charged for water puts you in a bad place considering how much water you use for irrigation."

"You insult me on what grounds?!" The farmer moved toward the detective.

Another man jumped between them, saying calmly, "Everyone has their needs." He used his palms against their chests to separate them and added quietly, "Not in Sofía's house." Each of the two men backed away while keeping a macho eye on the other.

"We need answers, not speculation!"

"Let's go to the Assembly!"

"No, let's go to the water bottling plant first."

"Sofía," they called for her to lead them. The group headed outside. She signaled that she would be with them in a moment, but the crowd was getting anxious.

"We need the public's eye on it!" one woman called out.

A man yelled, "We need answers. Bring the reporter! He needs to witness and document what happens."

Neighbors began to join the group out front. Detective González tried to slow the people, "Let me conduct my investigation. I'll bring you answers."

"Your investigation is about payroll fraud. Our movement is about protecting the water supply." Their voices could be heard growing louder; their numbers increasing.

"No, go to the bottling plant. It was Alejandro who told me about the privatization scheme. We need him to join our group. We should demonstrate their first. If Alejandro and Madera and his brother are good men, they will march with us."

The detective made his way to Caleb's side again, "Too many people have motives. The Americans, the farmers, the people. Everyone should be ready to fight." The house was clearing as the people made their way outside. The detective followed them.

"You two," Sofía said to Caleb and Miguel as if they were both boys. "Stay here. I mean it!"

"But mamá," Miguel protested.

"Sofía," Caleb said calmly, but emphatically. "This may be why Tracker sent me here. He may know something about the water scheme."

"I don't care. You'll be seen as an outsider, an agitator, an American. Our demands to know what is going on will be dismissed. Don't come to the bottling plant and stay away from the National Assembly building! Do you understand? Don't be a part of the crowd," she repeated her demand to Caleb.

"Yes, but—"

"I have to go," she turned to Miguel. "You've had enough adventures for now," she kissed him. Sofía turned to Caleb who now stood under the *bucayo* tree. A red petal fell to the ground. "Stay here. Take care of him. Understand? I don't want either one of you in that crowd." Caleb didn't answer.

"We're just going to get some answers. So stay here. I'll be back soon. Don't go. Don't even think about joining the crowd, okay?"

"Okay," Caleb finally agreed. Sofía turned and left them standing in the courtyard. It grew very quiet for a moment.

Caleb rubbed his chin, considered the situation, and finally asked Miguel a question.

"How did you know about Hunter S. Thompson and Gonzo?"

"My father's magazines," Miguel said. He led Caleb inside and pointed to a two-foot-high stack of *Rolling Stone* magazines in the corner of the room, behind a small table stand. Caleb seemed to be studying the unexpected stack of magazines. "John Lennon is on the cover of the first edition," Miguel said proudly. Without bridging the distance, Caleb looked at the stack of magazines, books had been set on top along with a candle and matches.

"What are the books?"

"Poetry books, mostly; some political books. Sometimes, my mother sits and reads them again and again."

Caleb remained quiet. He thought of the poem that Sofía had written and included in the notes for him. *Or had she,* he wondered again. *Had it been left in there quite by accident?*

"Well, are we Thompson and Gonzo, or what? You're not really going to stick around here are you?" Miguel demanded of Caleb. Caleb pursed his lips in thought.

"C'mon, let's also be Che and Ernesto again. We can drive your motorcycle. I know a place where they won't see us, but we'll be able to see them. C'mon. You want the real story, don't you?"

"But your mother said—"

"My mother said not to mingle with the crowd. I know a place where we can see them but they won't see us. We won't join the demonstration. How can you be a reporter if you stay away?!"

"I promised—"

"You promised not to get mixed up with the crowd. I swear to you on my honor as a baseball player that we won't get into the crowd."

"Do you think they went to the bottling plant or to the Assembly building?"

"Definitely the bottling plant. When that man gives them no answers, which he won't, then they'll go to the old Congress building. They'll be fired up."

"They're that predictable?" Caleb asked wondering if the boy could be right.

"Come with me and you'll see."

At that, Caleb dismissed his concerns, but knew they were breaking a promise. "Okay, but remember, as Thompson said, 'There is no sympathy for the devil; keep that in mind."

"If you mean that my mother will punish me for not listening to her, you're wrong. She'll never know we were there. We'll take the motorcycle; we'll get there before them since they're on foot. They're marching through the streets gathering people as they go. That takes time. They'll be a true force when they get there. And we'll be well hidden.

"So Cowboy, 'You drive. You drive. …Or else buy a ticket and take the ride.'"

"Okay, Gonzo," Caleb headed back to the patio where he'd left his backpack. He grabbed it and swung it over his shoulder. "Let's ride!" As he swung the backpack, a breeze blew through the air and another flame-red flower petal fell from the *bucayo* tree and floated to the ground.

CHAPTER 44

A TERMINATION PLAN

Madera and Chambers stood within the barren warehouse on the Agua Managua property. Madera glanced around at the emptiness of the warehouse, a warehouse that no Nicaraguan workers had ever entered. Chambers had been the only one to run the forklift. Other than Chambers and Madera, only the security team members had known the real contents of the tunnel and the warehouse. Two of those men had arrived long before the workers were ever hired and the others were brought in after the holiday bonus money was stolen. They were well paid for their work and their silence.

"It's loaded and ready to leave port," Madera told Chambers, adding, "I had my doubts as to whether we could pull this off without any glitches. But—"

"Me, too. I worried from time to time as I saw your plan unfolding. Yer could've told me a few more details on logistics."

"Need to know basis, my friend. Need to know only. It's always better that way." Madera smiled before asking about the final clean up. Chambers detailed the exit plan.

"We've pulled all the hydraulic equipment out, disassembled it and had it loaded onto the ship this afternoon. There will be no trace of it. Yer know what I mean?"

"Good," Madera said. "That should be the last of it then. I oversaw the barrels being loaded before sunrise."

"I liked the rain barrels," Chambers complimented Madera.

"It was Gail Kurts' idea," Madera told him with a smirk. "To use old wine barrels as rain barrels filled with spring water. The gold at the bottom of the barrels gives them even further stability. And customs won't notice the weight." They both smiled wider. The Mylar water balloons that Renée had suggested hadn't made as much sense as they first thought. But expensive oak barrels from the winery, which are only used for three years in wine making, could be repurposed to carry water by simply adding interior liners. So much more gold could be moved. And although Renée, the creative advertising and marketing executive, had been jealous of Gail's idea, Madera knew it was far better for him. If anything went wrong it would look like Gail and Mannie were in cahoots, not him and Chambers. Chambers and his small crew had added the gold. What Gail Kurts didn't know is that she had given them the best cover of all for moving gold nuggets on board a cargo ship, through customs, and into L.A. "It's handy when you can get other people to do your thinking," Madera said, thinking his dissemblance clever; *whenever anybody accidentally aids and abets it lightens the load of accountability, as well.* Madera was always storing such information in the back of his mind. Any little nugget that might come in handy in the game of life. *Nugget*, he thought. *Hahha.*

"You should really give her a bonus," Chambers said sarcastically. Madera smiled and scoffed at the same time but then changed his mind, sounding sincere at first, "Maybe I should be more generous, but for some reason the more I have, the more I want." But in his head he considered the possible bonus and how it could be used to his advantage in the future, if anything went sideways.

"I sent her home early, that's bonus enough. Leaves more for us."

Chambers laughed.

"I couldn't agree more. The more I have, the more I want." He repeated Madera's words. But Madera knew that Chambers was different. Chambers loved the prospecting. The discovery. The claim. Not the finer things in life that money can buy. Madera returned his thoughts to the final plan.

"So what's left to do?" Madera asked. "Are we leaving much of a footprint?"

"Well, we can either leave the rest down there or release it."

"Release what?" Madera asked Chambers.

"The slurry," Chambers said. Chambers then remembered that Madera hadn't been down in the mine since they started the high-powered water jets. He explained, "We built a small sluice, it's like a water slide, with a holding pond for the runoff water."

"Contaminated?"

"Probably, but not too bad."

"Why release it?"

"If we break down the holding wall, the water will wash through the maze of caves and take any evidence of our being down there with it."

"Any fall out from that?"

"No, there's a labyrinth of tunnels. It'll go in all directions and eventually just soak into the ground. Maybe a little mercury or arsenic residue, but not a big deal."

"Okay, let's do it," Madera gave approval. "Then the warehouse is completely empty?"

"Yes," Chambers confirmed. "But you know," Chambers paused thinking of a new idea, "I could have our backup generator explode. A small explosion. Just a little bang. We do have some empty gasoline containers in there. It'd take down the warehouse and close off the tunnel."

"Hmm."

"There's nothing else left in the warehouse, except a bunch of old cardboard boxes and a few leftover wine barrels. Everything else is on the ship. It would keep authorities from snooping around."

"Hmm. A small explosion. Nothing too big. Right?" Madera tentatively agreed, but then added, "Make sure all the security guys are in the front of the building, the bottling plant. I don't want anybody getting hurt. And break down the holding wall first, release the water and any sign of being down there. Just to be on the safe side."

"Of course," Chambers nodded and started to walk away. Madera stopped him.

"How do we explain the explosion?"

"On hot days, like today, if the fuel tank on the generator is overfilled, the gas will expand and can explode. It's a common mistake. I'll say we were emptying the warehouse after our first big shipment to sweep it out and wash it down and get ready for the next shipment of water bottles, canteens, and rain barrels. We have the containers in a sanitary holding area, right? If anybody asks, I'll tell 'em we decided to put the last of the gas in the generator tank to get rid of the containers, that I didn't realize how full it was and I didn't expect it to get so hot today. It is winter. They are sure to agree that the weather is extraordinarily hot for December."

"Sounds good, great idea, Chambers. How big would the explosion be?"

"Likely just enough to seal the hole and then knock down one warehouse wall which will leave the other walls to topple. I'll run a rope from the generator to the excavation tunnel. That should take care of everything."

"Okay then, release the slurry this afternoon. The guys can help you with that part. Then, later, you can handle the explosion. Say around sunset. And make sure the guys are out of here. I don't want anybody to get hurt."

"You sound so caring."

"Do I?" Madera turned away from Chambers, thinking the only thing he cares about is pulling this off without any snafus. When people get hurt that draws attention. Bringing down the warehouse was a great idea. It could explain slow-down in production and provide a cover story for ending the Nicaragua operation. If the explosion damages the bottling plant a little, all the better. "Slurry first. This afternoon. Explosion a little later today. Make sure the security team is in front of the bottling plant in case some of the bottling plant gets damaged. Sometimes explosions are bigger than expected," Madera concluded with a pensive tone.

"Sure, slurry first, explosion later. Sounds good," Chambers agreed.

CHAPTER 45

DELTA AT THE EDGE OF A DIG

Delta arrived at the Augusto C. Sandino International Airport and after clearing customs she spotted a small woman with dark blonde hair and large brown eyes, holding a sign that said *Prof. Delta Quinn.*

"I'm Delta," she told the young woman.

"I'm Loretta, a graduate student working on the archeological dig. It's a pleasure to meet you. I'm so excited to be here. Well, not here at the airport, but here in Nicaragua working on this project. I'm from Guatemala, originally."

"My guide on the Tikal trip was from Guatemala." Delta was reminded of the talented graduate student who spent part of his time uncovering mass graves and part of the year giving eco-archaeology tours. She had learned a great deal about the relations between the countries of Belize and Guatemala and between the two friends, one from Belize and one from Guatemala, but nothing of the relations between Nicaragua and surrounding countries.

"How are the relations between the two countries, Guatemala and Nicaragua, I mean?" Delta asked.

"All seven Central American countries have been working together since the 1990s to try to improve trade and economic conditions. Not all of them are on board with CAFTA. Nicaragua was slowest to get on board of those who joined?"

"Why is that?"

"Each country had to elect twenty delegates and send them to joint meetings to hammer out the details of trade within Central America and between it and the U.S."

"Were the Nicaraguans opposed to elections?"

"Oh, no. That wasn't it. They were simply one of the poorest nations. Elections are costly and sending representatives to meetings is expensive, too, but they eventually met the requirements, it simply took them the longest to do so. Now we have several joint ventures within Central America and with the U.S. It's just that rules and laws had to be made to protect the countries from any corporate colonization. You can imagine, what with the U.S. history."

Delta was not very well versed on the politics and economics of Central America or its relationship to the U.S. She had envisioned the countries as poor and infested with gang violence. And those summations weren't wrong, but they weren't the whole story, she was beginning to realize. In addition, she felt her privilege when she considered that the country was too poor to easily send delegates to a meeting. She didn't give her attendance at academic conferences across the country a second thought, hotel rooms, air fares, and more; the university paid for it.

"Anyway, it's wonderful that you're here." Delta could hear the excitement in Loretta's voice. "The project is so exciting!" the young woman declared.

Her enthusiasm reminded Delta of Mona Barthes, Caleb's sister and her advisee. The last time she'd seen Mona was when Mona had dropped her off at the airport to leave for Belize. It seemed like a lifetime ago, especially considering all she had experienced in Belize and Guatemala; but of course, it had been barely two weeks since she'd left the university in search of a Mayan adventure. A 'distraction,' she had called it when talking to her friend, P. J. But it had grown into much more than that.

"We were so sorry to hear about the accident you were in," Loretta sympathized.

"Thank you," Delta murmured as she limped slightly.

"We heard that you were quite the hero."

"Who me? Oh no," Delta contradicted her as they walked out of the airport terminal.

"Well, the way we heard the story, is that the van had flipped on its side and that everyone was trapped inside with a gushing river below and you climbed out and brought the rescue team. We heard that you went for help even though your ankle was badly injured."

Delta remembered feeling the raindrops against her face and tasting blood in her mouth as she ran for help. If it could be called 'running,' more like speedy limping with her ankle throbbing.

"Loretta, I was nearest to the passenger window and the smallest person in the van. I managed to make my way through the window and went for help. A group of very wonderful people did the rest; they pulled the others safely out of the van. I played a very small part."

"I don't know about the small part, but being *small* enough to get through the window is what's going to let you get down into the cave," Loretta quipped as she guided Delta to the car. "Everybody else okay?"

"Yes, the driver, Barlow, had a broken arm and one young woman had a concussion. Otherwise, fine. The birdwatchers even joked about having enough fat on them to bounce without getting hurt," Delta added with a smile.

"The upside to obesity, I guess," Loretta, a small Latina, quipped. They hadn't walked far under the stinging sun before Loretta pointed to a car and added, "This one." She then loaded Delta's bags into the dusty vehicle. They left the airport and drove along *Carretera Norte* highway.

Delta stared out the open window, feeling the warm breeze and soaking in the greenness of the view along the edge of the highway. She watched the foliage whiz by with low buildings and high billboards interspersed. Palm trees intermittently jutted upward. Turning forward, straight ahead of her, she saw the brightest blue sky on the planet. Pure white clouds popped out of cerulean skies straight ahead. She absorbed it all in a panoramic view, especially noting how the Managua highway median was not only lined with leafy tropical green trees, but also every one hundred feet or so the indigenous foliage was interrupted by a sculptor's rendering of a tree. These saffron painted, metal structures, with trunks rising into curling lace branches, gleamed like gold in the noon light and stood several feet higher than the natural trees that came before them and followed after.

"What are the tree statues all about?" Delta asked. Loretta smiled before answering.

"Everybody asks. Maybe that's the point. Rosario Murillo, the First Lady of Nicaragua, wife of Daniel Ortega, created them. Each is called the *Tree of Life*. They light up at night."

"No kidding?"

"Costs a fortune in electricity. People either love them or hate them."

"The trees or Ortega and Murillo?"

"She's quite a figure, Murillo."

"Why is that?"

"Oh, besides being Daniel Ortega's partner in life and politics; you know, he's the famous Sandinista, from the revolutionary days, some say that she changed him to make him more electable. She's brought him back from Atheism to Catholicism, from political revolution to Bohemian art, from communism to socialism slash capitalism. Anyway they took control again in 2007, I think, and have held power ever since. Term limits were abolished under their rule. If that tells you anything." Loretta made a dubious face before continuing. "Sandinistas started off loving them, thinking they were going to make the world right again, but now the Nicaraguans complain that the electricity is used to light the metal trees and not their homes. Love her or hate her, she's a powerful first lady, very intelligent. She and Ortega are negotiating a deal with the Chinese to build a canal across the country."

"Really?"

"That could be a game changer in trade.

"That's a good bet."

"And the Ortega's have eight children, so the Nicaraguans might be in for a long dynasty. The Ortega dynasty." Loretta turned off the highway.

"Where are we headed?'

"Oh, the plan is to let you drop your things off at the hotel and then we'll head over to the site and join the others."

"The hotel?"

"The Hilton, right there," Loretta told her pulling into the large contemporary hotel's drive. "We made a reservation for you. Watch your purse and your back. Tip if you can, not too much. Yankees are not especially liked, but their money is appreciated."

"Okay, I'll be right out."

"Great," Loretta added, already checking her phone for messages. Delta grabbed her bag from the back seat and jumped out of the car.

"Hey, Prof. Quinn," Loretta called out. Delta turned. "I recommend long, light-weight pants if you have them and a long-sleeved shirt. And," she said extending her water bottle to Delta, "would you mind refilling my water bottle? We're running a bit low at the site. The Hilton should have potable water somewhere."

Delta took the water bottle. "No problem." She was reminded momentarily of her cottage in the rain forest of Belize which had no potable water, but her thoughts quickly shifted. Excited to be in Nicaragua, Delta registered quickly at the front desk, went to her room, and changed clothes. She filled the water bottle. After packing a light backpack, she stood at the door considering whether she had forgotten anything, glanced around the room—contemporary with all the modern conveniences—and determined she had what she needed and she liked what she was coming back to later that day. She quickly made her way back to Loretta.

On the way to the site, Delta asked Loretta about what they had found and what they know so far about Lady Ikoom and her possible travels to Nicaragua.

"Really, we don't know much about the life and travels of Lady Ikoom. She came from the Snake Clan, and seems to have married someone of little ambition or is not well-known for anything, but she on the other hand is thought to have ruled the city near Tikal, strategized ways to make the Maya stronger through intermarriages and gave birth to a line of historic descendants. One of her granddaughters is believed to have been a famous warrior. Some stelae indicate that Lady Ikoom may have been an advisor to the royalty of Tikal."

"And here in Nicaragua?"

"Yes, we don't know for sure yet. What we have seen so far may only be a mention of the Lady Ikoom or something that belonged to her, but if we do find artifacts related to her so far south, it will be significant. It's possible that early Mayan groups or precursors to the Mayan's did carving and sculpting here and moved stone stelae north or columns north for building or for monument making. Some of those may have been made during her lifetime or shortly after and may have been made here. Nobody's really sure yet. Anyway, you'll get your look at it soon. It's incredible. That's it up ahead. We'll park the car, and walk the rest of the way, over that hill and along the ledge. We could drive, and we do have one van up there, but it's not a hard walk. See, over there," Loretta said pointing as she swung the car into a shaded area.

They exited the car and began the short hike up the hill. "The team leader isn't here yet today. She took some of the artifacts to the museum for carbon dating. We don't like to leave anything unprotected overnight. She'll be back later. But we'll get you started. We know your time is short, just being on winter break. So you'll go down into the labyrinth for a bit of a look around today."

Delta swallowed hard, both excited and nervous.

CHAPTER 46

PREPARATIONS

Delta smiled as she climbed uphill; the walk seemed more exhilarating than exhausting. Upon reaching the summit, she looked up to the clear cerulean sky with its touch of cumulus clouds, puffy and bright white, the sun turning toward late afternoon. Her thoughts on the majesty of the sky above her veered sharply to the deepness below, as Loretta announced, "We're here," and indicated the entrance to a cavern just a few feet away by looking ahead and downward. The opening of the cave yawned expansively.

"It's larger than I thought it'd be."

"The tiny opening is inside that cave. You'll see."

The perimeter of the area had been roped off, supplies set to the side, archeological equipment and small cameras piled neatly near the entrance to the cave. Delta followed Loretta's lead by stepping under the rope to join the other two women, who waited for them.

"Welcome, welcome," the taller of the two women called out with open arms.

"We're so glad you could make it. How was your trip?" the other, shorter woman asked.

"I'm Dee Dee," the taller woman interjected as she gave Delta a welcoming hug.

"Gloria," the smaller woman introduced herself, giving and taking the second hug with Delta. Loretta stood by Delta's side during the exchange.

"The flight was fine, thanks."

"And how are *you?*' Dee Dee remarked with more emphasis.

"Oh, we heard about the accident, the van accident that you were in crossing back into Belize. How are you?" Gloria echoed Dee Dee's sentiment.

"Fine, fine. Really. But it did set me back a bit."

"Sure. Sure, of course. No worries," Dee Dee assured her.

"Is everyone else okay?" Gloria added.

"Everyone is coming along nicely."

"Is your ankle strong enough to withstand a small jump?" Dee Dee questioned with concern.

"Absolutely," Delta told her. "Practically good as new. But because of the accident, I didn't get to take my scuba lessons in Belize. I'm not sure how to use the gear."

"It's okay. It's really just a precaution. We haven't seen any deep water, yet," again Dee Dee Penfield, professional scuba diver from California, assured her. "That's my specialty for the team. I do cave diving, aquarium diving, oceanic diving, you name it, if it has a tank associated with it, I do it. Anyway, this cave is dry as a bone. But I'll walk you through the safety precautions and the basics. And then I'll go with you. We're just about to go into an area we haven't explored yet. Although we took a peek at it and it looks like there might be a number of artifacts on an interior ledge. It'll be your job to photograph them. And from what I understand, you're familiar with glazes and Native American pottery styles."

"We won't remove anything without Dr. Pérez's okay. Feel free to get a good look at them," the other woman said and then provided a more formal introduction. "I'm Gloria Díaz from the *Museo Maya de Cancún*. Formerly, I worked in Mexico City as Head of the Mayan collection."

"I'm still surprised that you accepted me as part of your team," Delta added without false humility.

"P. J. Turner is a friend, and she explained that you also have expertise in natural glazes and in narrative. We want to gather soil samples and see if you can match the glazes to the local soil. It might be that the artifacts come from here or they could have been glazed here, but not made here or they could have been brought here, traded or something like that. As for narrative, everyone is still trying to piece the narrative of Ikoom's life together. So the more the merrier. Plus, the vases all seem to have different stories in pictorial form. The more brainstorming, the better," Gloria told her. "So when P. J. recommended you, I said, if she's a friend of yours, she's a friend of mine. And then I called Dr. Peréz and told her about your qualifications."

"Oh, you mean my 32 inch hips?"

They all laughed.

"Yes, that did keep poor P. J. from being included in the group. She's a curvaceous woman. God blessed her with hips that men love to look at, but she'd never fit through the opening that we'll maneuver. You'll see."

After guiding Delta through the use of the archeological equipment, Dr. Díaz explained that this excavation is preliminary, but if they find evidence of significant importance, then Dr. Pérez will write a grant and submit it to one of the foundations. "We'd try to get enough money to brace the entrance and enlarge the opening so that archeological anthropologists like P. J. could also survey the area and the contents of the cave." And then Dee Dee walked her through the basics of the scuba gear, gave her brief breathing lessons, and reminded her that the cave was as dry as a hangover throat on a Sunday morning. Loretta handed Delta a camera.

"High resolution digital photography will allow us to create 3D images later. We also wear GoPros," Dee Dee said handing one of the sets of head gear to Delta before adjusting her own camera. "Your boots are good, but you need gloves. These are thinner than what most cavers would wear."

"Why's that?"

"They are protecting their hands from what might be on ledge or wall that they can't see, a sharp edge, a snake, a bat, could be anything. These gloves have less protection but more flexibility for handling artifacts and can give you a solid grip on a rope if need be." Delta pulled on the thin, leather gloves.

"Ready?"

Delta nodded enthusiastically. "Just one question: How do we get back up?"

CHAPTER 47

MIGUEL AND CALEB'S BROKEN PROMISE

Miguel climbed high into the thick and sturdy arms of the *bucayo* tree. His young legs and strong but skinny arms holding and switching up as he moved from lower to higher branches, eventually seating himself high and behind the deep green leaves and bright red flowers. His red and yellow striped shirt offered him a colorful camouflage. "C'mon! C'mon!" Miguel called to Caleb with excitement.

Although Caleb's longer legs gave him an advantage in reaching and swinging onto branches, his flexibility was far from that of the young Miguel. Nevertheless, Caleb climbed into the heart of the tree and made his way upward, not as high as Miguel but high enough to see the entrance to the bottling plant.

"How long will it take them to get here?"

"Oh, they will stop along the way. My mother will speak, others will speak, and they will move to the next place."

"You've seen this before? Does your mother often lead such rallies?"

"My mother has some causes. She helped the Nico Maya fight for their land in Guatemala. She helped the children here in Nicaragua who were being used to mine minerals. She wanted them all in school. My mother is all about education. I told you she is a Sandinista. That's what they do."

"Between washing and writing poetry?"

"*Sí.*"

There was a lull in their conversation. Caleb wanted to ask about Miguel's father. He hesitated but then broached the subject, "Miguel, how old were you when your father died?"

"I never met him. He died before I was born."

The boy became quiet; so did Caleb. They listened to the birds. Caleb eventually said, "Sorry."

"*Gracias*. I know him through his books, poetry, and through my mother's stories." The boy said no more on the subject. They were each quiet again.

"Look! There are men heading toward the warehouse in the back. Keep an eye on them." Four men did indeed appear and disappear around the corner of the bottling plant to the warehouse. A fifth opened a door for them. They may have been inside for no more than twenty minutes when they all reappeared, except the fifth man. *Are there others in the bottling plant?* Caleb wondered.

Just then a car pulled into the drive of the bottling plant. Caleb and Miguel saw the man exit his car and hurriedly make his way to the handsome man standing in front of the building. The man called out to the others who responded to his command. Without realizing it, they were watching it all unfold: Alejandro Martínez, the Nicaraguan partner telling Manny Morales and Robert Madera that the marchers were coming. Madera waving to Chambers, giving him the sign to release the sluice with the help of the former Blackwater operatives.

Caleb and Miguel wished they could hear what was being said. They watched intently. The men seemed to scurry in different directions. Several minutes later, six armed-security forces stood at the front of the building. Four unarmed others stood with them—Martínez, Chambers, Morales and Madera.

"They have assault rifles!" Miguel called to Caleb with concern. "We have to warn my mother!"

"I'll do it! You wait here. Keep an eye on them. Watch to see if there are more men and where they're positioned. I'll be back soon. Stay here, you hear me?! Out of sight. You'll be our secret weapon. And safe in the branches." Caleb was already swinging himself out of his hiding place in the tree. "Which way should I go?" Caleb called up to Miguel.

Miguel pointed. Caleb jumped on the motorcycle and took off.

When Miguel turned back again to watch the scene, one man had disappeared from sight.

CHAPTER 48

DELTA EXPLORES A CAVE

Delta dropped through the opening with ease but her ankle hit the floor of the cave abruptly and she felt pain shoot through her leg. She winced.

"Here comes your tank," Loretta called down the narrow opening. The opening in the floor of the front cavern, that Griselda had slipped through months earlier, was as narrow as Delta had envisioned. The drop from top to bottom was 6 feet. Delta had sat at the lip of the opening and lowered her legs in first before she let go, thus cutting the drop distance almost in half. She had expected to bounce back up to a standing position as she had seen her companion do, but her ankle crumpled slightly. It jarred her.

Delta looked up. The shaft of light was broken only by the silver oxygen tank being lowered toward her. The face mask had been looped around its air hose.

"And here comes the anchor rope," Loretta yelled downward. "I'm going to attach the other end to the van, now."

The rope had knots every six inches or so apart, designed as hand holds, Delta noticed.

"If we have an emergency, drop the tank and go up the rope. But if everything is fine and going according to plan, they'll lower a basket for us to set the tanks in and they'll pull them up before we climb up," Dee Dee informed Delta. Delta nodded, now she knew how they were getting back up.

Dee Dee had gone down first, received her tank, and was now pushing it ahead of herself through the next narrow passageway. Once through she turned to Delta again and instructed her.

"Okay, push your tank ahead of you toward me. Once I can touch it, I'll pull it the rest of the way. Then you crawl through the first opening that you see. Come forward about twenty feet. The cave gets bigger after that and you can stand, sort of, and put the scuba gear on. There you'll see several openings, some smaller, some larger. It's like a labyrinth of tunnels. So don't get too far behind me or go too far in any direction. Keep me in view at all times. We'll turn 90 degrees from our starting point and go 40 feet into the tunnel.

"How do you know when you're 40 feet in?" Delta interrupted.

"I literally use my feet to pace it off. But we'll have far more precise measurements once the professional cavers have come down and mapped it for us. Anyway, as I was saying, then we'll go through a narrow opening that we haven't explored yet. It'll be to our right. It's a tight squeeze, but we can do it. I know it's kind of hard to see down here, but make sure you have the GoPro turned on. We could use new LED lights for these things," Dee Dee wished aloud.

Delta followed Dee Dee's instructions. Within a few moments she handed off her tank, made her way through the passageway, and found herself in a section of the cave where they could just barely stand in a crouching manner and lift the tanks onto their backs, one arm at a time. Delta scanned the outer chamber; there she saw the stela.

"This is it! Right?"

"Yes," Dee Dee answered with a smile.

The two walked carefully around the stela remarking on the hieroglyphs as they circled it. Delta was amazed at the intricate carving. She stared in awe. She smiled and a sparkle came to her eyes as she viewed the treasure.

"Don't get turned around. It's easy to get lost in these tunnels. Over there, that way is where we came in. Note the rock formation above that opening. And especially look at the quartz vein. See how it sparkles like a white river running through hills and valleys against the grey igneous rock. That's quartz. The old saying, *find the quartz, and gold follows*," Dee Dee said with a smile and then turned her head. "Now, look over there," she said pointing in the opposite direction, "that's the tunnel we haven't explored yet. Shall we?" Dee Dee invited her companion.

"Have you found any gold?" Delta asked.

"No, some cavers say you won't find gold around here, but a few say that limestone intermingled with quartz and gold here long ago. They say it was mined in this region for many years. They're probably right. I mean, the Aztecs and the Maya, both had gold."

Delta followed Dee Dee through the narrow archway. They moved slowly, feeling their way with their feet on the floor of the cave and their hands along the rocky sides. They moved and angled their heads to shine a light in front of and around them. Delta, felt the rough side of the cave wall turn into a ledge, it felt like a stone mantle above a fireplace. She moved her fingers forward, carefully. The shelf turned inward. She extended her reach, letting her glove-covered fingertips carefully explore the expanding ledge that now turned into an opening. *An alcove.* She felt something, something smoother than the rock inside the opening.

"Dee Dee, I think I have something."

"Really? What've you found?" She turned to look at Delta. "Ooh, aren't you the brave soul, sticking your hand in there. I'd be afraid of coming up with a snake or waking a bat." Dee Dee hadn't seen any snakes so far, but it was possible in the Yucatán as some snakes sought out caves with bats.

Delta hadn't thought of snakes or bats and she most certainly wasn't going to focus on that right now as she pulled the Mayan drinking vessel from the crevice. They turned their headlamps on the object. Delta studied it before handing it to Dee Dee.

"Oh my god! Is this what I think it is?"

"Is that a carving of Chaac on a goblet?" Delta asked.

Dee Dee turned the vessel in her hands. She studied it with great care.

"Incredible! Look, it appears to be Ikoom's mark on the other side. We'll have to get Dr. Pérez or Gloria to confirm, but I think that's what it is. Oh my gosh, what a find! But I'm no expert on this, remember." Dee Dee was the specialist in cave diving and mapping; and yes, she had a degree in archeology, but she wasn't a Mayan expert or an art specialist. Dee Dee's knowledge of Mayan culture had come from a crash course given by the team leader.

Delta reached in again, thinking to hell with spiders, snakes, or bats. She pulled another vessel from the small alcove within the cave. Delta studied the second artifact with disbelief. Turning it around, reading the hieroglyphic story. A story she had read before. She shook her head in both disbelief and amazement.

"Incredible," Delta announced.

"What is it?" Dee Dee asked.

"I've seen one almost identical to this one."

"Where?"

"In the Smithsonian," Delta told her. "Look, it's the story of a hunter who is hungry and makes offerings to the gods and spies a deer; and then look, he's carrying it over his shoulder. The deer is dead, indicated by this little puff of air, a cloud with three lines coming from its mouth, as though it has taken its last breath. And then the hunter praises the gods again in gratitude for fruitful hunt." Delta held the piece of pottery and gazed with amazement.

"Dee Dee," Delta added with a serious pause, "It was among the Maya collection!"

Delta handed the vase to Dee Dee and reached into the opening again. This time she extracted a water vessel. She turned it slowly. It was a portrait of a girl praying to Chaac and when she turned the vessel there was a picture of her holding the vessel upside down with one single drop of water falling from the lip of the vase. The drop of water had three little lines coming from it. As if it was the last drop of water.

"And that mark," Dee Dee added. "I am pretty sure that is the mark of the Lady Ikoom."

They looked at it, and then at each other. "Could Lady Ikoom have traveled this far in search of water for her people? Do you think she died here?" Delta asked, and as she asked, she let her gaze move from the vessel upward to Dee Dee's face and then beyond. Her eyes widened.

They both heard it. Like distant thunder. And then a rumbling as if the thunder was unending and moving toward them.

"What's that sound?" Delta said with trepidation.

Dee Dee knew. "Holy shit!" she said turning to see it.

A wall of water came rushing at them with a force beyond description. "Move, move, move!" Dee Dee yelled while putting the artifact back on the ledge. "Get your equipment on!"

Dee Dee pulled her mask over her face and put the snorkel mouthpiece in her mouth. Ready to help, she assisted Delta. Delta didn't let go of the priceless artifact in her hand and wasn't used to the scuba gear. Dee Dee pulled Delta's mask up from around her neck, knocking the GoPro a kilter. All Delta could think was to move, but the water around her knees seemed to be rushing in circles, making her legs feel tied together.

"When it gets deep enough, waist high, swim!" Dee Dee held her own air hose out and gave more instructions, "But you can't keep the gear on all the way back, the last tunnel is too narrow, remember?" The water continued gushing and rushing faster than they could move; it was over their waists and they were having to swim through the blackness of it all. Just two slim lights coming from their head gear. The noise was echoing all around them like a great waterfall. "Use your tank to get one last breath of air and then dump the tank, swim for the anchor rope, when you get there. Try to follow me. You have to get up the—"

Dee Dee's last instructions were cut off as the water now rolled over their heads. Delta could no longer see Dee Dee. All she could see was a swirling darkness with a stream of light. She tumbled against rocks. Her tank hit hard. She refused to let go of the artifact. With her free hand, she held the mouth piece and sucked in, but no air came to her. She felt for the hose. It was punctured; she could feel the leak. Bubbles rose, circling violently, from the punctured spot toward the surface. The surface. Delta followed the bubbles and swam frantically, searching for Dee Dee's light. But she couldn't see it. She searched the shaft of light, the light from above. She couldn't see it either. Gushing water now moved less like a swirling waterfall and more like a river with strong undercurrents. She started to panic. She threw off the useless tank. Thirty pounds she didn't need. She saw it swirling and sinking. At least now she knew top from bottom of the cave. She pushed herself upward. And she found a small pocket of air along the ceiling of the cave. She was in the chamber with all the different entrances. *Thank god*, she thought. She remembered the rock formation above the portal that Dee Dee had pointed out. She scanned the area. She held tight with one hand to a rock as she continued to breathe from the pocket of air at the ceiling of the cave. She spotted the rock formation that she knew led to the shaft, it was the one they had had to crawl through before getting into this chamber. She sucked in a last breath of air and swam for the egress.

The water was both pulling and pushing her. She fought to get through the cave's causeway. She knew the shaft opening would be just beyond it. She tried to swim with the artifact still in her hand. She wouldn't drop it. She wouldn't—

A sudden resurgence of the water whipped her hand against a rock. The artifact with the painting of the last drop of water fell from her hand and was swallowed by the churning water. Delta felt the loss as a wave of depression. She had to force herself to look away. She saw the light from above. The water pushed her half-way up the shaft. She felt her lungs were about to burst. Dee Dee was already above, yelling down to her. Loretta was in the van. Gloria was yelling something now, too. The rushing water blocked her from hearing. Delta felt as though she were a rag doll in a washing machine, spinning in the churning waters in the lower part of the shaft. At last, Delta made out what they were saying:

"Grab the rope! Grab the rope!"

Delta seized the rope with both hands.

"She's got it!" They both yelled to Loretta who put the van in reverse. The rope pulled Delta upward into the fullness of daylight. Dee Dee and Gloria helped her over the edge. Delta now lay under a serene blue sky. Not even a drop of water in the air. Coughing repeatedly, she spat out water, eventually breathing in relief and exhaling gratitude to be alive.

Later, Delta sat in the passenger seat, soaking wet, as Gloria drove them toward the hotel. Delta vigorously insisted that she would have stayed with them in the tent at the archeological site if she'd known they were all staying there.

"No, it's not a problem. I'll drive you back to the hotel and you can change into dry clothes. We can all regroup tonight for dinner or tomorrow morning when Dr. Pérez returns. What a day, eh? So much good fortune and so much bad luck. Dr. Pérez will be heart broken when she hears of what we found and what we've lost."

"I held it in my hands, so close; and, I let it go." Delta softly reiterated, "I can't believe that I let it go."

Gloria turned the van right and drove another few blocks, before turning left.

"Hey, what's going on here?" Gloria broke the remorseful musing.

"Some kind of parade?" Delta wondered aloud as she saw the crowd moving down the street.

"It's the season of feasts and festivals," Gloria said with a smile. "So you could be right." She stopped the car to let the people pass. The crowd was expansive. Delta and Gloria heard the chanting. Gloria translated for Delta, "Water is from God; God's gifts should be free."

"Ah, some kind of political march," Gloria reconsidered. And then the crowd came to a standstill. Gloria sighed. "Someone is probably giving speeches. The hotel is just another couple of blocks, but it looks like we're stuck for a while."

"Oh, no worries then. I can walk from here. Maybe I'll see what's going on after I change."

"Are you sure?"

"Absolutely," Delta assured her as she exited the car, her hair dripping into wet strings, her shirt sticking to her, her long pants hanging longer. And not a drop of rain in the air. But no one noticed her, their concerns consumed their focus.

MADERA'S BUSINESS' FRONT DOOR

"The people are coming!" Alejandro announced.

"What people? What are you talking about?" Robert Madera queried impatiently.

"There is a crowd convening and they plan to converge here at the plant," Alejandro told Madera.

"What's their problem?" Madera asked his Nicaraguan business partner.

"They think you are part of the water privatization plot. I told them about a possible plot but never mentioned you. I swear! I don't know how it got turned around."

That rumor was supposed to distract them from us. Not bring them to our front door, Madera couldn't conceal his anger. "Alejandro, I told you that was for your ears only. Who did you tell?" Yes, he had wanted the rumor to spread but never to point the finger at him.

"I told a couple of workers. This is not the kind of thing that should be kept a secret. Those companies can be profiteers worse than pirates," Alejandro defended himself with plaintive appeals.

"Some of the workers?" Madera yelled.

"*Sí.*"

Madera hadn't vetted the workers with any intensity. His assumptions, grounded in stereotypes, defined them all as poor, uneducated, not a threat to him, not worthy of concern.

Chambers was the only one he thought might challenge his own superiority. *Chambers had too much money to lose if he tried to blame Madera's company for the privatization. How had the people figured this out?* Madera was frustrated but not terribly worried. *There really isn't anything left for the crowd to discover,* he thought. *The gold was packaged and on the cargo ship, ready to leave port. Chambers had reported taking care of the sluice and holding tank. The run-off water had been freed to rush through the labyrinth of caves. Perhaps a medium-size explosion would be the final deterrent that would get the group to dispel. Making it look like I am also being attacked. Ah, I could claim to have been sabotaged by another company, an imaginary company, that wants to privatize the water. That would make sense,* he thought. They would be his competitors and he their competitor. Madera himself was almost thinking of the fictitious company as real by the time the people's chants reached his ears. He moved closer to where the crowd was coming into view. Alejandro followed. Morales joined the two. Madera saw the marchers coming down the street. Chanting. People shouting, "Water is Life—*¡El agua es vida!*"

A couple hundred or more Nicaraguans. His workers among them.

"Why would they think badly of me? I am the man who paid their bonuses. I have been good to the workers. They are like family," Madera continued his charade, lying to Alejandro.

"Speak on my behalf, Alejandro. Tell them they are like family to me. Tell them I'll meet with them. Where is Chambers? I'll be right back." He left his business partner and his brother-in-law to face the crowd.

Madera headed to the warehouse. He decided to make the small, spontaneous explosion more likely and a bit bigger than previously planned. He moved the generator, situating it over the trap door that had led to the mine. Then he disconnected the ground wire. Finally, he poured the last of the gasoline into the generator. He started to leave, stopped short, turned and pulled a board from the warehouse wall allowing the equatorial sun to shine directly onto the generator. Should it look like an accident or more clearly like sabotage? He reconsidered, it didn't matter. Even a saboteur might try to make it look like an accident. He wouldn't overthink it. If it looked like an accident, fine; if it didn't, no big deal; he'd blame it on his supposed competitors or on the sun.

Madera knew he could talk his way out of anything. *People are stupid; and, they hear what they want to believe.*

DESPERATION

Caleb dumped the motorbike by the side of the road, when he saw how large the throng of people had grown. He started to make his way through the crowd. He shouted her name, "Sofía! Sofía!" But he couldn't be heard over the crowd's rhythmic chanting. Just when he was within distance of being heard, the whole crowd seemed to turn like a tsunami and move toward the bottling plant. He was now headed away from Sofía. And she was headed toward men with repeating rifles. The crowd would be there in minutes. He had to get closer to her. He had to warn her that Madera's men have guns, assault-style weapons. That these were no amateurs. The crowd stopped again. This was his chance.

Delta came around the corner from the other direction just in time to see a beautiful Nicaraguan woman step forward from the crowd and onto a crate. The throng came to a halt, standing still, but shouting in unison and in response to the woman, with the exception of one figure weaving his way frantically toward the beautiful woman at the head of the marchers. Suddenly the crowd stopped chanting, getting ready to move again. Caleb called out, "Sofía, Sofía." Delta recognized the voice, the man, immediately—Caleb Barthes. Delta tried to take in the whole scene, to understand it all. But there was too much happening.

The marchers were on the move again, led by the woman. They made their way toward the bottling plant. The people swarmed the area. Delta followed the flow, but from the other side. Sofía gathered the crowd in front of Azteca's bottling plant. Their anger spilling forth in words demanding the water be left free. Madera, Morales, and Alejandro standing in front of the crowd. Armed guards between the people and the owners. A sudden surge of workers caught the guards off balance. One guard raised his rifle. Alejandro pleaded with the workers.

"Go home! Go home!"

Madera shouted, "I am with you. I am innocent of the charges."

And then it all went from bad to horrific with a ghastly explosion, from the generator.

The explosion even surprised Madera. He hadn't thought it would happen so fast or be so loud. They ducked or covered their heads. Madera had thought he'd have time to talk the crowd down, to explain to them that he wasn't part of privatization scheme. He thought he'd have it all under control, his control. But when the generator exploded chaos rained down. Bits of broken walls sprayed the area. People screamed. They ran helter-skelter. One security officer thought they were being attacked. He pulled his automatic rifle up and shot warning bullets over the heads of people in the crowd. The bullets sprayed high and wide, back and forth.

Madera shouted, "Stop! Stop!"

Some people in the crowd had ducked, others screamed, some charged and others retreated.

Madera yelled again, "Hold your fire! Hold your fire."

The shooting stopped.

A strange silence, like the eye of a storm, held them all in place. They listened to the silence and the one noise, the one sound, that turned their attention toward a tree. They all heard it. The cracking of a branch. And they all turned to see it. The body of a boy falling from limb to limb from a bucayo tree. Until a nauseating noise, a thud, made even the birds go silent.

It was as if the world stood still. The people turned their heads again. Toward Sofía.

"¡Miguel! ¡Miguel! ¡Mi Miguel!" Sofía screamed. She knew that shirt. The red and yellow one that she laundered and mended. The one she drew to her nose to smell the fragrance of Miguel; she knew it was her son and refused to accept it. "No, no. This cannot be!"

Caleb was closer to the tree, and ran for the boy. The crowd separated quickly for Sofía, coming from the other direction. She reached her son in time to push Caleb away from him. She looked down. The boy's eyes already stared into heaven. Sofía turned to see Caleb. Caleb tried to reach out to Miguel and to Sofía.

She shoved Caleb away, over and over. Pushing against his chest, pushing him away from Miguel's body, she yelled.

"What have you done?! What have you done?! He's not your son! I told you not to come. You let him come here! Why?! Why?! You just had to have your story. This is not your story! This is my life. He's not your story! He's my son!" She beat her own chest now. You promised me, you would stay away," she sobbed.

Sofía turned her back on the stunned Caleb. She bent down and drew Miguel into her arms. She sobbed and called out to God. She cradled the boy's head. Sofía felt it, then turned her blood-soaked hand over; the blood wasn't hers, but she wished it were.

"Please, no, he is everything to me. He is all I have. Dear God, no, no, don't take my baby!" Grief came in great heaving sobs and heartbreaking gasps for air. She could barely breathe as she rocked Miguel in her arms and watched as his last breath escaped his lips. "Miguel, Miguel."

Caleb tried once more; he reached out his hand. She slapped it away.

DELTA RETURNS TO THE FOREST MOTHER

Delta sat in the living room of Mona's house. The Christmas decorations were still hanging although the New Year holiday had come and gone. Mona's foster daughter, Abigail, played quietly. The girl poured imaginary water from a plastic watering can onto the plants and as she did so, she talked softly—*you need water, and you need water, and you need...* Mona brought Delta a cup of tea. She had a cup for herself, as well. Delta had remained in Nicaragua long enough to help with recovering some of the mud-soaked, broken artifacts and during that time she had pieced together much of Caleb's story by talking with others, and of course, having seen the tragic moment with her own eyes. She had explained as much as she could to Mona. Now, she had just a couple of things left to say.

"They must have loved each other. Clearly they both loved the boy. Caleb looked as grief stricken as she. The mother's loss was beyond description. I can't even tell you how heartbroken..." Delta broke away from the sentence and took a long sip of the tea. "I can't even imagine what it must be like to lose one's child."

Mona went still. She glanced at Abigail. Abigail looked up. Mona gathered herself and said to Delta, "You love my brother, too. I can tell."

"Yes," Delta agreed. And now, for the first time since witnessing the whole scene, Delta let tears loose. Slowly at first, but then they turned into sobs. Mona reached out to her, touched Delta's shaking shoulders. Delta forced her tears back as she saw the little girl look her way with concern.

"Mona, your brother, he—"

"He, what?"

"He needs you. You should go to him. I can watch Abigail for you."

"Do you know where he is? He's not answering my calls."

"I asked around and at first, no one knew, although one man said he is living with the cockroaches, where he belongs. Later, I thought of Tracker. Tracker would know how to find Caleb. So I called him. He gave me the name of the motel where Caleb would likely be staying," she explained, handing Mona a slip of paper with Geovany Vellejo's motel's address. "But Tracker added that he did get a text from Caleb that said, *No story. Leave me alone.*

"Maybe Tracker should go," Mona suggested.

Delta shook her head. "I think he needs you."

MONA'S ARRIVAL

Two texts were exchanged. Mona's text to Caleb was succinct: *Don't bother telling me not to come. I fly into Nicaragua tomorrow.* Caleb's text even briefer, yet far more enigmatic: *Bring my baseball mitt.*

Delta handled finding a driver to meet Mona at the airport and take her to Geovany Vallejos' motel. Delta had thought of Loretta, the graduate student whom she had met on the archeological dig. Loretta was more than agreeable. And this time, when roles were reversed, with Delta dropping Mona at the airport, Delta handed her an envelope with a thank you note and some money for Loretta.

"Will you give this to Loretta for me?"

"Of course," Mona said taking the envelope. This time Delta lifted a small carry-on bag out of her trunk for Mona and passed it to her. Mona set it down momentarily and gave Delta a hug. Then she leaned into the car where Abigail was belted in for the ride in the backseat. "Be a good girl for Delta while I'm gone."

"Come back, okay?" the child's voice had a tinge of concern.

"I will."

Then Mona turned around, picked up her suitcase, thanked Delta and started toward the terminal entrance.

"Hey, Mona,"

Mona turned around.

"Don't drink the water," Delta advised with a smile.

***

Mona also listened to Loretta's advice when she arrived in Nicaragua.

Loretta had given Mona a good deal of advice on how to find a hotel after seeing her brother and offered to take her back to the airport whenever she was ready. She had added, "This motel is a bit seedy, as

313

they say. You might want a more American-style hotel." Loretta tried to be helpful. Mona simply nodded.

They made small talk on the way to the motel, although Mona was having some trouble focusing on what Loretta was saying, and she didn't really want to go into any details on why she was there. Somehow Mona knew that Loretta was aware of her mission to find her brother and bring him back. And she knew that Loretta was politely avoiding the topic of the American reporter. Eventually, Mona asked Loretta, "Who is this Augusto C. Sandino that the airport is named for?"

"He was a famous revolutionary. He protected the country from the U.S. invasion."

"When was this?" Mona had hoped for small talk, nothing that would reinforce the negative situation. *Perhaps, it was a long time, this American invasion,* she thought hopefully.

"Early 1930's. He is considered a national hero for his efforts. Heroes are fewer and farther apart these days. Invaders closer all the time."

Mona nodded. She remained quiet.

"He was assassinated. The U.S. was said to have supported the assassination."

Mona was quieter still. They rode in silence. Each thinking very different thoughts.

"Well, here we are," Loretta announced as the car tires crunched across the dirt and gravel drive of the motel parking lot. "I'll wait for you."

RECOVERING CALEB

Geovany Vallejos led Mona to the motel room door. In his usual manner, he knocked, or rather banged twice, didn't wait, and swung the door open.

Mona viewed the scene.

Light from the open doorway sent roaches scattering along the floor toward dark corners. A figure in the single bed, threw his forearm over his eyes. The other arm dangled over the side of the bed. The nightstand had a bottle of cheap whiskey more than half gone. A used glass sat next to the bottle. Several small, red ants went up and down the glass. They also climbed over and around what may have been the remains of some food, perhaps a rice and chicken taco at one time, sitting on an old waxed paper wrapper. An uncomfortable wooden chair, half-hidden under discarded dirty clothes, sat in the corner. A knapsack lay at the foot of the bed. A small suitcase to the side.

"Your room stinks," Mona announced.

"Go away," Caleb groaned and rolled over onto his side, turning away from the light and his sister.

"Your sister is here; a little respect for her would be nice," Vallejos informed and chastised Caleb. He turned and left brother and sister to their difficult reunion, but not before saying to Mona, "Take him home. He doesn't belong here."

His back still to her, Caleb said, "I'm not going home."

Mona waited in silence.

"Just leave the mitt," he added.

She still stood in the doorway.

"Kafka or Hemingway?" she finally asked.

Caleb moaned a low noise and remained with his back to the door. He didn't answer. But he was mulling it over in his hangover-inflamed head, a cockroach or an adventurous alcoholic, those were

315

good choices, he thought. Leave it to Mona to sum things so succinctly, and accurately. He rolled over on his back continuing to keep the light out of his eyes with his arm as cover.

"Maybe both," he said at last.

"Have you written anything since it happened."

"Shut the door. The light is too bright." He turned again to his side.

"No."

"My head hurts. Shut the door."

"No."

Caleb sat up, keeping his eyes shut against the light. "Close it and come in or leave and shut it."

"No."

"Jesus, Mona." Caleb got up. "Here, I'm not going to face the light. You sit on the bed." He brushed the dirty clothes to the floor and swung the chair around to face the bed. He sat with his back to the door.

"Bite me," she said. "I am not sitting on that bed."

"Kafka reference again?" he said with a dry cough as he rubbed the stubble on his chin.

She pulled his suitcase from near the bed and set it against the sunny disposition of the day, facing the dialectic of Caleb's dark countenance and mood. As she perched herself on the suitcase, he reached for the bottle. She didn't try to stop him. He poured a shot's worth into the dirty glass. She let him drink without a word.

"Did you bring the mitt?"

"Yes."

He reached for the bottle a second time. This time she intervened. "A friend is waiting. Let's go."

Mona pushed the bottle away from Caleb's reach. She picked up the clothes on the floor, shook them out and shoved them into his knapsack. She swung the bag over her shoulder and grabbed him by the arm. He pulled away.

"They don't want you here, my brother." She stared the truth into his face. "It's hard to hear, I know." Caleb became very still; tears moistened his eyes.

"And I need you," she added.

"Nobody needs me."

She looked pointedly into his eyes, repeating the sentiment, "I do. I really do. And I need your help with something." She too had tears in her eyes. "You think you're the only one with problems?" He looked closely into his sister's eyes; he looked beyond himself for the first time in a long time, and saw that she really did need him.

"Okay," he acquiesced. She led him to the car in the parking lot where Loretta was waiting. Mona started to load his bag and the suitcase.

"Can you give me the mitt?" Caleb asked.

She unzipped her carry-on and pulled out his old baseball mitt. The redolent smell of leather brought back memories of their childhood.

He tucked the mitt under his arm and climbed into the back seat of Loretta's car.

"I need to make one stop," he told her.

A DIFFERENT KIND OF FUNERAL

"I'll wait here," Loretta told Mona, as the brother and sister exited the car.

The cemetery had been easy to find. Loretta knew its location, as did most of the people of Managua, Nicaragua. She drove them and even gave them directions to the burial site. By now, the boy was famous; Caleb was infamous. Mona walked down the cement sidewalk with Caleb, viewing the above ground tombs, most covered in ceramic tiles, some more colorful than others. Interspersed were the graves of the less fortunate, the poor who had no money for spectacular sepulchers with ceramic tiles, mosaic or Terrazzo marble; instead, they had dirt mounds or simple cement coffins painted white.

When they reached Miguel's grave they found a well-kept, colorful-tiled tomb. The colors were bright—yellow and red, the flowers on it—magenta, yellow, orange, pink, and red with green leaves on their stems. The people of Managua honored the boy hero, a martyr, and the son of a martyr with the colors he loved, with the spirit and energy with which he had lived. No one let a day go by without bringing flowers to the grave. And the boy's mother never went a day without visiting the grave. She too brought a flower or *sapodilla* or a *zapote* that his strong white teeth had so loved to sink into when he was vibrant. When he was alive.

Today, Sofía stood in the distance. She stopped abruptly when she saw Caleb approaching the tomb. She moved behind a tree. He hadn't seen her, but Mona had caught sight of the beautiful woman just as she ducked behind the trunk of a tree. Somehow, Mona knew who it was without being told. The living mother martyr of Managua hid herself. Mona watched Sofía. Sofía watched Caleb.

Caleb went close to the tomb. He touched it. He lowered his head and tears rained down his cheeks. After a long time, he spoke.

319

Neither woman could hear what he said to the boy who lay entombed in white and yellow, and covered in flowers. The two women could only imagine. They watched as Caleb laid the baseball mitt on Miguel's tomb.

Mona looked to the mother. Questioningly. Sofía's shoulders, once tense, drew down. Anger had held them in place; perhaps, forgiveness released them.

Mona walked closer to Caleb. She placed a hand on his shoulder.

"It's time to go, *mon frère*." The words were spoken softly.

Caleb lifted one red petal and placed it inside the palm of the baseball mitt before leaving Nicaragua forever.

PART 10

THE EPILOGUES

CHAAC CRIED

Chaac followed the life of Ikoom, watching from his position in the skies above. He saw her return to Tikal on the day that he returned to his celestial home. On that day, he cried not only for the forgiveness that he received from his brother and sister-in-law but also for the joy that Ikoom felt and that he felt for her.

Chaac witnessed Ikoom's victorious return to her people, a grateful people who received her with welcoming arms and bestowed upon her honors and gifts. Chaac watched as she became the ruling Queen of the nearby city. Occasionally, Chaac felt a twinge of remorse whenever Ikoom thought longingly of Ku'tl. Those times, he shed a few tears. But often he relished more in her resourcefulness.

She had learned well from Ixchel on the *Island of Women* and even more while acting as Chaac's companion. He watched as she solidified relations between the various clans. She moved groups of people toward sources of underground water that bubbled up in springs or flowed from cave walls which he had shown her during her days in the deep underground labyrinths with him.

He marveled at how she could set one enemy against another to place her people in the most strategic position. He became furious when he discovered that her enemies had killed Ikoom's husband and tried to take her land *and water*. That day, Chaac cast his heavy axe and threw bolts of lightning, but gave them no rain. When she enacted her revenge, he smiled.

Not until the day she died, did Chaac cry again with intensity. He had nearly forgotten that she was mortal, so much so that her death caught him off guard. His loss brought more than moisture to his eyes; on that day, Chaac cried mighty tears that restored the reservoirs, made the rivers rush from the mountains and out to sea, and filled the lakes, even those closest to the volcanos. When Chaac thought he had cried his last tear, he once again looked to the earth and watched as the people carved a stela to the legacy of Ikoom, whom he thought of as his little sister and loving companion. At that moment, one last enormous teardrop fell to earth.

CHAPTER 56

CALEB'S STORY

Tracker handed the sheets of paper to his editor at the *Chicago Tribune*. The editor read the first few lines:

> *Fourteen-year-old Miguel Rodríguez was killed trying to protect his country from corporate pirates. He was a boy with a dream looking for an adventure; he was also a hero who climbed a tree, spotted armed mercenaries and sent me to warn his family, his neighbors, and his community that they were walking into a trap.*

> *Following the Feast of the Immaculate Conception but preceding the Christmas celebrations of 2019 in the Catholic country of Nicaragua, a plot to strip the people of their water and gold was carried out by radical capitalist forces in the form of an American 'business deal.' What the Nicaraguan business partner, Alejandro Martínez, did not know, is that his U.S. partner, Robert Madera, the wine magnet of Azteca wines, along with his brother-in-law, Mannie Morales and other key players, had concocted a secret plan to build a water bottling plant in Nicaragua that would act as a fake front for him to move vast amounts of gold out of the country.*

The editor of the *Chicago Tribune* continued to read the free-lance article that provided the details of how Madera had schemed and plotted, legally gaining access to all mineral and water rights on the land for the duration of the business operation. How he had used a select team to create advertising and marketing materials that cleverly both disguised and declared that he was moving water and gold out of the country via *Gold 'n Water* labels on casks, canteens, old wine barrels, and other opaque containers, which held both water and gold nuggets. Quotes from Madera's lawyer, Jackson Jackson, made Robert Madera out to be a saint and a man completely within his rights. With regard to the death of Miguel Rodríguez, no one disagreed that Madera was the one to tell the former Blackwater operatives to stop shooting. That he tried to calm the situation. That he had absolutely nothing to do with any water privatization scheme and as for the gold and water, well the water was coming from a spring on the property to which he held the rights, Madera claimed the water simply had a high gold content. He wasn't smuggling anything. The article reported Madera's position.

However, as the editor read on he learned that the water did not have a naturally high gold content as claimed by Madera; instead, according to water expert, Professor López, the water had little to no gold, maybe a trace, but nothing like the amount that Madera was accused of exporting. Indeed, Professor López agreed to testify to the mineral content of the water in a court of law. The free-lance article explained that it was Madera himself who hired López to test the water under the pretense of assuring that it was safe for consumption. Little did Madera know that the professor would do his job all too well. It proved that smuggling had taken place.

The editor reading the free-lance article began to wonder how Madera could have extracted the gold without workers knowing about it. The article answered the question before the editor could even put it to Tracker. Geologists were interviewed and they explained how the gold may have been extracted. The editor continued reading:

> *Generally, the gold to ground, or dirt, ratio is so extreme that uncovering gold requires massive excavation, heavy equipment, large spaces for dumping earth, explosives, to separate minerals from each other and so much more. Since the area was deemed a crime scene, geological and archeological experts were allowed to examine the remains of the earth, while forensic experts investigated the murder of Miguel Rodríguez.*

Computer reconstructions revealed how Chambers had master-minded the take by resurrecting ancient methods used before the common era (BCE) in areas now known as northern Spain, Wales, and the Alps. Some specialists pointed to the mountains of Ethiopia as another place where gold had been mined BCE, while other specialists argued that Aztecs had their own methods and the Maya traded for gold. Whichever the case may be, geologists agree that Chambers had used some "hushing" but mostly "fire-setting" to crack the gold free. The gold was not alluvial, but rather a massive vein shot forth from a volcano centuries ago, standing like a column that Chambers submitted to high temperatures from oxy-fuel welding torches, repeatedly heating the surface all the way around the column and then flashing it with cold water from the original sluice that had been used to uncover the column of gold in the first place. This allowed him and his men to chip nuggets away from the column. Chambers probably thought the last explosion would free the thin column that remained, he was wrong. The gold column, thin as a shovel handle, by the time Chambers was done with it, but strong as a diamond, must have had a core that included quartz, or calcite, or corundum, or maybe even diamonds, all else washed away through the labyrinth of tunnels. The Nicaraguan government refused to allow experts to drill to the center of the column to reveal its mineral structure.

The article continued, providing additional details on how the gold had been hidden in the false bottoms of the rain barrels, before it returned to the story of Miguel Rodríguez. It ended on a note of sorrow from the author, free-lance writer:

I went to warn the people, but I left the young Miguel Rodríguez to keep an eye on the armed guards. I followed the parade of people, marching for their water rights, human rights. I couldn't stop them. An explosion erupted from the warehouse. It blew wood and rocks into the sky that then rained down upon the chanting crowd. Chaos ensued. And then one of the security force operatives shot into the air to quiet the crowd. He sprayed bullets over their heads. But when the shooting ceased, the boy's body fell through the tree branches, the sound of cracking limbs preceded and announced his final fall onto the volcanic encrusted earth below. His mother rushed to his aid, but it was too late. She had lost her son before she could even tell him one last time how he was the morning, the dawn of her life.

The editor leaned back in his seat. "It's good," he announced. "Who is the reporter?" he asked Tracker.

A LONG SIP OF TEA

At the start of the winter semester, Professor Delta Quinn met for the first time with the students enrolled in her narrative course, a part of 'Cornerstone,' a new program at Purdue University that encouraged reading and discussing transformative texts. She began the lecture in the following way:

> We will begin with the oldest written epic poem, the story of *Gilgamesh*. A man who is described as one with a restless heart who fails to think of those around him, who has been blamed for the death of his companion, Enkidu. We will ask ourselves, was Gilgamesh a hero or perhaps an anti-hero. Was he selfish and self-centered? Taking bride right, as it is called. Misogynist, criminal or great hero? Was his legacy, the Wall of Uruk, a monument to him or a means to protect the people? Does one exclude the other? Is the ultimate theme about mortality, friendship, or leadership? What parallels exist today?

> We will follow this with the reading of *Antigone,* whose heroic stance could cost her dearly, but she is so determined to see that what is right and noble prevail that she would place her own life in jeopardy. We will ask, how does her heroism compare and contrast to Gilgamesh's acts of courage. Is she a hero or a martyr? Does one exclude the other? Is the ultimate theme about morality, loyalty, or resistance?

> We will read these classics and others over the course of the semester.

Delta's lecture continued to preview other readings, as well as projects proposed in the syllabus for the course titled, "Transformative Texts" Cornerstone, SCLA 101. When she was done and had answered all the questions that the students had asked, she turned to a little girl who had been sitting in an over-sized, for the child, college desk, coloring pictures as she waited for the professor to finish. Together, they made their way across campus and met Delta's friend, Professor P.J. Turner in the cafeteria.

"Well, who is this?" P.J. asked Delta as Delta settled the girl in with a glass of juice and a coloring book and crayons. P.J. slid a cup of tea toward Delta and then took a sip of her coffee, thinking how nice it is to have her friend back from winter break. P.J. was looking forward to hearing all about Delta's adventures in Belize, Guatemala, and Nicaragua. P.J. wanted to hear everything especially about the archeological dig. What had they learned about Lady Ikoom, she wondered. So many questions swirled in her mind, like the cream in her coffee.

"This is Mona's foster child, Abigail Newton. I'm taking care of her while Mona is in Nicaragua."

"What? How did that turn of events happen?" P.J. asked. "What's Mona doing in Nicaragua?"

"It's a long story," Delta sighed. Her sigh held the sorrow of someone who had held a treasure in her hand, a love in her heart, only to have it swept away. She then took a slow sip of warm tea before breathing in and beginning the story.

FROM FOREST MOTHER TO WIND MOTHER

Following the completion of his sure-to-be award-winning investigative exposé, which Tracker presented to an editor at the *Chicago Tribune*, Caleb Barthes embarked on a very different mission—to help his sister, Mona. Mona had brought her brother back from Nicaragua and from the bottom of a bottle. She needed his help in finding Abigail's biological mother.

Since the time that Abigail began speaking again, she spoke about things from the past, things that her wind mother had done. Mona asked Abigail one day, "Why do you call her the wind mother?"

"Because she whispers, like the wind, so that we wouldn't make my father angry," Abigail had explained. "Because she loved me and didn't want me to feel the storm."

From that answer, Mona knew that she needed to find this woman and reunite the two. Mona knew that her brother, being one of the finest investigative reporters would be able to help her. Caleb took up the challenge.

After searching, Caleb found a woman named Wendy Nichols who had formerly been married under the name of Wendy Newton. She had been maligned by her former husband, and lost custody of her daughter Abigail. She had hidden in plain sight, never leaving the area and always trying to regain visitation with her daughter, but bureaucratic hurdles had again and again left her bereft. All she knew was that her daughter Abigail was being cared for by a foster mother. Caleb found the mother and Mona coordinated the meeting.

On May 15, 2020, Abigail Newton once again climbed into the arms of her biological mother, the 'wind mother,' as the girl called her. She did this, as Mona, her foster mother, whom the girl called her 'forest mother,' watched the two reunite. Mona understood, without a word being spoken, that the mother and daughter belonged together. Still, it broke her heart to lose the child.

"You've done the right thing, *mon frère*," Caleb assured his sister Mona, inserting the inside joke—his calling her my brother. He tried to lift her spirits.

"As have you, *mon frère*. As have you."

Whether Mona was referring to his helping to reunite the mother and child, didn't matter. The moment reminded him of Miguel and Sofía. The mother and son would never be reunited. He could never forgive himself for Miguel's death. Never. Mona knew what he was thinking as his face dropped. Now it was her turn to try to lift his spirits.

"You didn't pull the trigger, but you did provide the scapegoat. All they had before you finished the research and published the article was an unnamed Blackwater operative and a corporate pirate who would have gotten away with murder, literally. And before that, you gave Sofía a place to put her anger and frustration. She needed that, and I believe that she has forgiven you. Now, it's time for you to forgive yourself."

"There would not have been anything to forgive, if I had kept my promise to her."

They watched as Abigail Newton stroked the cheek of her wind mother.

CHAPTER 59

"LIFE IS OFTEN SAD"

The heavy tropical rains of early fall pelted against the pavement, sending up the fragrance of earth and humidity. Large drops fell sporadically at first, and then began to close in on each other. Sofía listened to the rain as she read the article about her son Miguel. It had come in the mail, no return address. She read the entire story, then folded the newspaper article and placed it inside a book of poetry. Her empty hand came to rest on her full and rounded abdomen, a life kicked from within. Sofía spoke softly, "Let us put our heroes to rest, shall we? And accept that life is often sad, *Y la vida es triste pero tenemos que seguir para adelante*, but we walk onward.

Tears speak our truth;
Water, washing
our souls."

The End

FACTS

FACTS CONCERNING THE 'BOLIVIAN WATER WARS'

The Bolivian Water Wars—the Cochabamba riots took place from November 1999 to April of 2000. The people struggled against the privatization of the water. Water treatment centers are relatively inexpensive in the U.S. and are held in public trust for the most part, but in some other countries water sanitation systems, proffered by private companies, have been extremely costly, especially to the citizens. Privatization of water led to the 'Bolivian Water Wars,' where the people marched on the government for allowing a private company to lay claim to the water and which in turn had the following tragic result:

> Just past noon, Victor Hugo Daza, an unarmed seventeen-year-old, was in one of the clusters of protesters gathered on a side street near the central plaza. A local television station captured footage of an army captain, Robinson Iriarte de La Fuente, firing live rounds into the crowd. A bullet exploded into Victor Hugo's face, killing him on the spot. A stunned crowd led by his older brother brought his bloody body to the plaza and held an angry, emotional wake. Iriarte would later be tried in a Bolivian military court, acquitted, and promoted the same day to major. (Schultz, 2010)

FACTS RELATED TO CONTEMPORARY NICARAGUA

Nicaragua has a rich history and a lengthy complicated past with the United States, one that readers might wish to explore through various historical sources. More recently, that history has included a social movement against government imposed cutbacks on social security and on demonstrations (whether physical or cyber) against the government. Protests against Daniel Ortega in 2018 were met with a brutal government crackdown. The protests arose claiming that the Ortega government was corrupt. The Nicaraguan government claimed the protesters were terrorists. The U.S. government placed sanctions on Nicaragua. Over 60,000 people have fled the country in the aftermath of the protests and continuing violence by the government. Human rights activists continue to keep a watchful eye so that the government police do not receive amnesty for their crimes of torture against protestors (see Rivas, 2018).

FACTS RELATED TO VARIOUS WATER ISSUES

"After the cost of packaging, shipping, and marketing, companies are usually left with a healthy 30% profit margin, and the average markup of water when bottled is 4,000%. We spend at least 10,000 times more on the packaged stuff than we would if we were to drink it straight from the tap" (Burns, 2015). The business relationships between U.S. companies and Nicaragua in the areas of water and bottled drinks such as coca cola products are of concern to activists not only in terms of profit margins, exploitation of workers, and general health, but also in terms of the environment. Studies indicate promises by corporations are not being met (McDonald, 2018).

FACTS RELATED TO FOSTER CARE

According to *Children's Rights* (Foster Care, 2020),

> Many of America's child welfare systems are badly broken—and children can suffer serious harm as a result. Some will be separated from their siblings. Others will be bounced from one foster care placement to another, never knowing when their lives will be uprooted next. Too many will be further abused in systems that are supposed to protect them. And instead of being safely reunified with their families—or moved quickly into adoptive homes—many will languish for years in foster homes or institutions.

In addition, the organization states that:

On any given day, there are nearly 443,000 children in foster care in the United States.

In 2017, more than 690,000 children spent time in U.S. foster care.

On average, children remain in state care for nearly two years and six percent of children in foster care have languished there for five or more years.

Despite the common perception that the majority of children in foster care are very young, the average age of kids entering care is 8.

FACTS ABOUT THE ARCHEOLOGICAL DISCOVERIES CONCERNING LADY IKOOM

"Early in March, [Griselda] Pérez was excavating a short tunnel along the centerline of the stairway of the temple in order to give access to other tunnels leading to a royal tomb discovered in 2012 when her excavators encountered Stela 44" (see Discovery, 2013). Stela 44 is dedicated to Lady Ikoom and was found in Guatemala, not Nicaragua (see Discovery, 2013; Washington, 2013).

FACTS RELATED TO ILLEGAL MINING

"The so-called '*war on drugs*' launched by the United States, and the drastic increase in the price of gold (between 2002 and 2012 gold increased by 500% worldwide) have made illegal mining one of the most lucrative businesses in the region [Central America]" (Bruner & Grande, 2018).

FACTS RELATED TO ANCIENT MINING TECHNIQUES

Ancient techniques in mining include "hushing" (2020) and "fire-setting" (2020) respectively.

FACTS RELATED TO U.S. MAJOR LEAGUE BASEBALL PLAYERS

Playing baseball in the United States is not a new dream for Nicaraguan players. Fourteen U.S. Major League Baseball player, who were born in Nicaragua, played between 1976 and 2018 (List, 2020).

BIBLIOGRAPHY

Achbar, M., Bakan, J., & Crooks, M. (2003). *The corporation* [Documentary]. Los Angeles, CA: Farrell Conlan Media.

Black, R. (2003, May 19). *Ancient Nicaraguan Society Found.* BBC. Retrieved October 19, 2013, from http://news.bbc.co.uk/2/hi/sci/tech/3035113.stm

Brunner, E., & Grande, R. (2018, January 26). Organized crime and illegal gold mining in Latin America. *Global Americans.* Retrieved from https://theglobalamericans.org/2018/01/organized-crime-illegal-gold-mining-latin-america/

Burns, A. (2015, February 19). 10 designer waters and their insane profit margins. *The Richest.* Retrieved from https://www.therichest.com/expensive-lifestyle/10-designer-waters-and-their-insane-profit-margins/

Clair, R. P., Carlo, S., Lam, C., Nussman, J., Phillips, C., Sanchez, V., Schnabel, E., & Yakovich, L. (2014). Narrative theory and criticism: An overview toward clusters and empathy. *Review of Communication, 14*, 1–18.

Clair, R. P., & Kunkel, A. W. (1998). "Unrealistic realities": Child abuse and the aesthetic resolution. *Communication Monographs, 65*, 24–46.

Clair R. P., & Mattson, M. (2013). From accident to activity: An ethnographic study of community engagement—From symbolic violence to heroic discourse. *Tamara: Journal of Critical Organizational Inquiry, 11*, 27–40.

Clair, R. P., Rastogi, R., Blatchley III, E. R., Clawson, R. A., Erdmann, C., & Lee, S. (2016). Extended narrative empathy: Poly-narratives and the practice of open defecation. *Communication Theory, 26*, 469–488.

Discovery of stone monument at El Perwaka. (2013, July 16). St. Louis, MO: Washington University. Retrieved from https://source.wustl.edu/2013/07/discovery-of-stone-monument-at-el-perwaka-adds-new-chapter-to-ancient-maya-history/

Egan, J. (2011). *A visit from the Goon squad.* New York City, NY: Knopf.

Fire-setting. (2020, July 21). In *Wikipedia.* Retrieved from https://en.wikipedia.org/wiki/Fire-setting

Foster Care. (2020). New York, NY: Children's Rights. Retrieved from https://www.childrensrights.org/newsroom/fact-sheets/foster-care/

Hushing. (2020). In *Wikipedia.* Retrieved from https://en.wikipedia.org/wiki/Hushing

Johns, C. (Ed.). (2010, April). Water: Our thirsty world (A special edition). *National Geographic.* Washington, DC: National Geographic Society.

List. (2020, July 13). In *Wikipedia.* Retrieved from https://en.wikipedia.org/wiki/Fire-setting

McDonald, C. (2018, May 21). Coke claims to give back as much as it uses: An investigation shows it isn't even close. *The Verge.* Retrieved from https://www.theverge.com/2018/5/31/17377964/coca-cola-water-sustainability-recycling-controversy-investigation

Nicaragua: Relations with Central American Countries. (n.d.). U.S. Library of Congress. Retrieved March 11, 2019, from http://countrystudies.us/nicaragua/59.htm

Rivas, O. (2019). Crackdown in Nicaragua: Torture, ill-treatment, and prosecutions of protestors and opponents. *Human Rights Watch*. Retrieved from https://www.hrw.org/report/2019/06/19/crackdown-nicaragua/torture-ill-treatment-and-prosecutions-protesters-and

Schultz, J. (2010). *The Bolivia water revolt, ten years later*. San Francisco, CA: The Democracy Center. Retrieved from https://democracyctr.org/the-bolivia-water-revolt-ten-years-later/

Schultz, J. (n.d.). *The Cochabamba water revolt and its aftermath*. San Francisco, CA: The Democracy Center.

Shiva, V. (2016). *Water wars: Privatization, pollution and profit*. Berkeley, CA: North Atlantic Books.

Tervalon, M., & Murray-García, J. (1998). Cultural humility versus cultural competence: A critical distinction in defining physician training outcomes in multicultural education. *Journal of Health Care for Poor and Underserved, 9*, 17–125.

Washington University in St. Louis. (2013, July 17). Discovery of stone monument adds new chapter to ancient Maya history: New World 'Cleopatra story' waits 1,000 years to be retold. *ScienceDaily*. Retrieved October 10, 2020, from www.sciencedaily.com/releases/2013/07/130717164133.htm

ABOUT THE AUTHOR

Robin Patric Clair (Ph.D.) is a Full Professor in the Brian Lamb School of Communication (BLSC) at Purdue University. She is an award-winning researcher, a two-time recipient of the Fellow to Creative Endeavors Center in the College of Liberal Arts, and has been named to the Book of Great Teachers. Clair is also a Purdue University Diversity Fellow which attests to her commitment to writing diverse characters in complex situations. Her novels are provocative and tackle contested social issues. She teaches rhetoric, organizational communication, ethnography, and diversity for the BLSC and teaches Transformative Texts for the Cornerstone Program at Purdue University.

Printed in the United States
By Bookmasters